A Level

PE
2ND EDITION

Keri Moorhouse

The Publishers would like to thank the following for permission to reproduce copyright material.

Photo credits

p.11 © Syda Productions/stock.adobe.com; **p.12** t © Tom Griffiths/ZUMA Wire/ZUMAPRESS.com/Alamy, b © jrroman/iStock/Thinkstock; **p.13** © kjekol/stock.adobe.com; **p.14** © Foodpics/stock.adobe.com; **p.15** © Stockbyte/Thinkstock; **p.24** l © Daxiao Productions/stock.adobe.com, c © Microgen/stock.adobe.com, r ALAN EDWARDS/Alamy Stock Photo; **p.45** © Crown copyright. Public Health England in association with the Welsh government, the Scottish government and the Food Standards Agency in Northern Ireland; **p.68** © junky_jess/stock.adobe.com; **p.69** © guruXOOX/iStock/Thinkstock; **p.78** © Bupa UK, PRICE infographic, http://www.bupa.co.uk/; **p.85** © t Aleksandar Kitanovic/123RF, b © Shariff Che'Lah/123RF; **p.107** © Ljupco/iStock/Thinkstock.

Every effort has been made to trace all copyright holders, but if any have been inadvertently overlooked, the Publishers will be pleased to make the necessary arrangements at the first opportunity.

Although every effort has been made to ensure that website addresses are correct at time of going to press, Hodder Education cannot be held responsible for the content of any website mentioned in this book. It is sometimes possible to find a relocated web page by typing in the address of the home page for a website in the URL window of your browser.

Hachette UK's policy is to use papers that are natural, renewable and recyclable products and made from wood grown in well-managed forests and other controlled sources. The logging and manufacturing processes are expected to conform to the environmental regulations of the country of origin.

Orders: please contact Hachette UK Distribution, Hely Hutchinson Centre, Milton Road, Didcot, Oxfordshire, OX11 7HH. Telephone: +44 (0)1235 827827. Email: education@hachette.co.uk. Lines are open from 9 a.m. to 5 p.m., Monday to Friday. You can also order through our website: www.hoddereducation.co.uk.

ISBN: 978 1 3983 6060 0

© Keri Moorhouse 2022

First published in 2017

This edition published in 2022 by
Hodder Education,
An Hachette UK Company
Carmelite House
50 Victoria Embankment
London EC4Y 0DZ

www.hoddereducation.co.uk

Impression number   10 9 8 7 6 5 4 3 2

Year   2026 2025 2024 2023

All rights reserved. Apart from any use permitted under UK copyright law, no part of this publication may be reproduced or transmitted in any form or by any means, electronic or mechanical, including photocopying and recording, or held within any information storage and retrieval system, without permission in writing from the publisher or under licence from the Copyright Licensing Agency Limited. Further details of such licences (for reprographic reproduction) may be obtained from the Copyright Licensing Agency Limited, www.cla.co.uk

Cover photo © Torsak Thammachote/123RF.com

Typeset in Caecilia LT Std 55 Roman by Integra Software Services Pvt. Ltd., Pondicherry, India

Printed and bound by CPI Group (UK) Ltd, Croydon, CR0 4YY

A catalogue record for this title is available from the British Library.

Get the most from this book

Everyone has to decide their own revision strategy, but it is essential to review your work, learn it and test your understanding. These Revision Notes will help you to do that in a planned way, topic by topic. Use this book as the cornerstone of your revision and don't hesitate to write in it — personalise your notes and check your progress by ticking off each section as you revise.

Tick to track your progress

Use the revision planner on p. 4 to plan your revision, topic by topic. Tick each box when you have:
+ revised and understood a topic
+ tested yourself
+ practised the exam questions, checked your answers and gone online to complete the quick quizzes

You can also keep track of your revision by ticking off each topic heading in the book. You may find it helpful to add your own notes as you work through each topic.

Features to help you succeed

Exam tips
Expert tips are given throughout the book to help you polish your exam technique in order to maximise your chances in the exam.

Now test yourself
These short, knowledge-based questions provide the first step in testing your learning. Answers are on pp. 166–174.

Definitions and key words
Clear, concise definitions of essential key terms are provided where they first appear.

Key words from the specification are highlighted in bold throughout the book.

Making links
This feature identifies specific connections between topics and tells you how revising these will aid your exam answers.

Knowledge and skills summary
These summaries highlight how specific knowledge and skills identified or applicable in that chapter can be applied to your exam answers.

Revision activities
These activities will help you to understand each topic in an interactive way.

Exam practice
Practice exam questions are provided for each topic. Use them to consolidate your revision and practise your exam skills. Model answers are given on pp. 175–183.

Online
Go online to try the quick quizzes at
www.hoddereducation.co.uk/myrevisionnotesdownloads

My Revision Planner

6 Introduction

Component 1 Physiological factors affecting performance

1.1 Applied anatomy and physiology
- 8 1.1a Skeletal and muscular systems
- 21 1.1b Cardiovascular and respiratory systems
- 35 1.1c Energy for exercise
- 41 1.1d Environmental effects on body systems

1.2 Exercise physiology
- 45 1.2a Diet and nutrition and their effect on physical performance
- 54 1.2b Preparation and training methods
- 73 1.2c Injury prevention and the rehabilitation of injury

1.3 Biomechanics
- 82 1.3a Biomechanical principles, levers and the use of technology
- 90 1.3b Linear motion, angular motion, fluid mechanics and projectile motion

Component 2 Psychological factors affecting performance

- 103 2.1 Skill acquisition
- 117 2.2 Sports psychology

Component 3 Socio-cultural issues in physical activity and sport

- 136 3.1 Sport and society
- 147 3.2 Contemporary issues in physical activity and sport

- 158 Glossary
- 166 Now test yourself answers
- 175 Exam practice answers

Try the quick quizzes online at:

www.hoddereducation.co.uk/myrevisionnotesdownloads

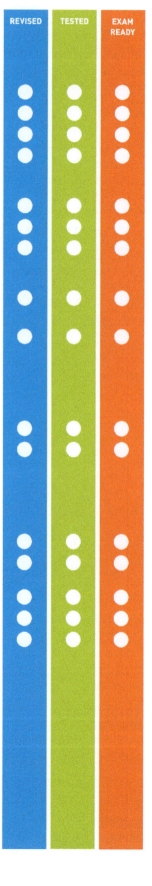

Quick quizzes at www.hoddereducation.co.uk/myrevisionnotesdownloads

Countdown to my exams

6–8 weeks to go

- Start by looking at the specification — make sure you know exactly what material you need to revise and the style of the examination. Use the revision planner on p. 4 to familiarise yourself with the topics.
- Organise your notes, making sure you have covered everything on the specification. The revision planner will help you to group your notes into topics.
- Work out a realistic revision plan that will allow you time for relaxation. Set aside days and times for all the subjects that you need to study, and stick to your timetable.
- Set yourself sensible targets. Break your revision down into focused sessions of around 40 minutes, divided by breaks. These Revision Notes organise the basic facts into short, memorable sections to make revising easier.

REVISED

2–6 weeks to go

- Read through the relevant sections of this book and refer to the exam tips, knowledge and skills summaries and key terms. Tick off the topics as you feel confident about them. Highlight those topics you find difficult and look at them again in detail.
- Test your understanding of each topic by working through the 'Now test yourself' questions in the book. Look up the answers at the back of the book.
- Make a note of any problem areas as you revise, and ask your teacher to go over these in class.
- Look at past papers. They are one of the best ways to revise and practise your exam skills. Write or prepare planned answers to the exam practice questions provided in this book. Check your answers on pp. 175–183 and try out the quick quizzes at **www.hoddereducation.co.uk/myrevisionnotesdownloads**
- Use the revision activities to try out different revision methods. For example, you can make notes using mind maps, spider diagrams or flash cards.
- Track your progress using the revision planner and give yourself a reward when you have achieved your target.

REVISED

One week to go

- Try to fit in at least one more timed practice of an entire past paper and seek feedback from your teacher, comparing your work closely with the mark scheme.
- Check the revision planner to make sure you haven't missed out any topics. Brush up on any areas of difficulty by talking them over with a friend or getting help from your teacher.
- Attend any revision classes put on by your teacher. Remember, they are an expert at preparing people for examinations.

REVISED

The day before the examination

- Flick through these Revision Notes for useful reminders, for example the exam tips, knowledge and skills summaries and key terms.
- Check the time and place of your examination.
- Make sure you have everything you need — extra pens and pencils, tissues, a watch, bottled water, sweets.
- Allow some time to relax and have an early night to ensure you are fresh and alert for the examinations.

REVISED

My exams

Paper 1: Component 1 Physiological factors affecting performance (2 hours)

Date:..

Time: ....

Location: ....

Paper 2: Component 2 Psychological factors affecting performance (1 hour)

Date:..

Time: ....

Location: ....

Paper 3: Component 3 Socio-cultural issues in physical activity and sport (1 hour)

Date:..

Time: ....

Location: ....

Introduction

How is A Level PE examined?

This book covers components 1, 2 and 3 (the theory elements of A Level PE). Component 4 is your practical and EAPI (Evaluating and Analysing Performance for Improvement).

Components 1, 2 and 3 are worth 70% of your A Level grade.

As a student of A Level PE it is important that you know these five things about the examination:
+ the structure of the exam
+ the assessment objectives
+ the quantitative skills needed
+ practical examples
+ the synoptic element within each paper.

The structure of the exam

REVISED

Each of the three papers consists of a mixture of objective response, short- and medium-length answers, and extended response items. Each paper may also include multiple choice questions. **You must answer all questions on each paper.**

Paper 1: Component 1: Physiological factors affecting performance

2 hours, 30% of total A Level

This paper will assess:
+ 1.1 Applied anatomy and physiology
+ 1.2 Exercise physiology
+ 1.3 Biomechanics

Total 90 marks

Paper 2: Component 2: Psychological factors affecting performance

1 hour, 20% of total A Level

This paper will assess:
+ 2.1 Skill acquisition
+ 2.2 Sports psychology

Total 60 marks

Paper 3: Component 3: Socio-cultural issues in physical activity and sport

1 hour, 20% of total A Level

This component will assess:
+ 3.1 Sport and society
+ 3.2 Contemporary issues in physical activity and sport

Total 60 marks

Quick quizzes at www.hoddereducation.co.uk/myrevisionnotesdownloads

Assessment objectives

Your answers will be marked by examiners who will consider how well you have met the three assessment objectives. These are explained in the table below.

Assessment objectives	Requirements	Comments
AO1: Knowledge and understanding	Demonstrate knowledge and understanding of the factors that underpin performance and involvement in physical activity and sport.	Usually 1- or 2-mark questions – recall of information.
AO2: Practical application	Apply knowledge and understanding of the factors that underpin performance and involvement in physical activity and sport.	Questions can range from 1 to 20 marks. Sometimes they assess AO2 alone, but often they combine this with AO1 and AO3.
AO3: Analysis and evaluation	Analyse and evaluate the factors that underpin performance and involvement in physical activity and sport.	Generally, questions range from 4 to 20 marks. Assessment of AO3 is often combined with AO2.
AO4: Practical performance	+ Demonstrate and apply relevant skills and techniques in physical activity and sport (practical performance). + Analyse and evaluate performance (EAPI).	Not covered in this book.

Quantitative skills

In the examinations 5% of the overall A Level marks will be from your quantitative skills, including:
+ interpretation of data and graphs (exercise physiology, sports psychology, contemporary studies)
+ ability to plot, label and interpret graphs and diagrams (biomechanics)
+ use of definitions, equations, formulae and units of measurement (biomechanics).

Practical examples

Throughout all three exam papers you will be asked for practical examples (AO2) from physical activities and sports to show how theory can be applied and to reinforce the understanding you demonstrate. It is important to learn as many practical examples as you can.

Synoptic assessment in each paper

Synoptic assessment tests your understanding of the connections between different elements of the subject. This involves the explicit drawing together of knowledge, skills and understanding within different parts of the A Level course. Synoptic links will be identified in the 'Making links' features, for example linking classification of skills to the best methods of practice.

Within examined components 1, 2 and 3, each assessment will contain an extended response question (marked with an asterisk, *). Here you must draw together knowledge from more than one topic within the component and demonstrate your understanding of how the topics interrelate. Look out for the 'Making links' feature throughout the book.

My Revision Notes: OCR A Level PE

1.1a Skeletal and muscular systems

Joints, movements, muscles and the analysis of movement

REVISED

Figure 1.1.1 shows the major bones of the skeleton.

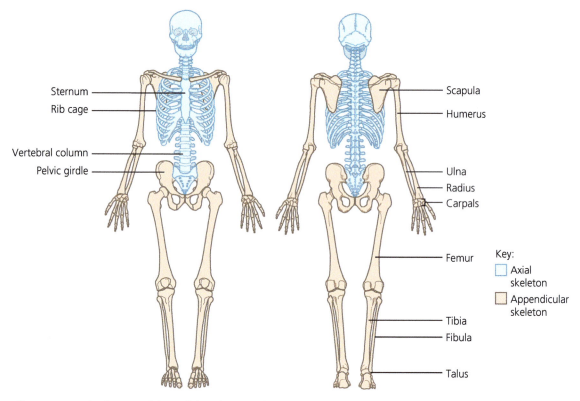

Figure 1.1.1 The bones of the axial and appendicular skeleton

Table 1.1.1 Structure and function of a synovial joint

Common features of a synovial joint	Structure	Function
Ligament	A tough band of slightly elastic connective tissue	Connects bone to bone and stabilises joints during movement
Synovial fluid	Lubricating liquid contained within the joint cavity	Reduces friction and nourishes articular cartilage
Articular cartilage	Smooth tissue that covers the surface of articulating bones	Absorbs shock and allows friction-free movement
Joint capsule	A fibrous sac with an inner synovial membrane	Encloses and strengthens the joint secreting synovial fluid
Bursa	A closed, fluid-filled sac found where tendons rub over bones	Reduces friction between tendons and bones

Joint: an area of the body where two or more bones articulate to create human movement.

Quick quizzes at www.hoddereducation.co.uk/myrevisionnotesdownloads

Planes of movement

If a person stands in an anatomical position, we describe their movement in three dimensions, based on three planes:
+ sagittal plane (vertical – divides body into left/right)
+ frontal plane (vertical – divides body into anterior/posterior)
+ transverse plane (horizontal – divides body into upper/lower).

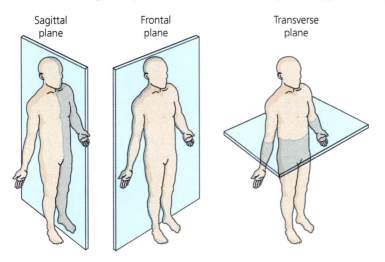

Figure 1.1.2 The three planes of movement

> **Plane of movement**: the description of three-dimensional movements at a joint.

Movement patterns

Table 1.1.2 describes the three types of plane and their movements.

Table 1.1.2 Planes and movements

Plane	Movement type	Example
Sagittal plane	Flexion	Bending arm at elbow
	Extension	Straightening arm at elbow
	Dorsi-flexion	Pointing toes up
	Plantar flexion	Pointing toes down
Frontal plane	Abduction	Moving arm at shoulder away from midline
	Adduction	Moving arm at shoulder towards midline
Transverse plane	Horizontal extension	Moving arm at shoulder away from midline parallel to ground
	Horizontal flexion	Moving arm at shoulder towards midline parallel to ground
	Rotation	Movement whereby articulating bones turn about their longitudinal axis in a screwdriver action

Table 1.1.3 provides an overview of joint types and movement patterns possible.

> **Movement pattern**: a description of the action taking place at a joint.

Table 1.1.3 Joints and movements

Joint type	Location	Plane of movement	Movement patterns possible
Ball and socket	Shoulder and hip	Sagittal plane	Flexion and extension
		Frontal plane	Abduction and adduction
		Transverse plane	Horizontal flexion, horizontal extension, medial and lateral rotation
Hinge	Elbow, knee and ankle	Sagittal plane	Flexion, extension, dorsi-flexion and plantar flexion
Condyloid	Wrist	Sagittal plane	Flexion and extension
		Frontal plane	Abduction and adduction

Shoulder

Joint type	Ball and socket joint	
Articulating bones	Humerus and scapula	
Movement	Sagittal plane	
	Flexion	Extension
Agonist muscles	Anterior deltoid	Posterior deltoid
Movement	Frontal plane	
	Adduction	Abduction
Agonist muscles	Latissimus dorsi	Middle deltoid
Movement	Transverse plane	
	Horizontal flexion	Horizontal extension
Agonist muscles	Pectoralis major	Posterior deltoid and teres minor

Shoulder *continued*

Movement	Transverse plane	
	Medial rotation	Lateral rotation
	Teres major and subscapularis *Anterior view*	Teres minor and infraspinatous *Posterior view*
Movement	Circumduction is characterised by shoulder circles and arm swings. It is a combination of flexion, extension, abduction, adduction and rotation.	
Practical application	To mobilise the shoulder joint as part of a warm-up, an individual may use star jumps. In the outward phase of a star jump, the agonist, the middle deltoid, concentrically contracts to abduct the shoulder joint.	

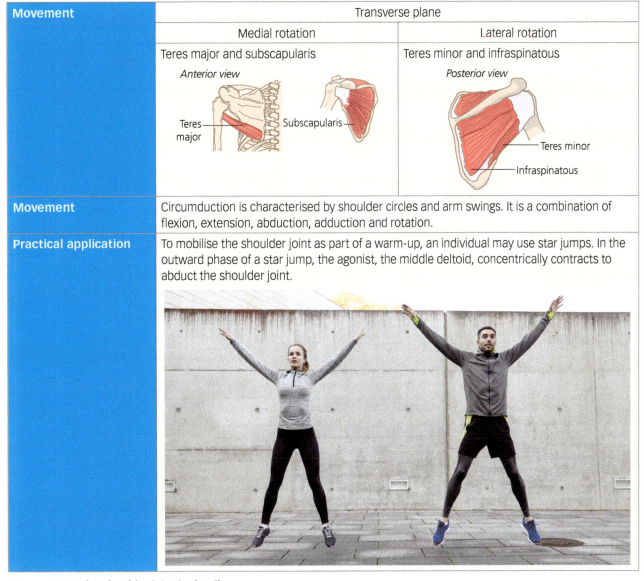

Figure 1.1.3 The shoulder joint in detail

Elbow

Joint type	Hinge joint	
Articulating bones	Humerus, radius and ulna	
Movement	Sagittal plane	
	Flexion	Extension
Agonist muscles	Biceps brachii *Anterior view*	Triceps brachii *Posterior view*

Elbow *continued*

Practical application	The elbow joint is essential for creating power in a netball shot. In the preparation phase, the biceps brachii will concentrically contract to flex the elbow, lowering the ball. In the execution phase, the triceps brachii concentrically contracts to extend the elbow joint through a large range of motion to generate a large force to apply to the ball. 

Figure 1.1.4 The elbow joint in detail

Wrist

Joint type	Condyloid joint	
Articulating bones	Radius, ulna and carpals	
Movement	Sagittal plane	
	Flexion	Extension
Agonist muscles	Wrist flexors	Wrist extensors
Practical application	Basketball players concentrically contract the agonist, the wrist flexors, to flex the wrist as the ball is released in a jump shot. This enables backspin to be put on the ball, causing the ball to 'pop up' from the back board rather than roll off. 	

Figure 1.1.5 The wrist joint in detail

Quick quizzes at **www.hoddereducation.co.uk/myrevisionnotesdownloads**

Hip

Joint type	Ball and socket joint
Articulating bones	Pelvic girdle and femur

Movement	Sagittal plane	
	Flexion	Extension
Agonist muscles	Iliopsoas 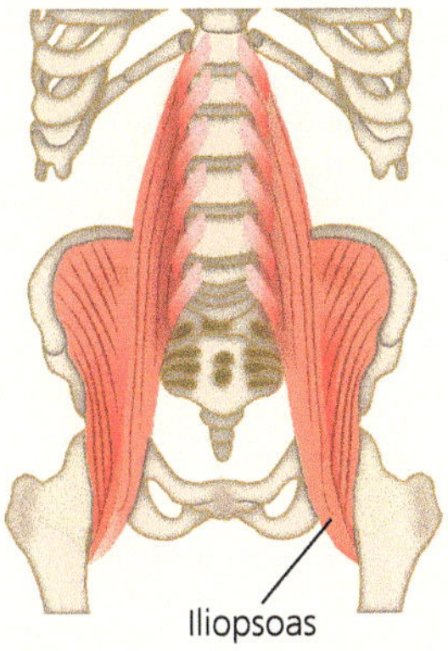	Gluteus maximus 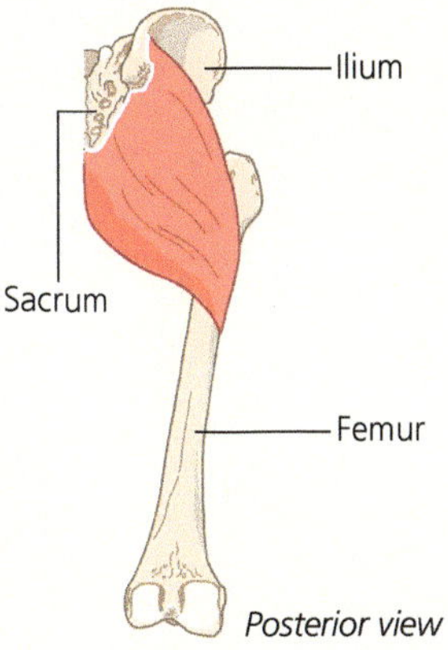

Movement	Frontal plane	
	Adduction	Abduction
Agonist muscles	Adductor brevis, adductor longus and adductor magnus 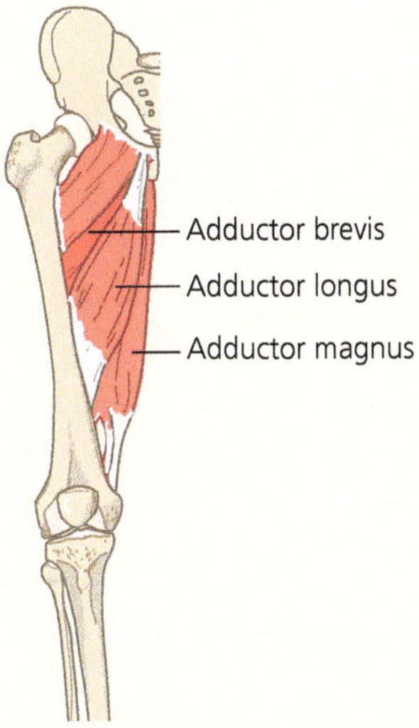	Gluteus medius and gluteus minimus 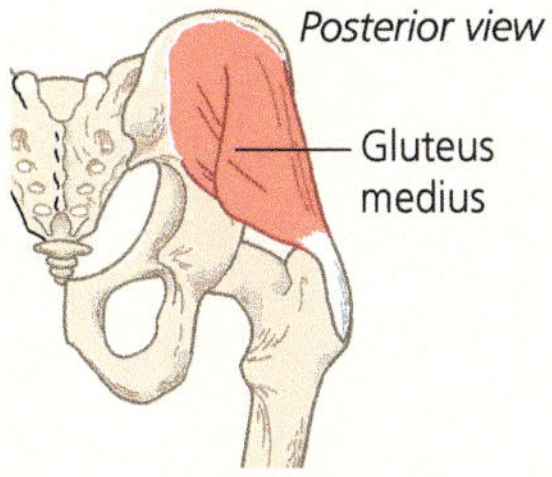 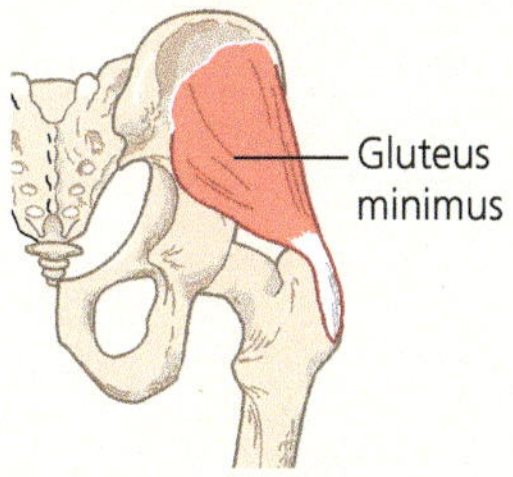

Movement	Transverse plane	
	Medial rotation	Lateral rotation
Agonist muscles	Gluteus medius and gluteus minimus (as above)	Gluteus maximus (as above)
Practical application	When weightlifting in the upward phase, the agonist, the gluteus maximus, will concentrically contract to create hip extension while the antagonist, the iliopsoas, co-ordinates the action. 	

Figure 1.1.6 The hip joint in detail

Knee

Joint type	Hinge joint
Articulating bones	Femur and tibia
Movement	Sagittal plane
	Flexion / Extension
Agonist muscles	Biceps femoris, semitendinosus and semimembranosus (hamstring group) / Rectus femoris, vastus lateralis, vastus intermedius and vastus medialis (quadriceps group) 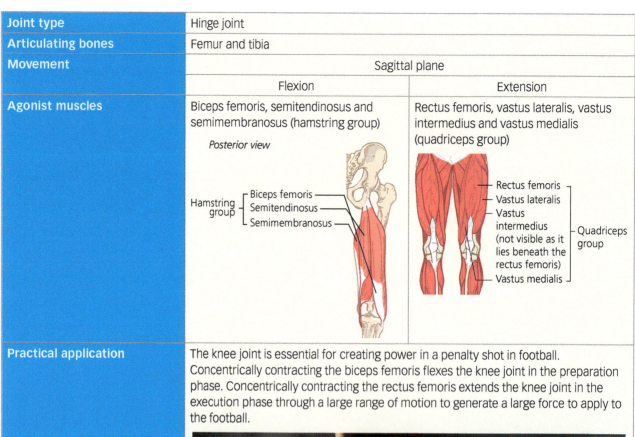
Practical application	The knee joint is essential for creating power in a penalty shot in football. Concentrically contracting the biceps femoris flexes the knee joint in the preparation phase. Concentrically contracting the rectus femoris extends the knee joint in the execution phase through a large range of motion to generate a large force to apply to the football. 

Figure 1.1.7 The knee joint in detail

Ankle

Joint type	Hinge joint	
Articulating bones	Tibia, fibula and talus	
Movement	Sagittal plane	
	Dorsi-flexion	Plantar flexion
Agonist muscles	Tibialis anterior	Gastrocnemius and soleus
Practical application	Contemporary dancers use their feet for shaping body movements. Concentrically contracting the gastrocnemius and soleus to plantar flex the ankle joint creates a fully extended finish to the leg in a split leap or when rising to the toes to go en pointe.	

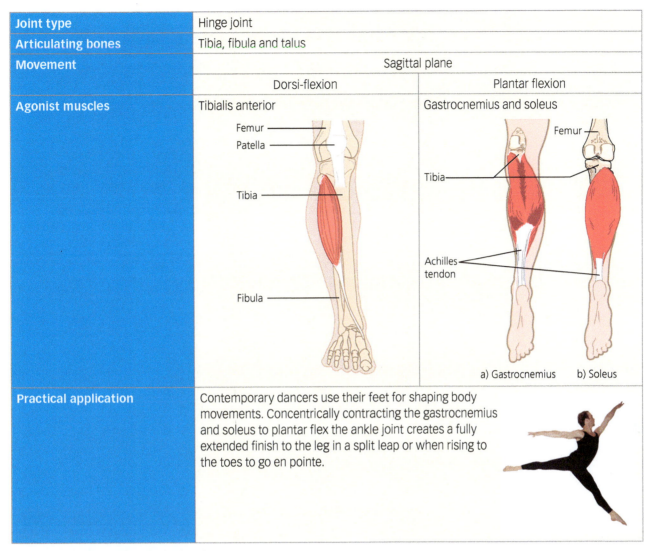

Figure 1.1.8 The ankle joint in detail

Functional roles of muscles and types of contraction

REVISED

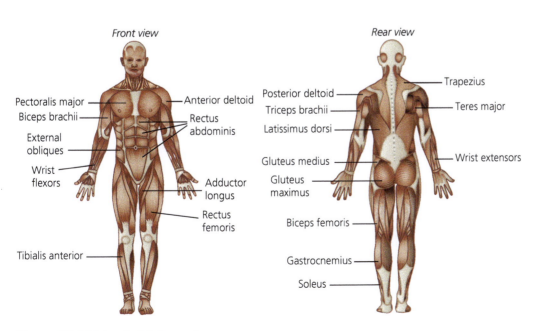

Figure 1.1.9 Major skeletal muscles

My Revision Notes: OCR A Level PE

- Muscles are made of up fibres that contain filaments.
- Thick filaments are made of the protein myosin and thin filaments are made of the protein actin.
- Myosin and actin filaments are arranged to form an overlapping pattern, which gives muscle tissue its striated appearance.
- During contraction, the myosin thick filaments grab on to the actin thin filaments by forming cross bridges.
- An increased number of cross bridges will increase the overall force of contraction.

Antagonistic muscle action

Muscles never work alone. They work in pairs or groups to produce co-ordinated movement. As the agonist shortens to create movement, the antagonist lengthens to co-ordinate the action. The fixator muscle stabilises one part of a body while another part moves.

It is important to understand the common muscle pairings for flexion at various joints, as shown in Table 1.1.4.

Table 1.1.4 The common antagonistic muscle pairings for flexion

Joint	Agonist	Antagonist
Wrist	Wrist flexors	Wrist extensors
Elbow	Biceps brachii	Triceps brachii
Shoulder	Anterior deltoid	Posterior deltoid
Hip	Iliopsoas	Gluteus maximus
Knee	Biceps femoris (hamstring group)	Rectus femoris (quadriceps group)
Ankle (dorsi-flexion)	Tibialis anterior	Gastrocnemius and soleus

> **Myosin and actin filaments**: proteins that form the contractile units of skeletal muscles.
>
> **Agonist**: a muscle responsible for creating movement at a joint. Also known as the prime mover.
>
> **Antagonist**: a muscle that opposes the agonist, providing a resistance for co-ordinated movement.
>
> **Fixator**: a muscle that stabilises one part of a body while another part moves.

Muscle contraction

A muscle uses energy to create force. Muscles create force by contracting. They can contract in the different ways shown in Table 1.1.5.

Table 1.1.5 Muscle contraction

Isotonic (changes length)	Concentric	Muscle shortens to produce tension, e.g. during the upward phase of a biceps curl, the biceps brachii concentrically contracts to lift weight
	Eccentric	Muscle lengthens to produce tension, e.g. during the downward phase of a biceps curl, the biceps brachii eccentrically contracts to lower weight
Isometric (does not change length)		Muscle contracts but does not change length and no movement is created, e.g. holding the press-up position still with arms and elbows extended

> **Exam tip**
>
> You need to be able to use all the information given so far to analyse different movements from sport. Always identify the joint type, articulating bones, movement pattern, agonist muscle, antagonist muscle and contraction type.
>
> Always refer to a joint when identifying a movement pattern, for example 'flexion at the shoulder'. 'Arm flexion' is too vague.

> **Revision activity**
>
> Choose a picture of an athlete playing football, hockey, netball or rugby. Complete a movement analysis of the knee, shoulder, hip, ankle, wrist and elbow. Refer to all the key points: joint type, articulating bones, movement pattern, agonist muscle, antagonist muscle and contraction type.

Quick quizzes at www.hoddereducation.co.uk/myrevisionnotesdownloads

Skeletal muscle contraction

REVISED

Skeletal muscle can only contract when stimulated by an electrical impulse sent from the central nervous system.

+ Motor neurons are specialised cells that transmit nerve impulses rapidly to a group of muscle fibres. They have a cell body in the brain or spinal cord with an extending axon that branches to connect motor end plates to a group of muscle fibres.
+ The motor neuron and its muscle fibres are termed the 'motor unit'.
+ Sending the nerve impulse to the muscle fibres is an electrochemical process that relies on a nerve action potential to conduct the nerve impulse as a wave of electrical charge down the axon to the end plates.
+ The point where the axon's motor end plates meet the muscle fibre is called the neuromuscular junction.
+ There is a small gap between the motor end plates and muscle fibre called the synaptic cleft. An action potential cannot cross a synaptic cleft without the neurotransmitter acetylcholine (ACh).
+ The neurotransmitter is secreted into the synaptic cleft to help the nerve impulse cross the gap.
+ If enough of the neurotransmitter is secreted and the electrical charge is above the threshold, a muscle action potential is created. This creates a wave of contraction down the muscle fibres.
+ If the stimulus is above the threshold, all the muscle fibres will give a complete contraction, but if the stimulus is below the threshold, none of the muscle fibres will contract at all. This is known as the all-or-none law.

Action potential: positive electrical charge inside the nerve and muscle cells that conducts the nerve impulse down the neuron and into the muscle fibre.

All-or-none law: depending on whether the stimulus is above the threshold, all the muscle fibres will give a complete contraction or no contraction at all.

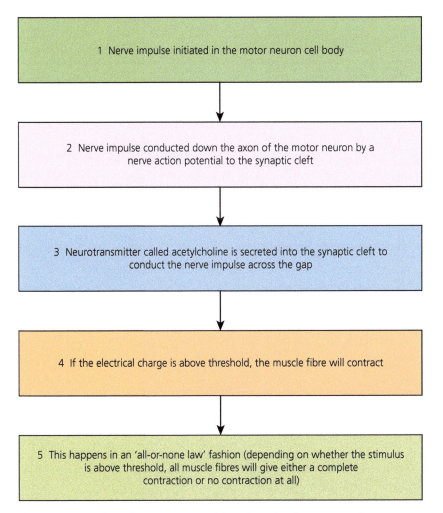

Figure 1.1.10 Flow diagram summarising the role of a motor unit

Muscle fibre type and exercise intensity

The strength of muscular contraction is dependent on the number of units recruited by the brain. The greater the number of motor units, the greater the force. As shown in Table 1.1.6, any one muscle contains three fibre types; the percentage of each fibre is dependent on genetics.

Table 1.1.6 The structural and functional characteristics of the three muscle fibre types

Fibre type	Slow oxidative	Fast oxidative glycolitic	Fast glycolitic
Structural characteristics			
Neuron size	Small	Large	Large
Fibres per neuron	Few	Many	Many
Capillary density	High	High	Low
Mitochondria density	High	Moderate	Low
Myoglobin density	High	Moderate	Low
Phosphocreatine store	Low	High	High
Functional characteristics			
Speed of contraction	Slow	Fast	Fast
Force of contraction	Low	High	High
Fatigue resistance	High	Moderate	Low
Aerobic capacity	High	Moderate	Low
Anaerobic capacity	Low	Moderate	High
Sporting application			
Highest percentage of fibres	Endurance athletes: + marathon + triathlon + cross-country skiing	High-intensity athletes: + 800–1500m + 200m freestyle	Explosive athletes: + 60–100m sprinting + javelin + long jump

Combining motor units and muscle fibre type indicates how the nervous system can produce movement for different activity requirements.
+ Small motor neurons stimulate relatively few muscle fibres. This is important for activities that require sustained muscle contraction, such as posture.
+ Large motor neurons stimulate many large muscle fibres. This is important for brief exertions of large force, such as jumping and throwing.

> **Revision activity**
>
> Using Table 1.1.6, copy out the information and colour code/add diagrams to help you learn it.

Muscle fibre type and recovery rates

Slow oxidative (SO) fibres
+ These are recruited and provide energy for sub-maximal aerobic work.
+ They contract intermittently to give overall low force of contraction.
+ Individual fibres will recover very quickly.

Application for training and recovery
+ 1:1 or 1:0.5 work:relief ratio, for example 3 minutes moderate-intensity running with relief of 90 seconds.
+ Training can be performed on a daily basis, as fibre damage is not associated with low-intensity training.
+ Low-intensity use of SO fibres is advised between heavy weight training sessions to increase blood flow and enhance the healing process.

Fast oxidative glycolytic (FOG) fibres
+ These are designed to produce a large amount of force quickly.
+ They have capacity to resist fatigue.

Application for training and recovery

+ They are more likely to be used in high-intensity activities lasting a few minutes, for example the 800 m.

Fast glycolytic (FG) fibres

+ These are recruited in the last 2–10 seconds of contraction when maximal efforts are needed quickly.
+ This will be accompanied by eccentric muscle fibre damage, which causes delayed onset muscle soreness (DOMS). This can be felt 24–48 hours after exercise and may worsen up to 72 hours after.

> **Delayed onset muscle soreness (DOMS):** pain and stiffness felt in the muscles, which peaks 24–72 hours after exercise, associated with eccentric muscle contraction.

Application for training and recovery

+ If fast glycolytic fibres have been used to exhaustion, they take 4–10 days to recover.
+ Maximal weight training sessions should leave 48 hours between using the same muscle group again.

> **Making links**
> + Consider the link between our muscle fibre types and the energy systems that are predominantly used (Chapter 1.1c, Energy for exercise).
> + Consider the recovery process and its impact on different muscle types (Chapter 1.1c, Energy for exercise).
> + These types of links are likely to feature in the 20-mark question at the end of Paper 1.

> **Now test yourself**   TESTED
>
> 1. Identify the agonist and antagonistic pairings for flexion in the:
>   a) wrist   d) hip
>   b) elbow   e) knee
>   c) shoulder   f) ankle (dorsi-flexion)
> 2. What are the three planes of movement and how do they divide the body?
> 3. What are the roles of the agonist, antagonist and fixator muscles?
> 4. What is the difference between concentric and eccentric muscle contraction?
> 5. What makes a motor unit?
> 6. Name the three types of muscle fibre.
> 7. State three structural characteristics of each muscle fibre type.
> 8. State three functional characteristics of each muscle fibre type.
>
> **Answers on p. 166**

> **Exam practice**
>
> 1. Ali kicks a football with her left foot. State the movement, at the ankle joint, of the striking foot at the point of contact and name the agonist muscle responsible for creating the movement. [2]
> 2. An athlete performs an upright row. Complete the table (A, B, C, D) for the athlete's shoulder joint while the bar is being raised. [4]
>
> | Joint | Joint type | Movement | Agonist | Antagonist | Type of muscular contraction |
> |---|---|---|---|---|---|
> | Shoulder | A | Abduction | B | C | D |
>
> 3. Explain the role of the triceps brachii in both the upward and downward phases of a press-up. [4]
> 4. Explain how a performer's mix of muscle fibre types might influence their reasons for choosing to take part in particular types of physical activity. [4]
> 5. Explain why a marathon runner predominantly uses slow oxidative muscle fibres. [4]
>
> **Answers on p. 175**

Knowledge and skills summary

By the end of this chapter, you should have the following knowledge (AO1):

- Joints, movements and muscles – including analysis of movement with reference to: joint type, movement produced, agonist and antagonist muscles involved, and type of muscle contraction taking place, at the:
  - shoulder
  - elbow
  - wrist
  - hip
  - knee
  - ankle.
- Planes of movement: frontal, transverse, sagittal.
- Roles of muscles: agonist, antagonist, fixator.
- Types of contraction: isotonic, concentric, eccentric, isometric.
- Structure and role of motor units in skeletal muscle contraction.
- Nervous stimulation of the motor unit: motor neuron, action potential, neurotransmitter, 'all-or-none' law.
- Muscle fibre types: slow oxidative, fast oxidative glycolytic, fast glycolytic.
- Recruitment of different fibre types during exercise of differing intensities and during recovery.

AO2 and AO3

- For application of knowledge (AO2), you may be asked to refer to muscle action or types of muscle fibre in specific practical examples.
- Sometimes you may be required to apply (AO2) your knowledge of the muscular system to another topic on the specification, for example explaining how the muscular system adapts after training.
- AO3 marks are for analysis or evaluation. In this topic an AO3 response may involve an analysis of reasons why different types of muscle fibre are used for different exercise intensities.

Quick quizzes at www.hoddereducation.co.uk/myrevisionnotesdownloads

1.1b Cardiovascular and respiratory systems

The cardiovascular system at rest

REVISED

The cardiovascular system refers to the heart, blood and blood vessels.

At the core is the heart, a dual pump moving blood through two separate circuits:
+ the pulmonary circuit
+ the systemic circuit.

> **Pulmonary circuit**: circulation of blood through the pulmonary artery to the lungs and pulmonary vein back to the heart.
>
> **Systemic circuit**: circulation of blood through the aorta to the body and vena cava back to the heart.

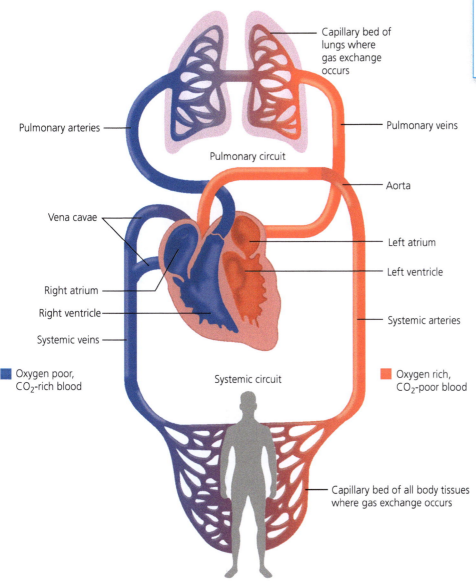

Figure 1.1.11 The heart: pulmonary and systemic circuits

The structure of the heart

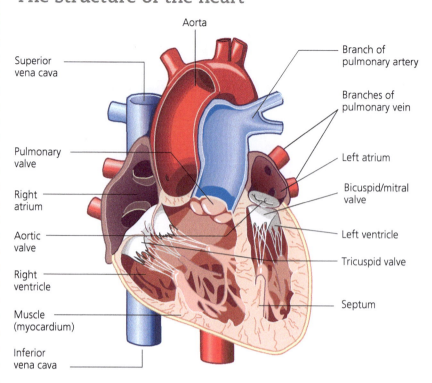

Figure 1.1.12 The structure of the heart

The left side of the cardiac muscle has a thicker wall than the right side, allowing it to forcefully contract to circulate oxygenated blood through the systemic system to the muscles and organs. The atrioventricular (bicuspid and tricuspid) valves and semilunar (aortic and pulmonary) valves prevent the backflow of blood. The right side of the heart circulates deoxygenated blood which enters the heart through the vena cava.

> **Oxygenated blood**: blood saturated with oxygen and nutrients, such as glucose.
>
> **Deoxygenated blood**: blood depleted of oxygen, saturated with carbon dioxide and waste products.

The path of blood through the heart

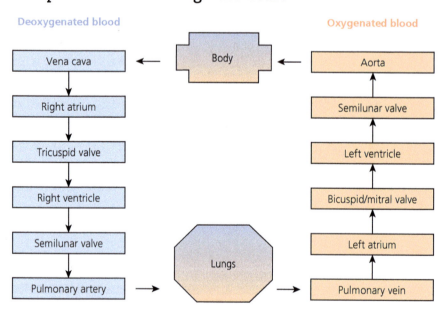

Figure 1.1.13 The pathway of blood

The conduction system

The cardiac muscle is myogenic. The conduction system is a set of five structures that pass the electrical impulse through the cardiac muscle:

1. SA node – this generates electrical impulses, causing the atria walls to contract. It is known as the 'pacemaker' and determines heart rate.
2. AV node – this collects the impulse and delays it by 0.1 seconds to allow the atria to finish contracting.
3. Bundle of His – located in the septum, this splits the impulse in two, ready to be distributed to the ventricles.
4. Bundle branches – these carry the impulses to the base of each ventricle.
5. Purkinje fibres – these distribute the impulse through the ventricle walls, causing them to contract.

> **Revision activity**
>
> Draw a flow diagram to help you learn the conduction system. Add small illustrations to each structure to create a visual learning medium or create a mnemonic to help you remember the order – SABBP.

Myogenic: the capacity of the heart to generate its own electrical impulse, which causes the cardiac muscle to contract.

Conduction system: a set of structures in the cardiac muscle that create and transmit an electrical impulse, forcing the atria and ventricles to contract.

Diastole: the relaxation phase of cardiac muscle where chambers fill with blood.

Systole: the contraction phase of cardiac muscle where blood is forcibly ejected into the aorta and pulmonary artery.

The cardiac cycle

The cardiac cycle refers to cardiac muscle contraction and the movement of blood through its chambers. One complete cardiac cycle is a single heartbeat. At rest, a complete cycle takes approximately 0.8 seconds. It has two phases, diastole and systole, as described in Table 1.1.7.

Table 1.1.7 Diastole and systole phases

Diastole (relaxation)	<ul><li>Relaxation of the atria and ventricles means lower pressure within the heart.</li><li>Blood then passively flows through the atria and into the ventricles.</li><li>AV valves are open, allowing blood to move freely from the atria to the ventricles.</li><li>Semilunar valves are closed at this time.</li></ul>
Systole (contraction)	**Atrial systole**<ul><li>Atria contract, forcing blood into the ventricles.</li></ul>**Ventricular systole**<ul><li>Ventricles contract.</li><li>AV valves close.</li><li>Semilunar valves open.</li><li>Blood is pushed out of the ventricles and into the large arteries leaving the heart.</li></ul>

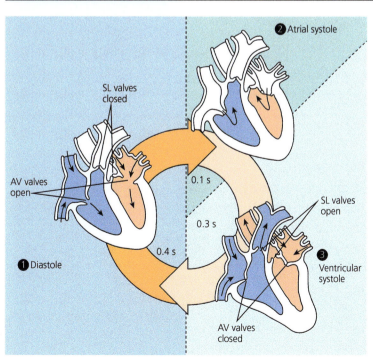

Figure 1.1.14 The stages of the cardiac cycle

Heart rate, stroke volume and cardiac output

Table 1.1.8 Definitions of HR, SV, CO, bradycardia and maximum heart rate

Key term	Definition	Typical resting value
Heart rate (HR)	The number of times the heart beats per minute	72 bpm
Stroke volume (SV)	The amount of blood ejected from the left ventricle per beat	70 ml
Cardiac output (CO)	The amount of blood ejected from the left ventricle per minute: HR × SV = CO	5 l/min
Bradycardia	A resting heart rate below 60 bpm	< 60 bpm
Maximum heart rate	Calculated by subtracting your age from 220	220 − age = HRmax (bpm)

Table 1.1.9 Comparison of HR, SV and CO of an untrained and trained individual at rest

	HR	SV	CO
Untrained	70–72 bpm	70 ml	5 l/min
Trained	50 bpm	100 ml	5 l/min

The cardiovascular system during exercise and recovery

REVISED

As we start to exercise, the demand for oxygen of the muscles increases rapidly. It is the role of the cardiovascular system to increase oxygenated blood flow to the muscles.

> **Exam tip**
>
> It can be helpful to include a sketch of a graph in an answer. Always label axes and take care to plot the resting value (not at zero).

Heart rate response to exercise

HR increases in proportion to the intensity of exercise until we reach HRmax, as shown in Figure 1.1.15.

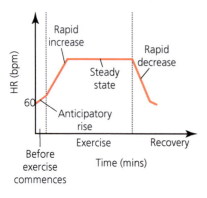
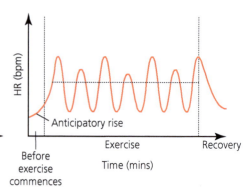

a) HR response to sub-maximal (aerobic) exercise

b) HR response to maximal (anaerobic) exercise

c) HR response to fluctuating intensities of exercise

Figure 1.1.15 HR response to exercise of different intensities

Stroke volume response to exercise

SV increases in proportion to exercise intensity until a plateau is reached at approximately 40–60% of working capacity. This corresponds to sub-maximal intensity exercise.

SV is able to increase due to:
+ increased venous return (due to skeletal muscle pump)
+ the Frank-Starling mechanism (Starling's law).

SV reaches a plateau during sub-maximal intensity because:
+ increased HR towards maximal intensities does not allow enough time for the ventricles to fill completely in the diastolic phase, limiting the Frank-Starling mechanism.

> **Exam tip**
>
> Knowledge of resting, sub-maximal and maximal values for HR, SV and CO will enable you to analyse, for example, the differences between untrained and trained performers when answering questions (AO3).

Sub-maximal: a low-to-moderate intensity of exercise within a performer's aerobic capacity.

Venous return: the return of the blood to the right atria through the veins.

Frank-Starling mechanism: increased venous return leads to increased SV, due to an increased stretch of the ventricular walls and therefore force of contraction.

Maximal: a high intensity of exercise above a performer's aerobic capacity that will induce fatigue.

Cardiac output response to exercise

CO increases in line with exercise intensity and plateaus during maximal exercise.

Table 1.1.10 Average HR, SV and CO at rest and during sub-maximal and maximal intensity exercise for an untrained performer

Untrained performer	Rest	Sub-maximal intensity	Maximal intensity
Heart rate	70–72 bpm	100–130 bpm	220 – age
Stroke volume	70 ml	100–120 ml	100–120 ml
Cardiac output	5 l/min	10–15 l/min	20–30 l/min

Table 1.1.11 HR, SV and CO at rest and during sub-maximal and maximal intensity exercise for a trained athlete

Trained athlete	Rest	Sub-maximal intensity	Maximal intensity
Heart rate	50 bpm	95–120 bpm	220 – age
Stroke volume	100 ml	160–200 ml	160–200 ml
Cardiac output	5 l/min	15–20 l/min	30–40 l/min

Heart rate, stroke volume and cardiac output in recovery

+ SV is maintained during the early stages of recovery as HR rapidly reduces. This will maintain blood flow and the removal of waste products while lowering the stress and workload on the cardiac muscle.
+ In recovery, there is a rapid decrease in CO followed by a slower decrease to resting levels.

Regulation of heart rate during exercise

When a situation arises where the heart rate needs to increase or decrease, the brain gets involved. This is known as cardiac control. The cardiac control centre (CCC) is:
+ controlled by the autonomic nervous system (ANS) and determines the firing of the SA node
+ located in the medulla oblongata of the brain
+ responsible for regulating the heart via motor nerves:
  + The sympathetic nervous system increases HR via the accelerator nerve.
  + The parasympathetic nervous system decreases HR via the vagus nerve.

Cardiac control centre (CCC): a control centre in the medulla oblongata responsible for HR regulation.

Sympathetic nervous system: part of the autonomic nervous system responsible for increasing HR, specifically during exercise.

Parasympathetic nervous system: part of the autonomic nervous system responsible for decreasing HR, specifically during recovery.

There are three factors that control the activity of the CCC: neural, intrinsic and hormonal, as shown in Table 1.1.12.

Table 1.1.12 Overview of neural, intrinsic and hormonal control of the CCC

Neural control	Proprioceptors	In muscles, tendons and joints, these inform the CCC that movement has increased.
	Chemoreceptors	Located in the aorta and carotid arteries, these detect a decrease in blood pH due to an increase of lactic acid and CO_2.
	Baroreceptors	Located in blood vessel walls, these inform the CCC of increased blood pressure.
Intrinsic control	Temperature	Changes will affect blood viscosity and the speed of nerve impulse transmission.
	Venous return	Changes will affect the stretch in ventricle walls, force of contraction and therefore SV.
Hormonal control	Adrenaline and noradrenaline	These are released from the adrenal glands and increase SV and HR.

The vascular system

The dense network of blood vessels and the blood they carry form the vascular system. Blood is approximately 45% cells and 55% plasma.

Blood vessels

Table 1.1.13 An overview of the blood vessels

Arteries and arterioles	Capillaries	Veins and venules
+ These carry oxygenated blood from the heart to muscles and organs. + They contain blood under high pressure. + They have a large layer of smooth muscle and elastic tissue. + Smooth muscle can **vasodilate** and **vasoconstrict**, regulating blood flow and pressure. + Arterioles have a ring of smooth muscle surrounding the capillary bed, called pre-capillary sphincters. These dilate and constrict to control blood flow.	+ Capillary walls are one cell thick. + This is where gas exchange takes place. Oxygen passes through the capillary wall and into the tissues; carbon dioxide passes from the tissues into the blood through the capillary wall.	+ These carry deoxygenated blood from the muscles and organs back to the heart. They have thin walls. + They have a smaller layer of smooth muscle, allowing them to **venodilate** and **venoconstrict**. + They contain blood under low pressure. + They have one-way pocket valves to prevent blood flowing backwards against gravity.

Venous return mechanisms

At rest, blood pressure and the structure of the veins maintain venous return. However, during exercise more oxygenated blood is needed, and therefore a far greater venous return is required to increase SV and CO. During exercise there are additional mechanisms that aid venous return:

+ Pocket valves – these are located within the veins and prevent the backflow of blood.
+ Smooth muscle – the wall of each vein contains smooth muscle that venoconstricts, helping push the blood back towards the heart.
+ Gravity – blood from the upper body, above the heart, is aided by gravity in its return to the heart.
+ Muscle pump – many veins are situated between skeletal muscles; during exercise they squeeze on the veins and help push the blood back towards the heart.
+ Respiratory pump – this helps return blood in the thoracic cavity and abdomen back to the heart. While exercising, we inspire and expire faster and more deeply; this rapidly changes the pressure within the thorax between high and low to help to squeeze the blood in the area back to the heart.

Vasodilation: widening of arteries, arterioles and pre-capillary sphincters.

Vasoconstriction: narrowing of arteries, arterioles and pre-capillary sphincters.

Venodilation: widening of the veins and venules.

Venoconstriction: narrowing of the veins and venules.

Quick quizzes at www.hoddereducation.co.uk/myrevisionnotesdownloads

Redistribution of cardiac output during exercise and recovery

Vascular shunt mechanism

As we start to exercise, our muscles demand more oxygen. Thus, blood flow is diverted to working muscles and away from non-essential organs. This is called the vascular shunt mechanism.

Table 1.1.14 How the vascular shunt mechanism works

At rest	During exercise
+ Arterioles to organs vasodilate, increasing blood flow. + Arterioles to muscles vasoconstrict to limit blood flow.	+ Arterioles to organs vasoconstrict, decreasing blood flow. + Arterioles to muscles vasodilate to increase blood flow.
+ Pre-capillary sphincters dilate, opening up the capillary beds to allow more blood flow to the organ cells. + Pre-capillary sphincters of capillary beds of muscle vasoconstrict.	+ Pre-capillary sphincters constrict, closing up the capillary beds to decrease blood flow to the organ cells. + Pre-capillary sphincters of capillary beds of muscle vasodilate.

Vasomotor control

- The vasomotor control centre (VCC) is located in the medulla oblongata of the brain.
- The smooth muscle in the walls of arterial blood vessels is always in a slight state of constriction, known as vasomotor tone.
- The VCC alters this level of stimulation sent to the arterioles and pre-capillary sphincters at different sites in the body, thus allowing the vascular shunt mechanism to operate.

The VCC receives information from:
- chemoreceptors – chemical changes such as CO_2 and lactic acid
- baroreceptors – pressure changes on arterial walls.

In response to this information, sympathetic stimulation is either increased or decreased.
- Increased sympathetic stimulation limits blood flow to an area.
- Decreased sympathetic stimulation increases blood flow to an area.

> **Vascular shunt mechanism**: the redistribution of cardiac output around the body from rest to exercise which increases the percentage of blood flow to the skeletal muscles.

> **Arterioles**: blood vessels carrying oxygenated blood from the arteries to the capillary beds, which can vasodilate and vasoconstrict to regulate blood flow.

> **Pre-capillary sphincters**: rings of smooth muscle at the junction between arterioles and capillaries, which can dilate or constrict to control blood flow through the capillary bed.

> **Vasomotor control centre (VCC)**: the control centre in the medulla oblongata responsible for cardiac output distribution.

> **Vasomotor tone**: the partial state of smooth muscle constriction in the arterial walls.

Now test yourself

TESTED

1. Name the two phases of the cardiac cycle.
2. Name, in order, the features through which the electrical impulse in the heart travels.
3. What is meant by the term 'myogenic'?
4. Define heart rate, stroke volume and cardiac output, and state resting values for both trained and untrained performers.
5. Sketch a graph showing the heart rate response to sub-maximal exercise.
6. Sketch a graph showing the heart rate response to maximal exercise.
7. Where are the CCC and VCC located?
8. Which factors affect the activity of the CCC?
9. Name the five mechanisms of venous return.

Answers on p. 166

The respiratory system at rest and during exercise

The respiratory system has two main functions:
1 Pulmonary ventilation – breathing of air into the lungs (inspiration) and out of the lungs (expiration).
2 Gaseous exchange:
   a) External respiration – exchange of O_2 and CO_2 between the lungs and blood.
   b) Internal respiration – exchange of O_2 and CO_2 between blood and the muscle tissues (cells).

> **Gaseous exchange**: the movement of oxygen from the alveoli into the bloodstream and carbon dioxide from the bloodstream into the alveoli.
>
> **Alveoli**: clusters of tiny air sacs covered in a dense network of capillaries which together serve as the external site for gaseous exchange.

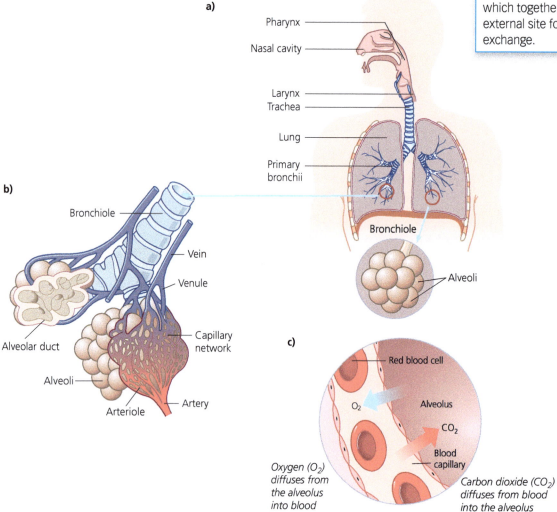

Figure 1.1.16 The respiratory system: a) the pathway of air through the respiratory organs, b) the dense capillary network on the surface of the alveoli, and c) gaseous exchange at the alveolar-capillary site

Gas transport

Table 1.1.15 How O_2 and CO_2 are transported

Gas	How is it transported?
O_2	97% in haemoglobin (HbO_2)
	3% in blood plasma
CO_2	70% dissolved in water carried as carbonic acid
	23% in haemoglobin ($HbCO_2$)
	7% dissolved in blood plasma

Quick quizzes at www.hoddereducation.co.uk/myrevisionnotesdownloads

Breathing rate, tidal volume and minute ventilation

Table 1.1.16 Overview of breathing rate, tidal volume and minute ventilation

Key term	Definition	Resting value (untrained)	Maximal value (untrained)	Resting value (trained)	Maximal value (trained)
Breathing rate (f)	The number of inspirations or expirations per minute	12–15 breaths/min	40–50 breaths/min	11–12 breaths/min	50–60 breaths/min
Tidal volume (TV)	The volume of air inspired or expired per breath	500 ml	2.5–3 litres	500 ml	3–3.5 litres
Minute ventilation (VE)	The volume of air inspired or expired per minute: VE = TV × f	6–7.5 l/min	100–150 l/min	5.5–6 l/min	160–210 l/min

During exercise

+ Breathing rate increases in proportion to exercise intensity up to a maximum of 50–60 breaths per minute.
+ Tidal volume increases initially in proportion to exercise intensity at sub-maximal intensities up to approximately 3 litres.
+ Minute ventilation increases in line with exercise intensity. During sustained sub-maximal intensity exercise, minute ventilation can plateau as we reach a comfortable steady state.

Mechanics of breathing at rest and during exercise

Table 1.1.17 Overview of inspiration and expiration

	At rest	During exercise
Inspiration	**Active process** + External intercostal muscles between the ribs contract, pulling the chest walls up and out. + The diaphragm muscle below the lungs contracts and flattens, increasing the size of the chest.	**Active process** + In addition to the external intercostal muscles and diaphragm: 　+ the sternocleidomastoid lifts the sternum 　+ the scalene and pectoralis minor contract and lift the ribs more. + Effect – the volume of the thoracic cavity increases, creating a larger concentration gradient between inside the lungs and outside the body, therefore more air enters the lungs more quickly.
Expiration	**Passive process** + External intercostal muscles between the ribs relax so that the chest walls move in and down. + The diaphragm muscle below the lungs relaxes and bulges up, reducing the size of the chest.	**Active process** + In addition to the external intercostal muscles and diaphragm: 　+ the internal intercostal muscles contract and pull the ribs down and in 　+ the rectus abdominus contracts and pushes the diaphragm up. + Effect – a decrease in the volume of the thoracic cavity increases pressure in the lungs, therefore air is forced out quickly because of the larger concentration gradient.

Respiratory regulation

Breathing rate and depth is continually adjusted to maintain the appropriate levels of O_2 and CO_2. The respiratory control centre (RCC) located in the medulla oblongata is responsible for respiratory regulation.

There are two centres within the RCC, the inspiratory centre (IC) and the expiratory centre (EC):
+ The IC stimulates inspiratory muscles to contract at rest and during exercise.
+ The EC is inactive at rest, but will stimulate additional expiratory muscles to contract during exercise.

Respiratory regulation at rest

At rest, the IC is responsible for the rhythmic cycle of breathing. Nerve impulses are generated and stimulate the inspiratory muscles, causing them to contract, via the:
+ intercostal nerve to the external intercostals
+ phrenic nerve to the diaphragm.

Respiratory regulation during exercise

Sensory nerves relay information to the RCC where a response is initiated by the IC and EC. The RCC receives information as shown in Table 1.1.18.

Table 1.1.18 Overview of how the RCC receives information

Chemical control	Chemoreceptors	Located in the aorta and carotid arteries; detect changes in blood acidity, increases in CO_2, decreases in O_2
Neural control	Thermoreceptors	Inform of increases in blood temperature
	Proprioceptors	Inform of motor activity in the muscles and joints
	Baroreceptors	Located in the lung tissue and bronchioles; inform of the state of lung inflation

Gaseous exchange

Gaseous exchange is the exchange of oxygen and carbon dioxide by the process of diffusion:
+ Diffusion is the movement of gas from an area of high pressure to an area of low pressure.
+ The difference between the high and low pressure is called the diffusion gradient.
+ The larger the gradient, the larger the diffusion/gaseous exchange that takes place.

Partial pressure (pp) is the pressure a gas exerts within a mixture of gases. Gas always moves from areas of high partial pressure to areas of low partial pressure.
+ pO_2 = partial pressure of oxygen
+ pCO_2 = partial pressure of carbon dioxide

> **Exam tip**
>
> Intercostals is not acceptable as an answer. You need to be more specific: external intercostals for inspiration and internal intercostals for expiration.

> **Exam tip**
>
> Don't forget to state whether inspiration is a passive or active process. This is often given as a mark in the exam.

Gaseous exchange at rest

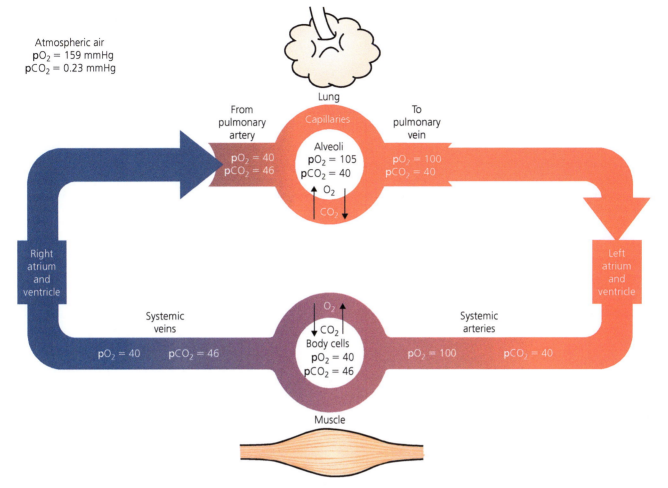

Figure 1.1.17 Resting partial pressures of oxygen (pO_2) and carbon dioxide (pCO_2) at various sites of the body

External respiration
External respiration is the exchange of gases at the lungs between the deoxygenated blood that arrives in capillaries and the oxygen-rich atmospheric air held in the alveoli:
- Oxygen moves from high pp in the alveoli to low pp in capillary blood down the diffusion gradient (alveoli pO_2 105 – capillary pO_2 40 = 65 mmHg).
- Carbon dioxide moves from high pp in capillary blood to low pp in the alveoli down the diffusion gradient (capillary pCO_2 46 – alveoli pCO_2 40 = 6 mmHg).

Internal respiration
Internal respiration is the exchange of gases at the muscle cells between the oxygenated blood that arrives in the capillaries and the carbon dioxide-producing muscle cells. Haemoglobin molecules dissociate (release) the O_2 as they pass the muscle cells.
- Oxygen moves from high pp in capillary blood to low pp in the muscle cell down the diffusion gradient (capillary pO_2 100 – muscle cell pO_2 40 = 60 mmHg).
- Carbon dioxide moves from high pp in the muscle cell to low pp in capillary blood down the diffusion gradient (muscle cell pCO_2 46 – capillary pCO_2 40 = 6 mmHg).

Gaseous exchange during exercise

External respiration
During exercise, muscle tissues use a greater volume of O_2 and produce a greater volume of CO_2. This means that the deoxygenated blood that returns to the lungs has a lower pO_2 and a higher pCO_2 than at rest:
+ The O_2 diffusion gradient steepens and O_2 diffuses from high pO_2 in the alveoli to lower pO_2 in capillary blood.
+ The CO_2 diffusion gradient steepens and CO_2 diffuses from high pCO_2 in capillary blood to lower pCO_2 in the alveoli.

Internal respiration
The more intense the exercise, the more the muscle tissue's demand for oxygen will increase. Therefore, the more intense the exercise, the lower the pO_2 and the higher the pCO_2 in the muscle tissue:
+ The O_2 diffusion gradient steepens and O_2 diffuses from high pO_2 in capillary blood to lower pO_2 in the muscle cell.
+ The CO_2 diffusion gradient steepens and CO_2 diffuses from high pCO_2 in the muscle cell to lower pCO_2 in capillary blood.

Dissociation of oxygen from haemoglobin
+ The oxyhaemoglobin dissociation curve informs us of the amount of haemoglobin saturated with oxygen.
+ Oxygen unloading from haemoglobin is termed dissociation.
+ Haemoglobin fully loaded with oxygen is described as being saturated (each haemoglobin molecule can carry up to 4 molecules of O_2).

> **Oxyhaemoglobin dissociation curve**: a graph showing the relationship between pO_2 and percentage saturation of haemoglobin.
>
> **Dissociation**: the release of oxygen from haemoglobin for gaseous exchange.

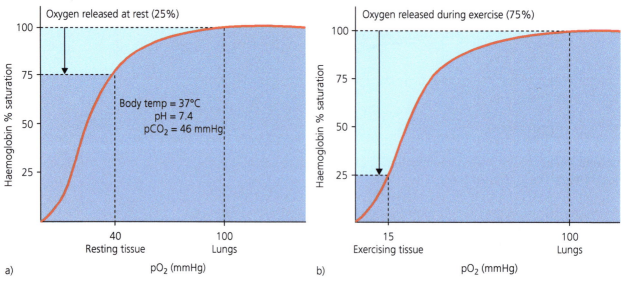

Figure 1.1.18 Oxyhaemoglobin dissociation curve showing the relationship between the pO_2 and % saturation of haemoglobin a) at rest and b) during exercise

> **Worked example**
>
> At rest the pO_2 in the muscles is 40 mmHg. Trace your finger upwards on the dotted line starting at 40 in Figure 1.1.18a). Stop when you reach the red curve. Trace your finger horizontally towards the y axis. Here you can see that in the muscles at rest, haemoglobin is 75% saturated (25% dissociated).
>
> Repeat this process for:
> + the lungs at rest (pO_2 100 mmHg) – identify saturation levels
> + the muscles during exercise (pO_2 15 mmHg) – identify saturation levels
> + the lungs during exercise (pO_2 100 mmHg) – identify saturation levels.
>
> Can you explain why the values differ?

The Bohr shift

In addition to the pO_2 lowering, there are three other effects of exercise that increase the dissociation of O_2 from haemoglobin. These effects move the oxyhaemoglobin dissociation curve to the right. This is known as the Bohr shift.

The effects are:
1 increase in blood and muscle temperature
2 increase in pp of carbon dioxide (raising pCO_2)
3 increase in production of lactic acid and carbonic acid (lowering pH).

> **Bohr shift**: a move in the oxyhaemoglobin dissociation curve to the right caused by increased acidity in the bloodstream.

Impact on performance

+ At any given pO_2 for exercising muscle tissue, the percentage saturation of oxyhaemoglobin is far lower and therefore dissociation of O_2 to respiring tissues is greater.
+ This enhances the volume of O_2 available for diffusion and therefore aerobic energy production for exercise.

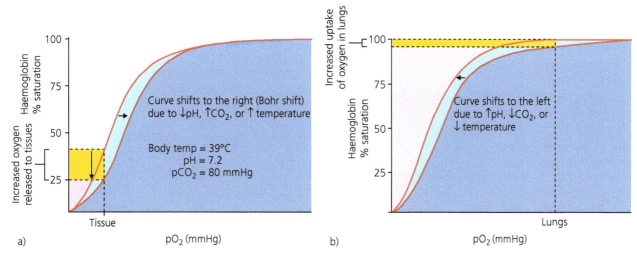

Figure 1.1.19 Oxyhaemoglobin dissociation curve showing the relationship between the pO_2 and % saturation of haemoglobin a) at the Bohr shift and b) in recovery

> **Making links**
> + Consider the links between extreme heat, heart rate and the dissociation of oxygen from haemoglobin (Chapter 1.1b, Cardiovascular and respiratory systems).
> + Consider the links between extended periods of training and the impact on the cardiovascular and respiratory systems and how they function (Chapter 1.1b, Cardiovascular and respiratory systems).

> **Now test yourself** TESTED
>
> 10 Define breathing rate, tidal volume and minute ventilation, and state how these change from rest to exercise.
> 11 Describe the differences between the mechanics of breathing at rest and during exercise for inspiration.
> 12 Describe the differences between the mechanics of breathing at rest and during exercise for expiration.
> 13 How does the RCC receive information?
> 14 What is partial pressure?
> 15 What is the diffusion gradient?
> 16 What is the Bohr shift?
>
> Answers on pp. 166–167

> ### Exam practice
>
> 1. Describe how the heart's conduction system controls the contraction and relaxation phases of the cardiac cycle. [5]
> 2. Explain how neural factors control heart rate at the start of exercise. [3]
> 3. Outline how oxygen is transported in the blood. [2]
> 4. Describe the process of oxygen diffusion at the alveoli during exercise. [3]
> 5. Describe the mechanics of expiration during exercise. [4]
> 6. Explain how redistribution of blood occurs during exercise. [3]
>
> **Answers on pp. 175–176**

Knowledge and skills summary

By the end of this chapter, you should have the following knowledge (AO1):

- Cardiovascular system at rest.
- Relationship between and resting values for: heart rate, stroke volume, cardiac output; methods of calculating these.
- Cardiac cycle: diastole, systole.
- Conduction system of the heart linked to the cardiac cycle.
- Cardiovascular system during exercise of differing intensities and during recovery.
- Effects of different exercise intensities and recovery on: heart rate, stroke volume, cardiac output; methods of calculating these.
- Redistribution of cardiac output during exercise of differing intensities and during recovery:
  - vascular shunt mechanism
  - role of the vasomotor centre
  - role of arterioles
  - role of pre-capillary sphincters.
- Mechanisms of venous return during exercise of differing intensities and during recovery.
- Regulation of heart rate during exercise: neural factors, hormonal factors, intrinsic factors.
- Respiratory system at rest.
- Relationship between resting values for: breathing frequency, tidal volume, minute ventilation; methods of calculating these.
- Mechanics of breathing at rest and the muscles involved: diaphragm, external intercostals, at the alveoli, at the muscles.
- Respiratory system during exercise of differing intensities and during recovery.
- Effects of differing intensities of exercise and recovery on: breathing frequency, tidal volume, minute ventilation.
- Mechanics of breathing during exercise of differing intensities and during recovery, including additional muscles involved.
- Regulation of breathing during exercise of differing intensities and during recovery; neural control, chemical control.
- Effect of differing intensities of exercise and recovery on gas exchange at the alveoli and at the muscles.
- Changes in diffusion gradient.
- Changes in dissociation of oxyhaemoglobin.

AO2 and AO3

- AO2 marks will ask for application of this knowledge, for example how exercise affects heart rate or blood flow, or application to aerobic events such as the triathlon.
- Sometimes you may be required to apply (AO2) your knowledge of the cardiovascular and respiratory systems to another topic on the specification, for example explaining how training at altitude can affect both systems (Chapter 1.1d).
- In this topic an AO3 response may involve an analysis of reasons why venous return changes during exercise and how these changes affect performance.

1.1c Energy for exercise

Adenosine triphosphate (ATP)

REVISED

- ATP is made up of one adenosine and three phosphate groups held together by bonds of chemical energy. This compound is the only immediately usable form of energy stored in our bodies. It is often called the 'energy currency' of the body.
- ATP is readily available as it is stored in the muscle cell.
- The energy is stored in the bond between the last two phosphate groups. When this bond is broken down by the enzyme ATPase, energy is released that can be used to make the muscle cell contract and cause movement:

    ATP → ADP (adenosine diphosphate) + P (phosphate) + energy

- This is a coupled reaction – it can be broken down and resynthesised, then broken down and resynthesised, and so on:
    - breakdown of ATP: ATP → ADP + P + energy
    - resynthesis of ATP: ADP + P + energy → ATP
- The only problem is that our body can only store a very small amount of ATP (85 g) – enough to last about 2 seconds.
- To maintain exercise beyond 2 seconds, ATP has to be resynthesised.

> **Coupled reaction**: where products of one reaction are used in another reaction.

ATP resynthesis

REVISED

- Depending on the intensity of the exercise, this is achieved by three energy systems: ATP/PC, glycolytic or aerobic.
- Energy systems do not work in isolation (separately).
- The amount of ATP resynthesised by each system will depend purely on the intensity of the exercise and two systems can be working at the same time.

Energy systems

Table 1.1.19 gives the key descriptors, strengths and weaknesses of each energy system.

Table 1.1.19 Overview of energy systems

	ATP/PC system	**Glycolytic system**	**Aerobic system**
Type of reaction (anaerobic/aerobic)	Anaerobic	Anaerobic	Aerobic
Chemical or food fuel used	Phosphocreatine (PC)	Glycogen/glucose	Glycogen/glucose or fat
Site of reaction	Sarcoplasm	Sarcoplasm	Stage 1 = Sarcoplasm Stage 2 = Krebs cycle – matrix Stage 3 = Cristae
Controlling enzymes	Creatine kinase	+ Glycogen phosphorylase (GPP) + Phosphofructokinase (PFK) + Lactate dehydrogenase (LDH)	+ Phosphofructokinase + Acetyl CoA
Energy yield	1 mole of ATP	2 moles of ATP	38 moles of ATP
Specific stages of system	+ PC → P + C + energy (exothermic) + energy + ADP + P → ATP (endothermic)	+ Glucose undergoes anaerobic glycolysis + Pyruvic acid/without O_2 → lactic acid	+ Aerobic glycolysis + Krebs cycle + Electron transport chain
Energy equations	+ PC → P + C + energy + energy + ADP + P → ATP	$C_6H_{12}O_6 \rightarrow 2C_3H_6O_6$	$C_6H_{12}O_6 + 6O_2 \rightarrow 6CO_2 + 6H_2O$ + energy

Table 1.1.19 continued

	ATP/PC system	Glycolytic system	Aerobic system
By-products formed	None	Lactic acid	$CO_2 + H_2O$
Intensity of activity	Very high intensity	High intensity	Low–moderate/sub-maximal intensity
Duration of system	2–10 seconds	Up to 3 minutes	3 minutes onwards
Strengths	+ No delay for O_2 + PC readily available in muscle cell + Simple and rapid breakdown of PC + Provides energy quickly + No fatiguing by-products	+ No delay for O_2 + Large fuel stores in liver, muscles and bloodstream + Provides energy for high-intensity activities for up to 3 minutes + Lactic acid can be recycled into fuel for further energy production	+ Large fuels: triglycerides, free fatty acids (FFAs), glycogen and glucose + High ATP yield and long duration of energy production + No fatiguing by-products
Weaknesses	Low ATP yield and small PC stores lead to rapid fatigue after 8–10 seconds	+ Fatiguing by-product lactic acid reduces pH and enzyme activity + Relatively low ATP yield and recovery can be lengthy	+ Delay for oxygen delivery and complex series of reactions + Slow energy production limits activity to sub-maximal intensity + FFAs demand 15% more O_2 for breakdown

> **Making links**
>
> + Consider how the predominant energy system can be linked to the training methods used when designing a programme (Chapter 1.2b, Preparation and training methods).
> + Consider how the use of energy systems affects the types of muscle fibre that are engaged (Chapter 1.1a, Skeletal and muscular systems).

> **Exam tip**
>
> Abbreviations for controlling enzymes, e.g. GPP, may not be accepted in an exam. Try to learn the full name, including the correct spelling.

Energy continuum

Intensity and duration of exercise

When we exercise, our energy systems do not work in isolation. Each energy system contributes to the overall energy production. How much each system contributes depends on the intensity and duration of the activity. This is referred to as the energy continuum.

> **Energy continuum**: the relative contribution of each energy system to overall energy production, depending on the intensity and duration of the activity.

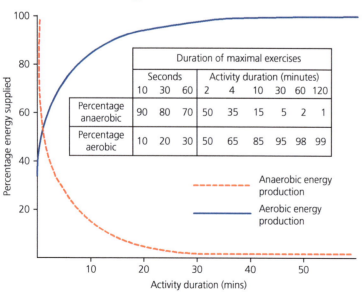

Duration of maximal exercises								
	Seconds			Activity duration (minutes)				
	10	30	60	2	4	10	30	60	120
Percentage anaerobic	90	80	70	50	35	15	5	2	1
Percentage aerobic	10	20	30	50	65	85	95	98	99

Figure 1.1.20 The relative contribution of aerobic and anaerobic energy production over time

Quick quizzes at www.hoddereducation.co.uk/myrevisionnotesdownloads

Intermittent exercise
+ An example of intermittent exercise is a rugby player who is required to alternate between various modes of activity such as standing, walking, running, sprinting, tackling and jumping.
+ Research has shown this type of exercise to have varying physiological demands as the player switches from one energy system's predominance to another.

Intermittent exercise: activity where the intensity alternates, either during interval training between work and relief intervals or during a game with breaks of play and changes of intensity.

Energy system thresholds
+ The threshold of any energy system is the point at which that energy system is unable to provide energy and therefore energy production switches to another system.
+ For example, the threshold of the PC system is the point at which PC can no longer provide energy to the working muscles. This threshold is about 10 seconds.

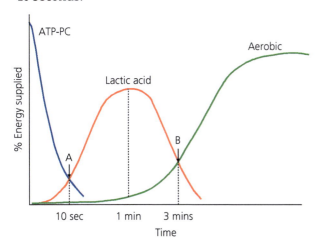

A = ATP-PC LA threshold
The point at which the ATP-PC energy system is exhausted and the lactic acid system prevails

B = LA O_2 threshold
The point at which the lactic acid system is exhausted and the aerobic system takes over

Figure 1.1.21 The percentage of energy supplied by each energy system over time

Revision activity

Note down the relative contributions of the various energy systems for your practical activity.

Recovery periods
+ Predominantly anaerobic activities, such as basketball and netball, rely heavily on ATP-PC and glycolytic energy systems.
+ Although **PC stores** deplete quickly, they are also replenished quickly: **50% in 30 seconds, 100% in 3 minutes**.
+ Oxygen stored in myoglobin can be fully replenished in 3 minutes.
+ Blood lactate levels can rise dramatically with prolonged high-intensity activity.
+ Correct **work:relief ratios** and sufficient oxygen supply allow lactic acid to be broken down and removed.
+ Time-outs and quarter- and half-time breaks aid recovery.
+ Recovery periods also allow for rehydration and glycogen replacement.

Myoglobin: a protein molecule that, similarly to haemoglobin, helps with the transport of oxygen.

VO_2max: maximum volume of oxygen inspired, transported and utilised per minute during exhaustive exercise.

Making links

Consider how the different training methods will impact the recovery process; work:relief ratios link closely with the energy system used (Chapter 1.2b, Preparation and training methods).

Fitness level
+ Once blood lactate values go **above 4mmol/l**, the **onset of blood lactate accumulation (OBLA)** has been reached.
+ OBLA will vary depending on the aerobic fitness of the performer:
  + In **untrained** individuals, this may occur at about **50% of their** VO_2max.

+ In **highly trained** individuals, this may occur at about **85% of VO$_2$max**. This is due to their increased ability to tolerate lactic acid and to remove waste products and supply oxygen to working muscles (buffering capacity).

Other factors that may contribute to the relative contribution of the energy systems include:
+ position of the player
+ tactics and strategies used
+ level of competition
+ structure of the game.

> **Now test yourself** TESTED
>
> 1 What is ATP?
> 2 Why do we need to resynthesise ATP?
> 3 Name the three energy systems that provide energy for the resynthesis of ATP.
> 4 Name the three stages of the aerobic energy system.
> 5 What is the energy continuum?
>
> Answers on p. 167

The recovery process

REVISED

To help the body return to its pre-exercise state, energy is required. Continued aerobic energy production fulfils this additional energy requirement. This is termed excess post-exercise oxygen consumption (EPOC). Recovery (EPOC) takes place in two stages:
1 fast (alactacid) component of recovery
2 slow (lactacid) component of recovery.

> **Excess post-exercise oxygen consumption (EPOC):** the volume of oxygen consumed post-exercise to return the body to a pre-exercise state.

Tables 1.1.20 and 1.1.21 detail what happens during the two stages of the recovery process.

Table 1.1.20 Fast alactacid component – first stage of recovery

Fast alactacid component	First stage of recovery – up to 3 minutes after exercise
Phosphocreatine (PC) stores restored	+ 3 minutes – PC stores to fully recover + 30 seconds for 50% of the recovery, 75% in 60 seconds + The process requires approximately 3–4 litres of oxygen
Replenishment of blood and muscle oxygen	Within the first minute, oxygen resaturates the bloodstream, associating with haemoglobin, and within 3 minutes restoring the oxymyoglobin link in the muscle cells.

Table 1.1.21 Slow lactacid component – second stage of recovery

Slow lactacid component	Second stage of recovery – from 3 minutes up to 24 hours after exercise
Elevated ventilation and circulation	Post-exercise respiratory rate, depth and HR remain elevated. These gradually decrease to resting levels to maximise the delivery of O$_2$ and the removal of by-products.
Elevated body temperature	Post-exercise elevated temperature increases metabolic rate, accounting for 60–70% of the slow lactacid component of EPOC.
Removal of lactic acid	Lactic acid is removed from the body. It can be removed in four ways: + 50–75% is converted back to pyruvic acid and enters the Krebs cycle; it is used in aerobic metabolism. + Approximately 10–25% can be converted back to glucose and glycogen (processes known as gluconeogenesis and glyconeogenesis). + It can be converted into proteins by the Cori cycle. + It can be removed via sweating and in urine. Lactate removal takes on average 1 hour, although it can take up to 24 hours.

> **Exam tip**
>
> Don't get the two components of recovery the wrong way around. The fast stage deals with restoring the body; the slow stage deals with removing waste products and getting the body back to normal.

Implications of recovery for training

At an elite level, each athlete's recovery is individually designed following these general principles:

1. **Warm-up** – this will minimise time spent using anaerobic energy systems, reducing oxygen deficit.
2. **Active recovery** – this maintains respiratory rate and HR, speeding up removal of lactic acid.
3. **Cooling aids** – these can be used post-event to speed up lactic acid removal and to reduce muscle soreness and DOMS.
4. **Intensity of training** – high-intensity training will: a) increase muscle mass, ATP and PC storage, boosting efficiency of the fast component; b) increase tolerance to lactic acid, increasing buffering capacity; and c) delay OBLA, reducing demand on the slow component. Low–moderate intensity will increase aerobic capacity, delaying OBLA, and maximise oxygen delivery during EPOC.
5. **Work:relief ratios** – based on the predominant energy system required in a physical activity, training intensity and the correct work:relief ratio can maximise recovery: a) speed/explosive strength 1:3+; b) lactate tolerance and high-intensity muscular endurance 1:2; c) aerobic capacity and endurance 1:0.5.
6. **Strategies and tactics** – time-outs and substitutions should be used. Lower-intensity set plays can delay OBLA and fatigue.
7. **Nutrition** – correct pre-event, during the event and post-event nutrition can help maximise fuel stores, delay fatigue, reduce lactic acid accumulation and speed up recovery.

> **Exam tip**
>
> It is worth considering the advantages/disadvantages and practicalities of the implications of recovery. If you can critically analyse these, you will be able to score highly in AO3.

> **Now test yourself** TESTED
>
> 6 Describe what is meant by an energy system threshold.
> 7 What does the abbreviation OBLA stand for and at what blood lactate level is this reached?
> 8 Outline the two stages of recovery.
> 9 What seven things should an athlete consider in order to maximise recovery?
>
> **Answers on p. 167**

> **Exam practice**
>
> 1 Explain the role of ATP. [3]
> 2 Explain the principle of a coupled reaction, giving an example. [4]
> 3 Evaluate the use of anaerobic energy systems to resynthesise ATP. [6]
>
> **Answers on p. 176**

Knowledge and skills summary

By the end of this chapter, you should have the following knowledge (AO1):

- ATP as 'energy currency'.
- The principle of energetically coupled reactions: breakdown of ATP to ADP (adenosine diphosphate) + P (phosphate).
- Resynthesis of ATP from ADP + P.
- Energy systems: ATP-PC (phosphocreatine) system, glycolytic system, aerobic system; for each system: type of reaction (aerobic or anaerobic), chemical or food fuel used, specific site of the reaction, controlling enzyme, ATP yield, specific stages within the system, by-products.
- How the energy continuum works, with the different energy systems being predominant during different types of exercise.
- The interplay of energy systems during intermittent exercise and factors that affect this interplay: intensity of exercise, duration of exercise, recovery periods and fitness levels.
- The recovery process.
- Excess post-exercise oxygen consumption (EPOC); fast components of EPOC, the processes that occur and the duration; slow components of EPOC.
- The effect of exercise intensity on EPOC and implications of the recovery process for planning exercise or training sessions.

AO2 and AO3

- An example of AO2 marks is applying the energy systems and implications of recovery to practical examples or physical activity.
- Sometimes you may be required to apply (AO2) your knowledge of energy systems to another topic on the specification, for example explaining how training methods can be adapted to suit a predominant energy system.
- In this chapter an AO3 response may involve an analysis of how an athlete should consider their recovery to improve performance.

Quick quizzes at www.hoddereducation.co.uk/myrevisionnotesdownloads

1.1d Environmental effects on body systems

Exercise at altitude

REVISED

Differing environmental conditions affect the efficiency of the cardiovascular and respiratory systems and can dramatically affect the performance and even the health of athletes and spectators. Athletes and coaches must prepare for these conditions and alter strategies to ensure peak performance.

Effect of altitude on the cardiovascular and respiratory systems

+ As altitude increases, barometric pressure decreases.
+ Even though the composition of air stays the same, the partial pressure of oxygen (pO_2) decreases, which has a severe impact on performance.
+ The greater the diffusion gradient, the faster oxygen will move from one area to another.
+ The greater the altitude, the greater the negative impact on the diffusion gradient.

Table 1.1.22 details partial pressures of oxygen and diffusion gradients at different altitudes.

Altitude: the height or elevation of an area above sea level.

Barometric pressure: the pressure exerted by the Earth's atmosphere at any given point.

Table 1.1.22 Partial pressures of oxygen and diffusion gradients at different altitudes

Sea level pO_2 = 159 mmHg	Diffusion gradient of 119 to capillary blood
3600 m above sea level pO_2 = 105 mmHg	Diffusion gradient of 65 to capillary blood (45% reduction)
8800 m above sea level pO_2 = 43 mmHg	Diffusion gradient of 3 to capillary blood

If an athlete competes at high altitude:
+ The rate of oxygen diffusion decreases, reducing haemoglobin saturation and resulting in poor transport of O_2. As a result:
  + Blood volume decreases – plasma volume decreases by 25% to allow increase in density of red blood cells (RBCs).
  + SV decreases, which increases HR.
  + Maximal CO, SV and HR decrease during maximum-intensity exercise.
+ **Impact** – there is a reduction in aerobic capacity and VO_2max, adversely affecting the intensity and duration at which an athlete can perform.

> **Exam tip**
>
> When referring to partial pressures, remember to include units (mmHg – millimetres of mercury).

Acclimatisation

Altitude starts to have an effect around 1500 m, and although different people acclimatise at different speeds, guidelines allow:
+ 3–5 days for low-altitude performance (1000–2000 m)
+ 1–2 weeks for moderate-altitude performance (2000–3000 m)
+ 2+ weeks for high altitude performance (3000 m+); athletes going above 3000 m should sleep no more than 300 m higher each day and have regular rest days to prevent altitude sickness
+ 4+ weeks for extreme altitude performance (5000–5500 m); for example, a climber will spend one month at base camp before making a summit attempt on Everest.

Acclimatisation benefits for the cardiovascular and respiratory systems are:
+ an increase in red blood cell production, due to increased release of erythropoietin (EPO)

Acclimatisation: a process of gradual adaptation to a change in environment (for example lower pO_2 at altitude).

Erythropoietin: a naturally produced hormone responsible for producing red blood cells.

- stabilisation of breathing rate and ventilation, although they remain elevated at rest, compared to at sea level
- reduction of SV and CO as O_2 extraction becomes more efficient
- reduced incidence of altitude sickness, headaches, breathlessness, poor sleep and lack of appetite.

> **Revision activity**
>
> Create a revision card detailing how to acclimatise for different altitudes. Use different colours for the different altitudes (see above) and include diagrams.

Exercise in the heat

REVISED

- The process of maintaining internal core temperature is called thermoregulation.
- Thermoreceptors deep in the core sense a change in body temperature.
- If core temperature rises, metabolic heat is transported by the circulating blood to the surface of the body and released mostly by convection and evaporation (sweat).
- An athlete exercising in the heat can lose around 2–3 litres of sweat per hour.
- Loss of sweat decreases blood volume and causes dehydration.
- The rate of heat loss through sweating is affected by humidity.

> **Thermoregulation**: the process of maintaining internal core temperature.
>
> **Thermoreceptors**: sensory receptors that sense a change in temperature and relay information to the brain.
>
> **Dehydration**: loss of water from body tissues, largely caused by sweating.
>
> **Humidity**: the amount of water vapour in the atmospheric air.

> **Exam tip**
>
> Remember: low humidity increases sweating; high humidity decreases sweating and the cooling process.

Hyperthermia is caused by:
1. high and prolonged exercise intensities
2. high air temperatures
3. high relative humidity.

> **Hyperthermia**: significantly raised core body temperature.

Cardiovascular drift

During prolonged exercise in the heat, a rise in core body temperature can cause cardiovascular drift. This is an upward drift in heart rate associated with a rise in body temperature (1 °C increases heart rate by 10 bpm).

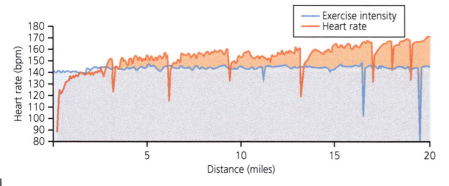

Figure 1.1.22 Cardiovascular drift: the upward drift in heart rate during steady state prolonged exercise

Quick quizzes at www.hoddereducation.co.uk/myrevisionnotesdownloads

The effects of heat and humidity and the body's thermoregulatory response

Table 1.1.23 summarises the effects of heat and humidity on the cardiovascular and respiratory systems.

Table 1.1.23 Effects of heat and humidity on the cardiovascular and respiratory systems

Cardiovascular system	
Effect	**Implication**
Dilation of arterioles and capillaries to the skin	+ Increased blood flow and blood pooling in the limbs
Decreased blood volume, venous return, SV, CO and blood pressure (BP)	+ Increased HR to compensate + Increased strain on the cardiovascular system + Reduced O_2 transport to the working muscles.
Respiratory system	
Effect	**Implication**
Dehydration and drying of the airways in temperatures above 32°C make breathing difficult	+ Increased mucus production + Constriction of the airways + Decreased volume of air for gaseous exchange
Increased breathing frequency to maintain oxygen consumption	+ Increased oxygen 'cost' of exercise
High levels of sunlight increase the effects of pollutants in the air	+ Increased irritation of airways, leading to coughing, wheezing or asthma symptoms

Strategies to maximise performance in heat and humidity

Table 1.1.24 summarises strategies to maximise performance in heat and humidity.

Table 1.1.24 Maximising performance in heat and humidity

Pre-competition	+ 7–14 days of acclimatisation in the same conditions to increase the body's tolerance to heat + Using cooling aids such as ice vests to reduce core temperature and delay effects of dehydration
During competition	+ Pacing strategies to reduce the feelings of exertion at low-exercise intensities + Wearing suitable clothing to maximise heat loss + Rehydrating as often and as much as possible with a hypotonic or isotonic solution
Post-competition	+ Using cooling aids such as cold fans + Rehydrating using isotonic solutions to replace lost fluids, glucose and electrolytes

> **Now test yourself** TESTED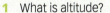
>
> 1. What is altitude?
> 2. Describe how the diffusion gradient is affected as altitude increases.
> 3. How does altitude affect an athlete's cardiovascular system?
> 4. How does altitude affect an athlete's respiratory system?
> 5. What are the benefits of acclimatisation for the cardiovascular and respiratory systems?
> 6. What is cardiovascular drift?
> 7. State three effects of heat and humidity on the cardiovascular and respiratory systems.
> 8. State one pre-competition, one during competition and one post-competition strategy to maximise performance in heat and humidity.
>
> **Answers on p. 167**

Exam practice

1. Explain the effects of altitude on the respiratory system and how these effects impact on the overall performance of an endurance athlete performing at altitude. [5]
2. What is altitude training? Evaluate whether it improves performance in endurance events. [6]

Answers on p. 176

Knowledge and skills summary

By the end of this chapter, you should have the following knowledge (AO1):
+ The effect of altitude on the cardiovascular and respiratory systems.
+ Acclimatisation, including the importance of timing arrival, at altitude (above 2400m).
+ The effect of heat on the cardiovascular and respiratory systems, including temperature regulation and cardiovascular drift.

AO2 and AO3
+ AO2 marks will ask for application of this knowledge, such as applying the principles of acclimatisation to specific examples.
+ In this chapter an AO3 response may involve an analysis of reasons why cardiovascular drift occurs in extreme heat and the impact this has on performance.

Quick quizzes at www.hoddereducation.co.uk/myrevisionnotesdownloads

1.2a Diet and nutrition and their effect on physical performance

Diet and nutrition

REVISED

A well-planned diet and nutritional strategy will aid any performer or athlete. Diet and nutrition can support fitness or performance gains, assist recovery and reduce the risks posed by overtraining.

Healthy, balanced diet

For 19–50-year-olds, the government recommends the following calorie guidelines:
+ men – 2500 calories per day
+ women – 2000 calories per day
+ for both – 55% carbohydrate (CHO), 15% protein, no more than 30% fats, a variety of foods including five portions of fruit and vegetables per day.

The amount of energy you need will depend on how old you are (e.g. growing teenagers may need more calories), how active you are, your height and weight, hormones, medication you may be taking and whether you are unwell.

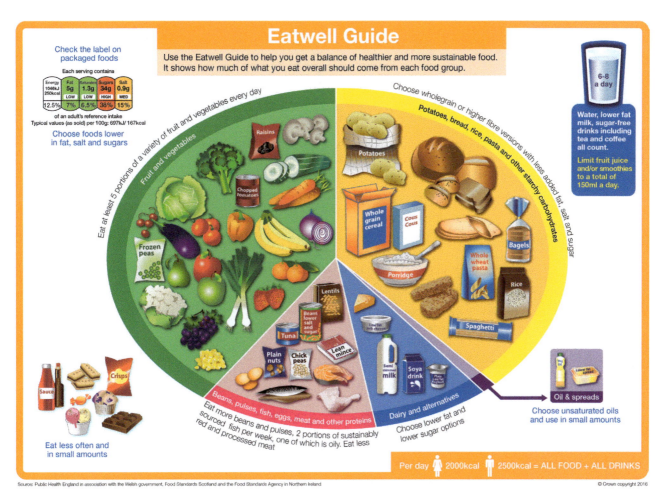

Figure 1.2.1 Public Health England guidelines on the composition of a healthy balanced diet

Carbohydrates (CHOs)

+ Carbohydrates (CHOs) are vital for energy production.
+ CHOs are the preferred fuel for exercise, accounting for approximately 75% of energy requirements.
+ CHOs can be consumed (eaten/drunk) in several forms, as shown in Table 1.2.1.
+ CHOs are converted into glycogen and glucose, providing energy for aerobic and anaerobic performers.
+ Surplus glucose, for example from a high-sugar diet, will be converted into triglycerides (the main constituents of body fat in humans) and stored in the body as fat.

Carbohydrates (CHOs): sugars and starches stored in the body as glycogen and converted to glucose to fuel energy production.

Table 1.2.1 Types of carbohydrates and where they are stored

CHO	Food example	Where?
Starches	Rice, potatoes	Stored as glycogen in liver and muscles
Sugars	Fruit, honey	Circulate in bloodstream as glucose

Proteins

Proteins (found in large quantities in milk, eggs, meat and soya) are essential for:
+ growth and repair of tissues and cells
+ making muscle proteins (increasing muscle size)
+ making haemoglobin
+ making enzymes, antibodies and collagen.

They can also be used as a fuel (when CHOs and fats are depleted).

Protein: amino acids essential for the growth and repair of cells and tissues.

Enzyme: biological catalyst that increases the speed of chemical reactions.

Fats: triglycerides that provide the body with fatty acids for energy production.

Fats

The role of fats is to:
+ insulate nerves, form cell membranes and cushion organs
+ provide an energy store – they can be broken down for aerobic energy production and have twice the yield of CHOs.

Table 1.2.2 Types of fat

Fat type	Example	Consideration
Unsaturated fatty acids	Avocado and soya beans Omega 3s (fish oil), olive oil	Can boost the delivery of oxygen, improve endurance recovery and reduce joint inflammation
Saturated fatty acids	Butter, bacon	Intake should be limited to reduce the risk of cardiovascular disease

Unsaturated fatty acid: a type of fat molecule that is typically liquid at room temperature and is found in sunflower, olive and fish oils. They can help lower cholesterol.

Saturated fatty acid: a type of fat molecule that is typically solid at room temperature and is mainly found in animal products. When consumed excessively, they can be associated with heart disease.

Exam tip

Ensure that you can apply knowledge about food fuels (CHOs, fats and proteins) to the relevant energy systems.

Making links

Food fuels link to energy systems and their thresholds (Chapter 1.1c, Energy for exercise).

Vitamins and minerals

Vitamins and minerals are essential to maintain healthy body functions. They can be consumed in adequate quantities through a balanced diet.

Table 1.2.3 summarises different vitamins and minerals and their uses in the body.

> **Vitamins and minerals**: essential organic and inorganic nutrients required for healthy body function.

Table 1.2.3 Vitamins and minerals and their functions in the body

Vitamin/mineral	Name	Essential for
Minerals	Calcium	Bone health, muscle contraction, nerve transmission, blood clotting
	Iron	Formation of haemoglobin, enzyme reactions, the immune system
	Phosphorus	Bone health, energy production
Vitamins	Vitamin A	Antioxidant properties, eye health
	Vitamin D	Bone health, protection against cancer and heart disease
	Vitamin E	Antioxidant properties, skin and eye health
	Vitamin K	Blood clotting, bone health
	Vitamin C	Skin, blood vessels, soft tissues
	Vitamin B	Breakdown of food, haemoglobin formation, skin and eye health

Fibre and water

+ Fibre is essential for the function of the large intestine.
+ Fibre is found in cereals, bread, beans, lentils, fruit and vegetables.
+ Adequate fluid intake allows fibre to work properly and to provide bulk in the bowel.
+ Water is essential for hydration before, during and after exercise.
+ Two-thirds of the body weight is water.
+ Dehydration can result in decreased plasma volume and SV, and increased temperature and HR (see p. 42 on cardiovascular drift).

> **Making links**
>
> Consider the link between diet and energy systems (Chapter 1.1c, Energy for exercise).

> **Revision activity**
>
> Create a table with three columns, headed: component of a healthy diet; importance and function; example of source. Complete the table by adding information for the seven components of a healthy diet.

> **Now test yourself** TESTED
>
> 1. What are the seven components of a balanced diet?
> 2. What is the difference between saturated and unsaturated fatty acids?
>
> **Answers on p. 168**

Energy intake, expenditure and balance in physical activity and performance

An athlete's diet provides them with energy. The amount of energy needed may differ from that needed by an inactive (sedentary) individual. Each performer has unique nutritional needs. Failure to consume sufficient calories will have a negative impact on training and performance, such as:

+ muscle loss (atrophy)
+ decreased intensity and duration of performance
+ increased risk of fatigue, injury and illness.

> **Energy**: the ability to perform work, measured in joules or calories.

> **Exam tip**
>
> Remember: energy expenditure = BMR + TEF + physical activity energy expenditure

Energy expenditure

Having accurate knowledge of an individual's energy expenditure allows accurate planning of the correct diet to facilitate training and performance.

Physical activity expenditure

This is the total number of calories required to perform daily tasks (often around 30% of total energy expenditure, but can be higher for a training athlete). Metabolic equivalent (MET) values are used to give a precise picture of expenditure. For example:

+ sitting quietly = 1 MET (1 kcal/kg/hr)
+ running at 11.5 minute/mile pace = 9 METs.

To calculate the total amount of energy an individual expends, we must add together basal metabolic rate (BMR), the thermic effect of food (TEF) and physical activity expenditure.

> **Exam tip**
>
> When calculating or describing energy expenditure, always include units (joules or calories): failure to do so will mean no marks.

Energy expenditure: the sum of basal metabolic rate, the thermic effect of food and the energy expended through physical activity.

Basal metabolic rate (BMR): the minimum amount of energy required to sustain essential physiological function at rest, which can account for as much as 75% of total energy expenditure.

Thermic effect of food (TEF): the energy required to eat, digest, absorb and use food taken in.

Energy intake: the total amount of energy from food and beverages consumed, measured in joules or calories.

Energy balance: the relationship between energy intake and energy expenditure.

Energy intake and energy balance

+ Energy intake is the total amount of energy from food and drinks, measured in joules or calories.
+ An average individual should have intake of approximately 55% CHO, 15% protein and no more than 30% fat.
+ An athlete's diet may differ significantly depending on the intensity and duration of their activity.

Energy balance is the relationship between energy intake and energy expenditure:

+ energy in > energy expenditure = weight gain
+ energy in < energy expenditure = weight loss
+ energy in = energy expenditure = weight stays the same.

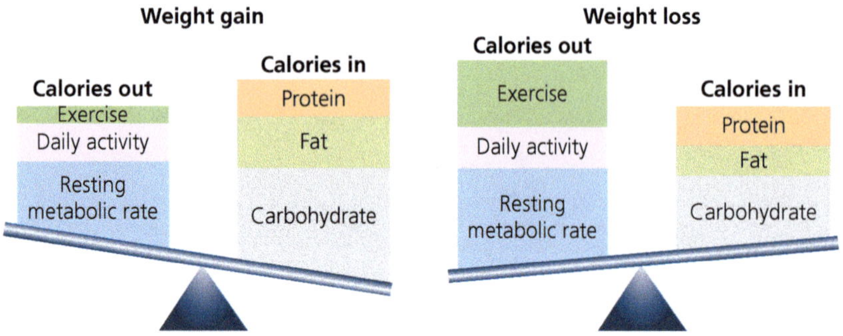

Figure 1.2.2 The energy balance scales

> **Now test yourself**
>
> 3 Define energy and explain what is meant by energy balance.
> 4 Explain how an athlete would calculate their overall energy expenditure and why this information is important for them.
>
> **Answers on p. 168**

Ergogenic aids

REVISED

A substance, object or method used to improve or enhance performance is called an ergogenic aid. There are three groups of ergogenic aids:
- pharmacological aids, taken to increase the levels of hormones or neural transmitters
- physiological aids, used to increase the rate of adaptation of the body
- nutritional aids, relating to diet and hydration.

> **Ergogenic aid**: a substance, object or method used to improve or enhance performance.
>
> **Pharmacological aids**: a group of ergogenic aids taken to increase the levels of hormones or neural transmitters.

> **Revision activity**
>
> Create a revision card for each ergogenic aid. Use colours to highlight benefits and drawbacks, and use diagrams to illustrate applications to practical examples.

Pharmacological aids

Table 1.2.4 outlines the benefits, drawbacks and practical applications of different pharmacological aids.

Table 1.2.4 Overview of pharmacological aids

Pharmacological aid	Legal or illegal	+ Benefits	− Drawbacks	Practical application
Anabolic steroids Synthetic derivatives of testosterone; tablets, capsules, cream, injected	Illegal	+ Increased muscle mass and strength + Increased recovery + Increased intensity and duration of training	− Irritability − Moods − Liver damage − Heart failure − Acne − Hormonal disturbances	+ Can be used for rehabilitation and to treat muscle wastage diseases + Used by weightlifters, body builders, sprinters and power athletes
Erythropoietin (EPO) A hormone made naturally in the body, secreted by the kidneys; RhEPO is the artificial version	Illegal	+ Increased RBCs and haemoglobin count + Increased O_2 transport and aerobic capacity + Increased intensity and duration of performance	− Increased blood viscosity − Decreased cardiac output − Increased risk of blood clots and heart disease − Decreased natural production of EPO	+ Difficult to detect as some athletes have a high concentration of RBCs + Used by endurance athletes, e.g. Tour de France cyclists
Human growth hormone (HGH) Synthetically produced HGH, used by some athletes in place of anabolic steroids	Illegal	+ Increased muscle mass and strength + Increased fat metabolism and decreased fat mass + Increased blood glucose + Increased recovery + Increased intensity and duration of training	− Abnormal bone and muscle development − Enlargement of vital organs − Increased risk of cancer and diabetes	Used by any type of athlete

1.2a Diet and nutrition and their effect on physical performance

Physiological aids

Table 1.2.5 outlines the benefits, drawbacks and practical applications of physiological aids.

> **Physiological aids**: a group of ergogenic aids used to increase the rate of adaptation of the body and thus increase performance.

Table 1.2.5 Overview of physiological aids

Physiological aid	Legal or illegal	+ Benefits	– Drawbacks	Practical application
Blood doping + Red blood cell volume is increased + Remove blood 4–6 weeks before + Body then compensates, replenishing lost RBCs	Illegal	+ Increased RBCs, therefore more haemoglobin + Increased O_2 transportation and aerobic capacity + Increased intensity and duration of performance	– Increased blood viscosity – Decreased cardiac output – Increased risk of blood clots and heart disease – Risk of transfusion infections (HIV/AIDS)	Used by endurance athletes
Intermittent hypoxic training (IHT) Athletes live at sea level but train under hypoxic conditions (low pO_2)	Legal	+ Allows acclimatisation for events at altitude + Increased RBCs, therefore more haemoglobin + Increased intensity and duration before fatigue + Increased mitochondria and buffering capacity, therefore delayed OBLA	– Benefits lost when IHT stops – May disrupt training patterns, leading to loss of motivation – Hard to reach normal work rates – Decreased immune function and increased risk of infection – Dehydration	Used by endurance athletes
Cooling aids + Pre-event: ice vests, cold towel wraps – used 10–30 mins before to reduce core body temperature + Injury: ice packs, sprays, PRICE (protect, rest, ice, compression, elevate) + Post-event: ice baths	Legal	+ Reduced core body temperature + Decreased sweating, dehydration and early fatigue + Decreased injury pain and swelling + Increased speed of recovery and repair + Decreased DOMS	– Difficult to perceive exercise intensity – Ice burns and pain – May mask or worsen injuries – Chest pain and decreased efficiency in older people – Dangerous for those with heart and blood pressure problems	+ All athletes use post-event + Used to speed up recovery – vessels constrict, capillaries dilate and oxygenated blood flows back to the muscles, bringing fresh oxygen

Nutritional aids

Dietary manipulation

Table 1.2.6 outlines the benefits, drawbacks and practical applications of different types of dietary manipulation.

Table 1.2.6 Overview of dietary manipulation

Dietary manipulation	Legal or illegal	+ Benefits	– Drawbacks	Practical application
Glycogen/carbohydrate loading (pre-competition) CHO loading starts one week before competition: + Day 1: intense exercise (deplete glycogen stores) + Days 2–3: high-protein/high-fat diet + Day 4: intense exercise (deplete glycogen stores further) + Days 5–7: high-CHO diet and tapering training or rest This super-compensates and muscles store more CHO than usual	Legal	+ Increased glycogen stores + Increased endurance capacity + Increased time to exhaustion (up to 30%) + Delays fatigue	– Hypoglycaemia and poor recovery rates in depletion phase – Lethargy and irritability – Gastrointestinal problems – Increased risk of injury – Affects mental preparation	+ Used for endurance events, e.g. marathon running, or all-day events, e.g. hockey tournament over a weekend + Used to ensure body has enough glycogen for aerobic glycolysis
Pre-event meal CHO meal 3 hours before event – food with low glycaemic index (GI), e.g. porridge 1–2 hours before event, a high-GI food (maintains blood glucose levels) **Pre-training meal** A small meal 30–60 minutes before an event	Legal	+ Tops up liver glycogen + Maintains blood glucose levels	– Avoid CHOs immediately prior to an event, as the body might try to counteract raised glucose levels – the athlete might become dizzy/fatigued	+ A CHO meal before event within timescale + Used by all athletes
During event meal/food Vital to eat small amounts in activity lasting longer than 1 hour	Legal	+ Tops up liver glycogen + Maintains blood glucose levels	– Can be difficult to eat during activity – Must be pre-planned to have best effects	Examples: + Energy gels in marathon + Banana at change of ends in tennis
Post-event meal Consume CHOs as soon as possible, within the first 30 minutes of finishing an event, and repeat at 2-hour intervals up to 6 hours post-event **Post-training meal** As soon as possible after, but within 2 hours of an event	Legal	+ Promotes faster recovery rate of glycogen	– Not always practical or possible within 30 minutes of finishing	+ Consume moderate and fast-digesting CHOs for faster recovery, e.g. white bread, white rice + Used by all athletes

Hydration

An athlete should be well hydrated prior to training/performance and replace all lost fluids throughout performance. Electrolytes lost through sweat must be replaced.

All dehydration decreases performance due to:
+ decreased heat regulation and increased temperature
+ increased blood viscosity
+ increased heart rate
+ increased fatigue
+ decreased cognitive function and skill level.

Table 1.2.7 outlines three types of sports drink that contain glucose and electrolytes.

> **Revision activity**
>
> Using the information about ergogenic aids, create ten revision questions about dietary manipulation. Write answers to the questions, then ask someone else to test you.

Table 1.2.7 Types of sports drink

Type of sports drink	Description	Practical application
Hypotonic	**Lower** concentration of glucose than blood	Vital during prolonged exercise
Isotonic	**Equal** concentration of glucose to blood	Used for events of over 1 hour
Hypertonic	**Higher** concentration of glucose than blood	Used during recovery. **Do not** use during activity as can increase dehydration

Supplementation

Table 1.2.8 outlines the benefits, drawbacks and practical applications of different dietary supplements.

Table 1.2.8 Overview of dietary supplements

Dietary supplement	Legal or illegal	+ Benefits	– Drawbacks	Practical application
Creatine supplements Taking supplement in the form of powder/tablet to increase phosphocreatine (PC) stores in muscle; used for very high-intensity energy production	Legal	+ Increased PC stores = more fuel for high-intensity energy production (ATP-PC system) + Increased intensity and duration of training + Increased maximum and explosive strength	– Increased weight gain – Increased water retention – Muscle cramps and gastrointestinal problems – Long-term effects unclear	Used by power athletes – weightlifters, sprinters
Caffeine Stimulates central nervous system and increases breakdown of FFAs for aerobic energy production	Legal	+ Increased nervous stimulation + Increased focus/concentration + Increased metabolism of fats + Preservation of muscle glycogen + Increased endurance performance	– Diuretic effect = dehydration – Insomnia and anxiety – Gastrointestinal problems	Found in tea/coffee, energy drinks or tablet form
Bicarbonate Alkaline that acts as a buffer to neutralise a rise in acidity in the bloodstream	Legal	+ Increased buffering capacity + Increased tolerance to lactic acid, delaying OBLA + Increased intensity and duration of performance	– Gastrointestinal problems – Unpleasant taste, causing nausea	Soda loading (ingesting large amounts of bicarbonate in advance of an event to make the blood more alkaline, therefore increasing anaerobic endurance by limiting lactic acid build-up)

Table 1.2.8 continued

Dietary supplement	Legal or illegal	+ Benefits	– Drawbacks	Practical application
Nitrates Inorganic compounds that dilate blood vessels and reduce blood pressure (BP)	Legal	+ Decreased BP + Increased blood flow + Increased intensity and duration of performance + Delays fatigue	– Headaches, dizziness, light-headedness – Long-term effects unclear – Possible carcinogenic risk	Consumed by eating root vegetables, beetroot and greens

Exam tip

When analysing the effect or use of an ergogenic aid, always give a brief description and a practical example and discuss benefits and drawbacks.

Revision activity

Create a mind map for each dietary supplement. Use green to highlight benefits and red to highlight drawbacks. Use diagrams where possible in place of written text (e.g. instead of writing the word 'fatigue', draw an image to represent it).

Now test yourself

TESTED

5 Describe the possible benefits and drawbacks of the dietary supplement caffeine, blood doping and cooling aids.

Answer on p. 168

Exam practice

1 How would you increase the muscle glycogen stores of an endurance athlete? [4]
2 Outline how a named pharmacological aid would benefit an endurance athlete, and identify the possible risks associated with it. [4]
3 When participating in physical activity, it is important to drink water to stay hydrated. What are the possible physiological effects of a lack of water on a performer? [3]
4 What is meant by the term 'balanced diet'? Explain how two different named classes of food in an athlete's diet will aid their performance. [3]

Answers on p. 176–177

Knowledge and skills summary

By the end of this chapter, you should have the following knowledge (AO1):
+ Components and functions of a balanced diet.
+ How to relate diet, hydration and dietary supplements to performance in physical activities and sports.
+ Ergogenic aids and how they are used to improve sports performance.

AO2 and AO3
+ For AO2 marks, you may be asked to suggest a diet/nutrition for a specific type of athlete (e.g. a marathon runner or netball player).
+ For AO3 marks, you may be asked to analyse and evaluate or compare different ergogenic aids.

1.2b Preparation and training methods

Training

Training programme design

It is important to include the following in any training programme:
1. evaluation test
2. warm-up
3. cool-down.

The basic building blocks of training programme design are called the principles of training. Correct use of the principles of training will result in desirable adaptation of the body.

> **Making links**
>
> Consider the application of the principles of training and how they may help to prevent chronic injury (Chapter 1.2c, Injury prevention and the rehabilitation of injury).

> **Principles of training**: the rules that underpin training programme design to ensure safe and effective fitness adaptation.
>
> **Adaptation**: a physiological change in response to training, e.g. increased RBC production.

Specificity
- To get the best results from training, it must be geared towards the demands of the activity.
- These demands could be the energy system that is predominantly used, the muscle groups involved or the fitness components that are crucial, for example maximum strength for a weightlifter.
- Training also needs to be specific to the person doing it: age, ability, current fitness level and so on.
- Specificity is applied in two ways:
  1. the individual
  2. the sport/activity.

Progression
- Our bodies adapt to the stresses and loads put on them, so training should gradually increase over time.
- After a while, the body will have adapted fully and no other changes will occur unless the training is made harder.

Overload
- To make the body adapt, it must be made to work harder than it normally does. This is known as overload.
- The body can be overloaded by manipulating:
  - frequency
  - intensity
  - time
  - type.

Variance
- To make the body adapt, a long period of training must take place. Boredom can become an issue.
- A variety of different training sessions are vital to avoid repetition and keep up concentration and commitment.

Moderation
- Although overload is vital for the body to adapt, caution must be taken not to overload too much.
- If overload is too great, overuse injuries can occur and in younger performers burnout is possible.

Reversibility
+ Fitness levels quickly drop when periods of inactivity occur.
+ It is vital that training programmes avoid any long periods of inactivity, even during off-season time.
+ The loss of fitness will be reduced if steady progression has been made throughout the training.

> **Exam tip**
>
> Always give relevant practical examples when referring to the principles of training. For example:
> + 'The athlete must consider specificity. For example, an 800m swimmer would conduct most of their training in the pool, focusing on aerobic training, as this targets the muscle movements and the specific energy system used in their event.'
> + 'An endurance runner (10,000m) must consider the principle of moderation. If they train too much, for example every day, they are likely to sustain an injury, such as a stress fracture of the foot.'

Periodisation

REVISED

Aims

Periodisation involves dividing training into specific blocks. The aims are:
1. to reach physiological peak at the correct time
2. to avoid injury and burnout
3. to structure training, to give realistic and achievable goals.

Cycles

The Olympic Games are held every 4 years; most athletes and coaches plan training on a yearly basis.

1. A macro-cycle is the whole training programme:
   + Often a calendar year is used.
   + For an Olympic athlete, it may be 4 years.
   + This is broken down into meso-cycles and is a long-term training plan.
   + This cycle includes the preparation, competition and recovery phases of the plan.
   + A macro-cycle provides an overview of the training regimen and allows the athlete to incorporate long-term planning in order to peak at competition time.
2. A meso-cycle is a phase of training:
   + It is often about a month or 6 weeks long.
   + The length of each meso-cycle will depend on its aim.
   + These cycles involve developing a particular component of fitness such as power, strength or endurance. The more important the component, the longer an athlete may spend on it.
   + Many performers will use six meso-cycles or phases.
   + A meso-cycle is broken down into micro-cycles and is a mid-term training plan.
3. A micro-cycle can be a typical week that is broken down into training units:
   + Any training sessions may contain one or more units.
   + This is a short-term training plan.
   + Micro-cycles may be similar from week to week. For example, a series of weight-training micro-cycles may involve the same exercises, but the weight lifted may increase across different cycles.
   + Micro-cycles may also be different from week to week. For example, a running programme may have cycles that vary in intensity, duration and training method guidelines.

> **Periodisation**: the organised division of training into blocks, each with a goal and time frame.
>
> **Macro-cycle**: a long-term training plan, typically over a year, to achieve a long-term goal.
>
> **Meso-cycle**: a mid-term training plan, typically over 6 weeks, to achieve a mid-term goal.
>
> **Micro-cycle**: a short-term training plan, typically over 1 week, to achieve a short-term goal.

Phases of training

There are three main training phases in a periodised year, as shown in Table 1.2.9.

Table 1.2.9 Main training phases

Phase	When	What happens
Preparatory 1	Off-season	General conditioning; aerobic and mobility training, strength conditioning
Preparatory 2	Pre-season, approaching competition	Training intensity increases; sport-specific fitness is central, e.g. anaerobic training for a 400m runner
		Training volume reduces; more competition-specific training, e.g. practice games
Competitive 3	During season	Training load reduces, allowing adequate rest; focus is on strategy, tactics and game-play; endurance performers still need high-intensity training
Competitive 4	2–3 weeks before main event	Tapering – maintaining intensity but decreasing volume by a third
Transition (T)	After season, before start of new season	Active rest or low-intensity aerobic work, e.g. swimming/cycling

> **Making links**
> + Training programme design and periodisation link together with all the components of fitness, activity demands, energy systems and the recovery process (Chapter 1.1c, Energy for exercise).
> + Consider the effectiveness of periodisation and how this may affect the motivation levels of a performer (Chapter 2.2, Sports psychology).

> **Tapering**: maintaining the intensity but decreasing the volume of training by one-third to prepare for competition.

> **Now test yourself** TESTED
> 1 What are the six principles of training?
> 2 Describe the three cycles used in periodisation.
>
> **Answers on p. 168**

> **Revision activity**
> Divide up your own practical activity into a periodised programme of training, using the suggestions above.

Annual periodised training programme

Month	January	February	March	April	May	June	July	August	September	October	November	December
Meso-cycle	8	9	10	11	12	1	2	3	4	5	6	7
Comp phase	Competitive league season – international fixtures occur in this time phase					Off-season		Pre-season		Season begins mid-September		
Training phase	Maintenance					General prep		Specific prep (includes technical, aerobic and tactical training)		Maintenance		
	Maintenance of technical and tactical training – decrease in strength training					Hypertrophy	Max strength development	Strength endurance development	Convert strength to power	Maintenance of strength and endurance training – decreased aerobic training volume – increased technical and tactical training		
Peaking	Key international period e.g Six Nations		Attempt to maintain performance levels – training levels adjusted 1–2 days before game so as not to affect physiological performance		HC final peak	No specific peaking during non-competitive season – training levels adjusted 1–2 days before game so as not to affect physiological performance				Start of season	Attempt to maintain performance levels – secondary weekly targets for matches	
Testing	Mid-season testing					Baseline tests and injury screening	Pre-season strength tests		Pre-season re-test			
Goals	Peak in physical condition for key international period		Maintenance of physical conditioning for season run-in, no specific peaking but aim for weekly preparation for matches			Hypertrophy	Development of optimum strength	Conversion of strength to rugby-related power		Maintain power and strength without causing performance-inhibiting fatigue due to training		

Figure 1.2.3 Complex and detailed periodised training programme for an elite rugby player

Aerobic training

REVISED

- **Aerobic capacity** is a key fitness component that underpins all endurance-based work, such as long-distance running, triathlon, open-water swimming and cross-country running.
- It is also an important contributor to many other sporting situations, such as football, hockey and rowing.
- It is reliant on the efficiency of the respiratory, cardiovascular and muscular systems.
- A key component of aerobic capacity is VO_2max.

> **Aerobic capacity**: the ability of the body to inspire, transport and utilise oxygen to perform sustained periods of aerobic activity.
>
> **VO_2max**: maximum volume of oxygen inspired, transported and utilised per minute during exhaustive exercise.

VO_2max

VO_2max is measured in millilitres per kilogram per minute (ml/kg/min).
- untrained individual = 40–50 ml/kg/min
- highly trained athlete = 90 ml/kg/min.

Factors that affect VO_2max

Table 1.2.10 outlines the factors that can affect the VO_2max of an individual.

Table 1.2.10 Factors that affect VO_2max

Factor	Effect on VO_2max	Explanation
Physiological make-up	The greater the efficiency of body systems to transport and utilise O_2 = higher VO_2max; can be determined by genetics	Stronger respiratory muscles, larger heart, higher SV, higher CO, increased number of RBCs, capillaries, SO fibres = higher VO_2max
Age	From age 20, VO_2max drops 1% each year	Efficiency is lost in elasticity of heart, blood vessels and lung tissue = lower VO_2max
Gender	Females lower than males	Females have higher body fat, smaller lung volumes, lower haemoglobin levels = lower VO_2max
Training	Aerobic training increases VO_2max up to 20%	Aerobic training causes long-term adaptations to heart, lungs, blood = higher VO_2max

Evaluation

Table 1.2.11 identifies the methods of evaluating VO_2max and lists the advantages and disadvantages of each method.

Table 1.2.11 Methods of evaluating VO_2max

Method	Advantages	Disadvantages
Direct gas analysis Expired air captured, results graphed and a calculation used	+ Direct measurement + Accurate and reliable + Uses different exercises, e.g. running, cycling, rowing	− Maximal test to exhaustion − Not suitable for older people/those with health problems − Specialist equipment required
Cooper 12-minute run Run as far as possible in 12 minutes; calculation used	+ Good for large groups + Can test yourself + Simple/cheap	− Only a prediction − Result affected by subject motivation − Not suitable for older people/those with health problems − Not sport-specific
NCF multi-stage fitness test 20m progressive shuttle run; results compared to standardised tables	+ Good for large groups + Simple/cheap + Published table of VO_2max equivalents	− Only a prediction − Result affected by subject motivation − Not suitable for older people/those with health problems − Not sport-specific
Queens College step test Stepping on and off box for 3 mins; HR recovery used to predict results	+ Sub-maximal test + Simple/cheap + HR easily monitored + Published table of data and simple VO_2max calculations	− Only a prediction − HR recovery affected by lots of factors – food, fluid, prior exercise − Not sport-specific − Shorter subjects may be at a disadvantage

Quick quizzes at www.hoddereducation.co.uk/myrevisionnotesdownloads

> **Revision activity**
>
> Create a fact card for each method of evaluating VO_2max. Give the card to a friend and get them to ask you questions.

Training zones

Training at the correct intensity is essential:
+ If intensity is too high, performers will experience fatigue quickly and adapt anaerobically.
+ If intensity is too low, no adaptations will take place.

Heart rate is often used as a prediction of training intensity. This can be done in two ways:
1 Heart rate training zones (Figure 1.2.4):

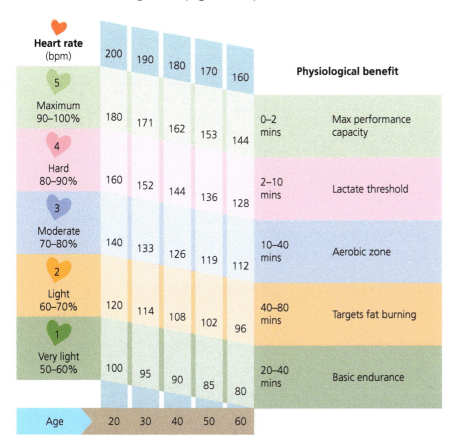

Figure 1.2.4 Heart rate training zones

2 Karvonen's principle:
+ HRmax = (220 − age)
+ training HR = resting HR + % (HRmax − resting HR)

> **Worked example**
>
> For example, for a 60% HR for a 17-year-old with a resting HR of 72:
>
> Training HR = 72 + (0.60 × (203 − 72))
> = 72 + 78.6
> = 150.6 bpm

Training methods: aerobic capacity

Table 1.2.12 identifies the key features of continuous training and high-intensity interval training (HIIT).

Table 1.2.12 Key features of continuous training and high-intensity interval training

Key feature	Continuous training	High-intensity interval training
Intensity of work	Low–moderate, 60% to 80% max HR	High, 80% to 95% max HR
Duration of work	20 to 80 minutes	5 to 8 seconds, repeated bouts of high-intensity work with varied recovery time – overall 20–60 minutes
Intensity of recovery	No recovery, non-stop activity	40% to 50% of max HR
Duration of recovery	No recovery, non-stop activity	Recovery interval = work interval (1:1)
Practical example	Jogging, swimming, cycling	Cycling, running, cross-training
Type of athlete suited to	Endurance athletes, as it stresses the aerobic system and slow-oxidative muscle fibres	Can be modified for most athletes with varying levels of fitness

> **Exam tip**
>
> If you are asked to compare methods of training, compare carefully point by point. Marks are only awarded for direct comparisons of similar points, e.g. work intervals of both, activities of both, practical example of both.

> **Now test yourself** TESTED
>
> 3 Define aerobic capacity and VO_2max.
> 4 Identify the factors that affect VO_2max and explain how they impact performance.
> 5 Outline the similarities and differences between continuous training and high-intensity interval training (HIIT).
> 6 Using Karvonen's principle, calculate the 70% training heart rate for an 18-year-old with a resting heart rate of 60 bpm.
>
> **Answers on p. 168**

Adaptations: aerobic capacity

After a prolonged period of aerobic training (12 weeks, 3–5 times a week), many long-term responses or adaptations will take place.

Respiratory system

Table 1.2.13 outlines the long-term adaptations in the respiratory system after 12 weeks of aerobic training.

Table 1.2.13 Overview of long-term adaptations in the respiratory system

Adaptation	Functional effects
Respiratory muscles become stronger	+ Increased efficiency of mechanics of breathing + Increased maximum-exercise lung volumes + Decreased respiratory fatigue
Surface area of alveoli increases	+ Increased external gaseous exchange
Overall effects	
+ Increased volume of O_2 diffused into the blood + Decreased breathing rate at rest and during sub-maximal exercise + Easier to perform exercise	+ Reduced onset of fatigue + Delayed OBLA + Increased intensity and duration of performance + Alleviates symptoms of asthma

Cardiovascular system

Table 1.2.14 outlines the long-term adaptations in the cardiovascular system after 12 weeks of aerobic training.

Table 1.2.14 Overview of long-term adaptations in the cardiovascular system

Adaptation	Functional effects

Cardiac hypertrophy	+ Increased SV at rest and during exercise and increased CO (at rest) due to:
	  + increased filling capacity and force of ventricular contraction
	  + decreased resting and sub-maximal HR (< 60 bradycardia)
	  + decreased HR recovery after exercise

Increased elasticity of arterial walls	+ Increased vascular shunt efficiency + Decreased resting BP
Increased number of RBCs/haemoglobin volume	+ Increase in O_2-carrying capacity + Increased gaseous exchange
Increased blood plasma volume	+ Lower blood viscosity aids blood flow and venous return
Increased capillarisation of alveoli and SO muscle tissue fibres	+ Increased surface area for blood flow + Increased gaseous exchange + Decreased distance for diffusion
Overall effects	
+ Increased blood flow and O_2 transport to muscles + Decreased BP + Easier to perform exercise	+ Reduced onset of fatigue + Delayed OBLA + Increased intensity and duration of performance + Lower risk of coronary heart disease, hypertension and stroke

Musculo-skeletal system

Table 1.2.15 outlines the long-term adaptations in the musculo-skeletal system after 12 weeks of aerobic training.

Table 1.2.15 Overview of long-term adaptations in the musculo-skeletal system

Adaptation	Functional effects
SO muscle fibre hypertrophy	+ Increased potential for aerobic energy production + Increased strength, decreased energy cost, which delays fatigue
Increased size and density of mitochondria	+ Increased utilisation of O_2 + Increased aerobic energy production + Increased metabolism of fats
Increased stores of myoglobin	+ Increased storage and transport of O_2 to mitochondria
Increased stores of glycogen and fats	+ Increased aerobic energy fuels + Increased duration of performance
FOG fibres become more aerobic	+ Increased aerobic energy production, fuel and O_2 utilisation
Increased strength of connective tissue	+ Tendons and ligaments strengthen + Increased joint stability + Decreased risk of injury
Increased thickness of articular cartilage	+ Increased synovial fluid production
Increased bone mineral density	+ Increased calcium absorption + Increased bone strength + Decreased risk of injury
Overall effects	
+ Increased capacity of aerobic energy production + Increased joint stability + Increased metabolic rate + Decreased risk of injury, osteoarthritis and osteoporosis	+ Easier to perform exercise + Reduced onset of fatigue + Delayed OBLA + Increased intensity and duration of performance

Metabolic function

Table 1.2.16 outlines the long-term adaptations made in metabolic function after 12 weeks of aerobic training.

Table 1.2.16 Overview of long-term adaptations in metabolic function

Adaptation	Functional effects
Increased activity of aerobic enzymes	+ Increased metabolism of fats and glycogen
Decreased fat mass	+ Increased lean mass + Increased metabolic rate + Increased breakdown of fats
Decreased insulin resistance	+ Increased glucose tolerance + Treatment and prevention of type II diabetes
Overall effects	
+ Increased use of fuel and O_2 to provide energy + Improved body composition + Easier to perform exercise + Reduced onset of fatigue	+ Delayed OBLA + Increased intensity and duration of performance + Increased metabolic rate, increased energy expenditure and better management of body weight

Now test yourself — TESTED

7 Describe the adaptations that would occur in the musculo-skeletal system after a sustained period of aerobic training. How would these impact health and performance?

Answers on p. 168

Power output: the amount of work performed per unit of time, measured in watts (W).

Strength training

REVISED

Table 1.2.17 identifies and defines the different types of strength.

Table 1.2.17 Overview of different types of strength

Type of strength	Definition	Practical example
Static	Force is applied against a resistance without movement occurring (isometric contraction)	Gymnastics – arabesque on the beam, handstand on the floor, crucifix position
Dynamic	Force is applied against a resistance with movement occurring; also known as power output	Hop, step and jump phases of triple jump
Maximum	The ability to produce a maximal amount of force in a single muscular contraction, e.g. 1RM (repetition maximum)	Olympic weightlifter performing a deadlift, a throw in judo, a push in a rugby scrum, putting the shot
Explosive (elastic)	The ability to produce a maximal amount of force in one or a series of rapid muscular contractions	Long jump or high jump run-up (sprint) and take-off, sprinting down the wing in rugby or hockey, driving for an interception in netball
Strength endurance	The ability to sustain repeated muscular contractions over a period of time	Swimming, rowing and wrestling, where muscles perform the same movement repeatedly

Quick quizzes at www.hoddereducation.co.uk/myrevisionnotesdownloads

Factors that affect strength

Table 1.2.18 identifies the factors that affect strength.

Table 1.2.18 Factors that affect strength

Factor	Effect on strength	Explanation
Cross-sectional area of muscle	Greater cross-sectional area of muscle = greater strength	Maximum of 16–30 newtons per cm^2
Fibre type	Greater % FG + FOG = greater strength over a short period of time	Fast twitch fibres contract with higher force = greater force of contraction
Gender	Males have higher strength than females	Males have higher muscle mass and cross-sectional area due to higher testosterone levels
Age	Peak strength: + females – 16–25 years + males – 18–30 years Thereafter strength decreases with age	Age-related decline due to decrease in efficiency of neuromuscular system, elasticity and testosterone, leading to reduction in muscle mass

Figure 1.2.5 shows how the type of muscle fibre affects the amount of force produced over a period of time.

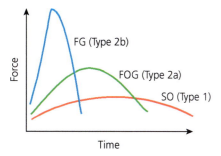

Figure 1.2.5 Effect of fibre type on force production

Evaluation

Table 1.2.19 identifies the different methods of evaluating strength, highlighting advantages and disadvantages of each method.

Table 1.2.19 Methods of evaluating strength

Test	Advantage	Disadvantage
Maximum strength One repetition maximum test (1RM; lifting a high weight for one repetition only)	+ Direct measurement + Easy procedure + Most muscle groups can be tested	– Difficult to isolate individual muscles – Trial and error may induce fatigue – Potential for injury
Maximum strength Grip strength dynamometer	+ Simple and objective measure + Inexpensive equipment + High reliability	– Only the forearm muscles are assessed – Not sport-specific
Strength endurance UK abdominal curl test – continuous sit-ups at progressive intensities to exhaustion (press-up or sit-up test)	+ Good for large groups + Simple/cheap + Abdominal muscles can be isolated + Valid and reliable	– Good technique needed – Safety concern over strain on lower back – Result affected by subject motivation as test to exhaustion – Not sport-specific
Explosive strength Vertical jump test – compared to standardised tables	+ Data can be converted to calculate a power output + Easy test/minimal equipment + Can test yourself	– Measure not isolated to one muscle group – Only estimates explosive strength in legs

> **Now test yourself** TESTED
>
> 8 Identify four factors that can affect an athlete's strength.
> 9 Name three types of strength and state how you would evaluate them.
>
> **Answers on p. 168**

Training methods to develop strength

There are many methods of training to improve strength, and design of these programmes will depend on the type of strength desired. All training programmes will manipulate several factors:
+ resistance (weight – measure as a % of 1RM)
+ repetitions (number of times an exercise is repeated)
+ number of sets (series of repetitions and relief period)
+ work-to-relief ratio (e.g. 1:1 – so you work for the same amount of time as you rest).

Table 1.2.20 Strength training guidelines for maximum, explosive and endurance strength

Type of strength	Intensity: % of one rep max	Repetitions	Sets	Work:relief ratio	Recovery between sets
Maximum	85–95%	1–5	2–6	1:3+	4–5 minutes
Explosive	75–85%	6–10	4–6	1:3	3–5 minutes
Endurance (advanced)	50–75%	15–20	3–5	1:2	30–45 seconds
Endurance (basic)	25–50%	15–20	4–6	1:2	60 seconds

Weight training and plyometric training

Figure 1.2.6 identifies the key features of weight training and plyometric training, and Figure 1.2.7 shows a plyometric circuit.

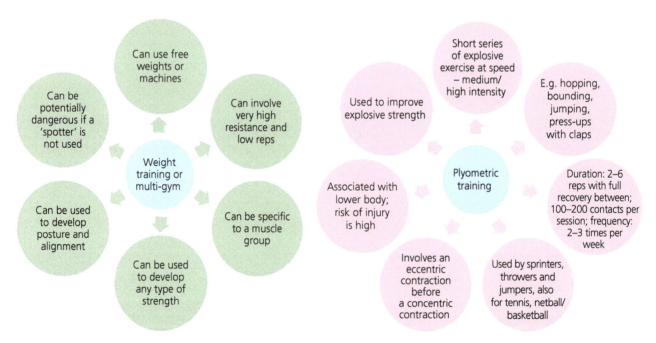

Figure 1.2.6 Key features of weight training and plyometric training

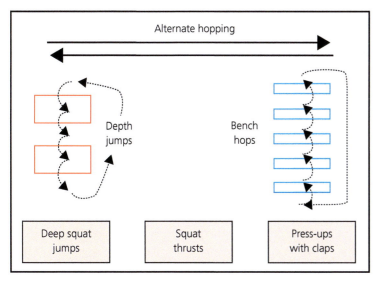

Rotate around the circuit twice, one minute on each exercise, stretch off during rest intervals

Figure 1.2.7 A plyometric circuit

Circuit and interval training

Figure 1.2.8 identifies the key features of circuit and interval training.

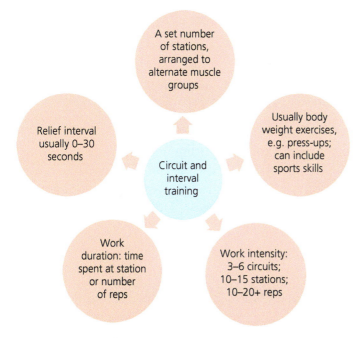

Figure 1.2.8 Key features of circuit and interval training

Physiological adaptations from strength training

Significant changes and adaptations will take place if an athlete follows a specific strength training programme at the correct intensity and duration:
+ 2 to 5 times a week
+ for at least 12 weeks.

Strength can increase 25–100% in 6 months due to improvements in neural pathways and muscle physiology.

Muscle and connective tissue adaptations

Table 1.2.21 outlines adaptations of muscle and connective tissue after 12 weeks of strength training.

Muscle hypertrophy: increased muscle cell size.

Muscle hyperplasia: increased number of muscle fibres.

Table 1.2.21 Overview of muscle and connective tissue adaptations after strength training

Adaptation	Functional effect
Muscle hypertrophy **Muscle hyperplasia**	+ Increased force of contraction + Maximum and explosive training = increased size of FG fibres + Strength endurance training = increased size of FOG fibres
Increase in number/size of contractile protein and myofibrils	+ Increased force of contraction + Increased actin–myosin filaments and cross bridges + Myofibrils become thicker due to increased protein synthesis
Increased strength of tendons and ligaments	+ Increased joint stability + Decreased risk of injury
Increased bone density and mass	+ Increased absorption of calcium + Decreased risk of osteoporosis
Overall effects	
+ Increased muscle mass + Increased speed, strength and power output + Increased intensity of performance + Hypertrophic physique – may increase self-esteem	

Metabolic adaptations

Table 1.2.22 outlines the metabolic adaptations after 12 weeks of strength training.

Table 1.2.22 Overview of metabolic adaptations after strength training

Adaptation	Functional effect
ATP, PC and glycogen stores within the muscle increase	+ Increased capacity for alactic (very high-intensity) energy production + Increased energy for speed- and power-based activities
Increased enzyme activity	+ Increased efficiency of anaerobic energy production + Increased activity of ATPase, creatine, kinase and glycolytic enzyme + Delaying of OBLA/fatigue
Increased buffering capacity	+ Increased tolerance and removal of lactic acid + Delaying of OBLA/fatigue + Increased anaerobic threshold
Increased muscle mass	+ Improved body composition + Increased metabolic rate
Overall effects	
+ Increased aerobic fuel stores + Increased intensity/duration of performance and delaying of OBLA/fatigue + Increased metabolic rate, increasing energy expenditure and helping to manage weight	

Neural adaptations

Table 1.2.23 outlines neural adaptations after 12 weeks of strength training.

Table 1.2.23 Overview of neural adaptations after strength training

Adaptation	Functional effect
Increased recruitment of motor units and FG and FOG fibre types	+ Increased force of contraction + Improved co-ordination and simultaneous stimulation of motor units
Decreased inhibition of the stretch reflex	+ Increased force of contraction from the agonist muscle, allowing the antagonist to stretch further and the agonist to contract with more force
Overall effects	
+ Increased speed, strength and power output	

Quick quizzes at www.hoddereducation.co.uk/myrevisionnotesdownloads

> **Worked example**
>
> Design two strength training programmes, one for a rower and one for a weightlifter. Refer to the types of strength to improve, frequency, intensity, duration, types of activity and work:relief ratios.
>
> It is useful to set this question out as a table or list. This will enable you to give the similarities and differences if needed.
>
> | | Rower | Weightlifter |
> | --- | --- | --- |
> | Type of strength to improve | Strength endurance | Maximum strength |
> | Frequency | 2+ times per week | 2+ times per week |
> | Intensity | 50–75% 1RM | 85–95% 1RM |
> | Duration | + 3–5 sets
+ 15–20 reps | + 2–6 sets
+ 1–5 reps |
> | Type of activity | + Circuit training
+ Weight training
+ Interval training | + Weight training
+ Multi-gym |
> | Work:relief ratio | 1:2 | 1:3+ |

Flexibility training

Flexibility is the range of motion (ROM) about a joint. High levels of flexibility are beneficial in most sports and physical activities, although they are especially important in some, such as ballet dancing and gymnastics.

Different sports make different demands on the flexibility of specific joints. For example, hip flexibility is important in hurdling, while shoulder flexibility is important in swimming.

> **Exam tip**
>
> Flexibility is a specific component of fitness. If a performer is flexible around the hip joint, this does not mean they are flexible around the shoulder joint.

Types of flexibility

There are two main types of flexibility:
1 static flexibility, for example holding a hamstring stretch:
    + static active flexibility – performer completes a voluntary contraction to move a joint just beyond its range of movement
    + static passive flexibility – assistance from a partner to move the joint just beyond its range of movement
2 dynamic flexibility, for example a gymnast performing a straddle vault.

> **Static flexibility**: the range of motion about a joint without reference to speed of movement.
>
> **Dynamic flexibility**: the range of motion about a joint with reference to speed of movement.

Factors that affect flexibility

Table 1.2.24 identifies the factors that affect flexibility.

Table 1.2.24 Factors that affect flexibility

Factor	Effect on flexibility	Explanation
Type of joint	A ball and socket joint has a greater ROM than a condyloid joint	The size and shape of joints and their articulating bones can aid and limit ROM; the presence of bony features such as processes will limit movement
Length and elasticity of surrounding connective tissue	The greater the length and elasticity of surrounding muscles, tendons and ligaments, the greater the ROM	The greater the length, the greater the distance before the stretch reflex is inhibited, preventing further ROM; the greater the elasticity, the greater the ROM possible
Gender	Females are generally more flexible than males	Females have higher levels of the hormones oestrogen and relaxin
Age	Flexibility is greatest in childhood and declines with age	Age-related decline is due to loss of elasticity in connective tissues

Evaluation of flexibility

Table 1.2.25 identifies the methods of evaluating flexibility, highlighting advantages and disadvantages of each method.

Table 1.2.25 Methods of evaluating flexibility

Test	Advantage	Disadvantage
Goniometry 360-degree protractor; difference between starting angle and full ROM calculated	+ Objective + Valid/accurate + Any joint can be measured + Can be sport-specific	− Difficult to locate axis of rotation − Training required for accurate measure
Sit and reach test Test box placed against wall, straight legs at full stretch, best score is recorded	+ Easy + Cheap, accessible equipment + Standardised data score	− Measures flexibility in lower back and hamstrings only − Not joint-specific − Need to warm up and hold position for 2 seconds

Training used to develop flexibility

There are two main types of stretching routine, based on whether a performer wants to maintain or improve flexibility:

1. maintenance stretching – performed as part of a warm-up to maintain current ROM and prepare for exercise
2. developmental stretching – designed to improve the ROM at a joint.

The stretching techniques that can be used to improve flexibility include:
+ static active stretching
+ static passive stretching (illustrated in Figure 1.2.9)
+ isometric stretching
+ proprioceptive neuromuscular facilitation (PNF)
+ dynamic stretching
+ ballistic stretching.

> **Static active stretching**: a performer moves the joint into its fully stretched position without any assistance and holds for 10–30 seconds.
>
> **Static passive stretching**: a performer moves the joint just beyond its point of resistance with assistance and holds for 10–30 seconds.
>
> **Proprioceptive neuromuscular facilitation (PNF)**: a stretching technique to desensitise the stretch reflex, whereby a performer completes a static passive stretch, isometrically contracts against the agonist, relaxes, then stretches further.

Figure 1.2.9 Static passive stretching technique

Static stretching and isometric stretching

Figures 1.2.10 and 1.2.11 identify the key points associated with static and isometric stretching.

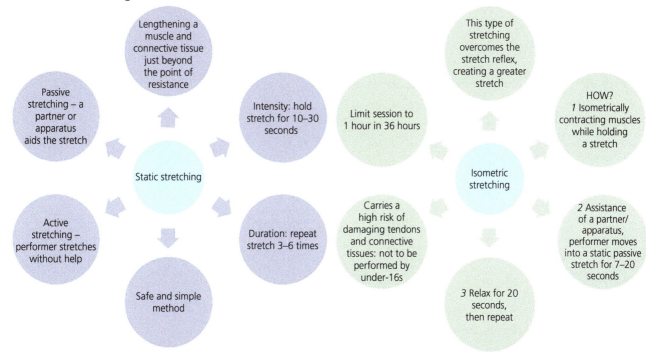

Figure 1.2.10 Static stretching

Figure 1.2.11 Isometric stretching

PNF, dynamic stretching and ballistic stretching

Figure 1.2.12 A proprioceptive neuromuscular facilitation (PNF) chest stretch

Figure 1.2.13 Ballistic high leg kick exercises

Figure 1.2.14 identifies the key points associated with PNF, dynamic stretching and ballistic stretching.

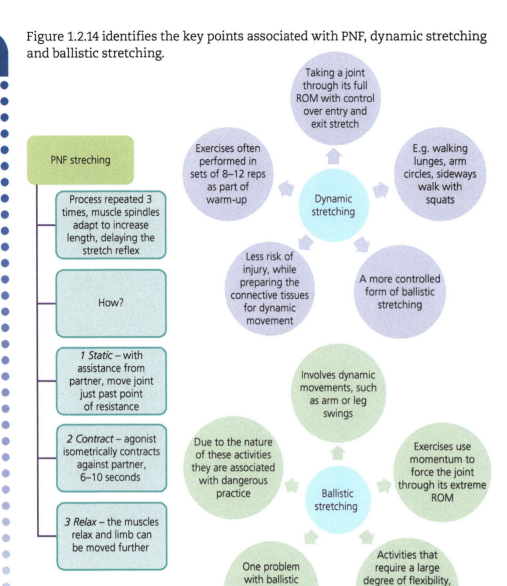

Figure 1.2.14 PNF, dynamic stretching and ballistic stretching

Physiological adaptations from flexibility training

Significant structural changes in muscle and connective tissue will result from following a specific flexibility training programme:
+ 3 to 6 times a week
+ for at least 6 weeks.

Table 1.2.26 summarises the effects of adaptations after flexibility training.

Table 1.2.26 Overview of adaptations after flexibility training

Adaptation	Functional effect
Increased resting length	+ Increased ROM about a joint + Muscle spindles adapt to increased length, reducing stretch reflex stimulus
Increased elasticity	+ Increased potential for static and dynamic flexibility + Decreased inhibition from the antagonist + Increased stretch of the antagonist
Overall effects	
+ Increased ROM about a joint + Increased distance and efficiency for muscles to create force at speed + Decreased risk of injury + Improved posture and alignment	

Quick quizzes at www.hoddereducation.co.uk/myrevisionnotesdownloads

> **Now test yourself**
>
> 10 Provide definitions of static flexibility and dynamic flexibility.
> 11 State the factors that affect an individual's flexibility.
> 12 Identify and briefly describe two methods of evaluating flexibility.
> 13 Identify the different types of training to develop flexibility.
>
> Answers on p. 168
>
> TESTED

Impact of training on lifestyle diseases

REVISED

Cardiovascular system

Cardiovascular disease (CVD) is a term for all diseases of the heart. Specific diseases include the following:

+ **Atherosclerosis** – a build-up of fatty deposits on arterial walls, leading eventually to chronic high blood pressure (hypertension).
+ **Coronary heart disease** – results from atherosclerosis of the coronary arteries. The reduction in blood flow and O_2 to the cardiac muscle can ultimately lead to angina (pain) or heart attack.
+ **Heart attack** – a blockage or clot in the coronary artery cuts off O_2 supply to the cardiac muscle, causing the death of cells or permanent damage.
+ **Stroke** – caused by a blockage in a cerebral artery, cutting off blood supply to the brain, or by a blood vessel bursting in the brain.

The effects of training

Exercise can reduce the overall risk of developing CVD by 30%. Regular training can:

+ reduce blood lipids (fats) and cholesterol and increase the proportion of HDL to LDL cholesterol
+ prevent hardening and loss of elasticity in arterial walls, slowing onset of atherosclerosis and hypertension
+ decrease blood viscosity, preventing blood clots and reducing BP
+ increase coronary circulation
+ lead to cardiac hypertrophy, increased SV and lowered resting HR
+ decrease body fat, reducing strain on the heart
+ increase blood flow and O_2 transport, reducing strain on the heart
+ reduce the risk of a stroke by 27% by lowering BP.

> **HDL** and **LDL cholesterol**: high-density lipoproteins (HDL) actively remove cholesterol from arterial walls and transport it to the liver, whereas low-density lipoproteins (LDL) deposit cholesterol in the arterial walls.

Respiratory system

Respiratory disease is characterised by one or several diseases of the airways:

+ **Asthma** – the constriction of the bronchial airways and inflammation of the mucus membranes, which limit breathing. It can also be exercise-induced (EIA).
+ **Chronic obstructive pulmonary disease (COPD)** – condition of the lungs where airways become inflamed and narrowed. Over time the inflammation causes permanent changes and can lead to an inability to exercise and a reduced quality of life.

Smoking is the biggest risk factor for respiratory disease.

The effects of training

Exercise can reduce the risk of developing respiratory disease. Regular exercise and training can:

+ increase respiratory muscle strength, alleviating symptoms of asthma
+ decrease resting and sub-maximal breathing rate
+ increase air flow
+ maintain full use of lung tissue and elasticity, decreasing the risk of infection
+ increase the surface area of the alveoli, maximising gaseous exchange.

> **Making links**
>
> Consider the physiological adaptations from extended periods of training and the impact these may have on the efficiency of the cardiovascular and respiratory systems (Chapter 1.1b, Cardiovascular and respiratory systems).

Now test yourself

TESTED

14 Explain how an active lifestyle can reduce the risk of lifestyle diseases associated with the cardiovascular system.

Answer on pp. 168–169

Exam practice

1 Identify and explain three physiological adaptations that take place after a strength training programme. [3]
2 A performer carries out a number of fitness tests. The table below gives the results of two of these tests.

Component of fitness	Test	Result	Evaluation by comparison norm tables
Aerobic capacity	**Test A**	Predicted VO$_2$max = 50 ml/kg/min	High
Fitness component B	UK abdominal curl test	Stage 6	Very good

a) Identify Test A and Fitness component B. [2]
b) Explain three physiological factors related to the heart and skeletal muscle that enable the performer to score so highly on Test A. [3]
3 Describe the effects of an unhealthy lifestyle and lack of training on the cardiovascular system. [4]
4 Training causes physiological adaptations. Explain how three structural adaptations in skeletal muscle benefit performance. [6]

Answers on p. 177

Knowledge and skills summary

By the end of this chapter, you should have the following knowledge (AO1):
+ Periodisation of training:
  + macro-cycle
  + meso-cycle
  + micro-cycle.
+ Phases of training.
+ Aerobic capacity and maximal oxygen uptake (VO$_2$max).
+ How VO$_2$max is affected by:
  + the individual
  + physiological make-up
  + training
  + age
  + gender.
+ Methods of evaluating aerobic capacity.
+ How intensity and duration of training is used to develop aerobic capacity:
  + continuous training
  + high-intensity interval training (HIIT).
+ The use of target heart rates as an intensity guide.
+ Physiological adaptations from aerobic training:
  + cardiovascular
  + respiratory
  + muscular
  + metabolic.
+ Sports in which aerobic capacity is a key fitness component.
+ Types of strength and factors that affect strength.
+ Methods of evaluating each type of strength.
+ Training to develop strength, referring to repetitions, sets, resistance, work intensity, work duration and relief interval.
+ Physiological adaptations from strength training.
+ Activities and sports in which strength is a key fitness component.
+ Types of flexibility and factors that affect flexibility.
+ Methods of evaluating flexibility.
+ Training used to develop flexibility.
+ Physiological adaptations from flexibility training.
+ Sports in which flexibility is a key fitness component.
+ How to plan personal health and fitness programmes for aerobic, strength and flexibility training.
+ Impact of training on lifestyle diseases of the cardiovascular and respiratory systems.

AO2, AO3 and quantitative skills
+ For AO2 marks within this chapter, you may be asked to design a training programme for a specific athlete.
+ For AO3 marks, you may be asked to compare different training methods and evaluate their effectiveness.
+ Quantitative skills may be tested in this chapter, for example interpreting data within fitness tests.

Quick quizzes at www.hoddereducation.co.uk/myrevisionnotesdownloads

1.2c Injury prevention and the rehabilitation of injury

Acute and chronic injuries

Acute injuries

Acute injuries happen suddenly after a stress to the body, such as a fractured eye socket after being hit with a ball in hockey.

A hard tissue injury involves damage to the bone, joint or cartilage, including fractures and dislocations.

> **Acute injury**: a sudden injury associated with a traumatic event.

Hard tissue injuries: fracture

Fractures involve a partial or complete break in the bone.
+ In simple (closed) fractures, the skin remains unbroken.
+ Compound (open) fractures are where the bone breaks through the skin.

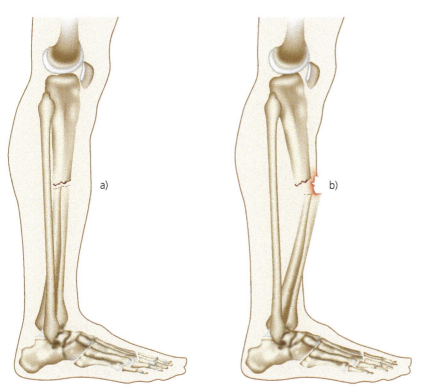

Figure 1.2.15 Simple (a) and compound (b) fractures

Table 1.2.27 sets out the signs and symptoms of fractures. Note that signs of an injury are things that you can see, whereas symptoms of an injury are things a performer may feel.

Table 1.2.27 Signs and symptoms of fractures

Signs	Symptoms
+ Deformity + Swelling + Discoloration	+ Pain + Inability to move injured area

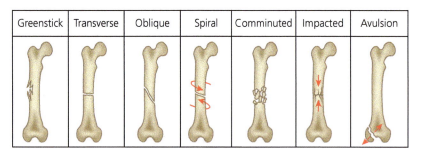

Figure 1.2.16 Additional types of possible fracture

Hard tissue injuries: dislocation

+ A dislocation occurs from a direct force (collision or object) or an indirect force (a fall) pushing the joint past its extreme range of motion.
+ A subluxation often causes damage to ligaments and increases the likelihood of recurrent dislocations. This may compromise an athlete's career.

Dislocation: the displacement of one bone from another out of their original position.

Subluxation: an incomplete or partial dislocation.

Table 1.2.28 Signs and symptoms of dislocation

Signs	Symptoms
+ Deformity + Swelling and discoloration	+ May feel a 'pop' + Severe pain + Loss of movement

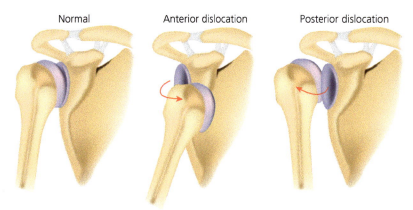

Figure 1.2.17 Anterior and posterior dislocation of the humerus from the shoulder joint

Soft tissue injuries: contusion and haematoma

+ A contusion (bruise) is an area of skin or tissue where the blood vessels have become damaged. Most contusions are minor; however, severe contusion can cause deep tissue damage and ultimately a haematoma.
+ Haematoma is internal bleeding, ranging from minor bruises under the skin to deep tissue bleeding.

Soft tissue injury: damage to the skin, muscle, tendon or ligament, including tears, strains and sprains.

Haematoma: localised congealed bleeding from ruptured blood vessels.

Sprain: overstretch or tear in the ligament that connects bone to bone.

Table 1.2.29 Signs and symptoms of contusion and haematoma

Signs	Symptoms
Swelling and discoloration	Pain (at touch in minor case)

Soft tissue injuries: sprain

Sprains are caused by a sudden twist, impact or fall that forces the joint beyond its extreme range of motion. They are common at the ankle joint of games players.

Table 1.2.30 Signs and symptoms of sprains

Signs	Symptoms
+ Swelling + Bruising	+ Inability to bear weight + Pain

Quick quizzes at www.hoddereducation.co.uk/myrevisionnotesdownloads

Soft tissue injuries: strain

Strains result from overstretching a muscle. They are commonly caused by dynamic lunging movements, for example lunging to return a drop shot in badminton. A very serious sprain or strain can result in a rupture.

Table 1.2.31 Signs and symptoms of strains

Signs	Symptoms
+ Swelling/discoloration + Bruising	+ Pain on movement

Strain: overstretch or tear in the muscle or tendon that connects muscle to bone.

Rupture: a complete tear of muscle, tendon or ligament.

Soft tissue injuries: abrasion

Abrasions are caused by falling or slipping, or by clothing rubbing on the body.
+ If an abrasion causes an open wound, it will need to be cleaned; severe abrasions may need stitching.
+ Most sports have blood rules; players must leave the game until the bleeding stops or is covered.

> **Exam tip**
>
> Be clear on the difference between a strain and a sprain. Strain = muscle, sprain = ligament.

Soft tissue injuries: blister

Blisters occur due to friction on the skin. They can be painful but may not stop participation. They are preventable with the correct footwear, equipment and training load.

Abrasion: superficial damage to the skin caused by scraping against a surface.

Blister: separation of layers of skin where a pocket of fluid forms, caused by friction.

Concussion

Concussion occurs after a trauma to the head. It can result in:
+ headaches
+ dizziness
+ balance problems
+ nausea
+ a loss of consciousness (sometimes).

A blow to the head can cause swelling and possibly a disruption in the electrical processes of the brain.

Concussion: a traumatic brain injury resulting in a disturbance of brain function.

Table 1.2.32 Signs and symptoms of concussion

Signs	Symptoms
+ Lying motionless/slow to get up + Possible post-traumatic seizure + Loss of consciousness + Balance problems + Disorientation/confusion	+ Lying motionless/slow to get up + Headache/dizziness + Visual problems/light sensitivity + Nausea/vomiting

> **Exam tip**
>
> Always give a relevant sporting example to describe how an injury may have occurred, for example, 'a hockey player may suffer a concussion after being hit in the head by a hockey ball'.

Chronic injuries

Chronic injuries develop by repeated continued stress on the body over a period of time, for example pain in a runner's knees or heels.

Hard tissue injuries: stress fracture

Stress fractures are common in distance running events, tennis, gymnastics and basketball, where the repetitive stress of the foot on the ground can cause a trauma.
+ Overtraining can cause stress fractures.
+ Pain will usually stop with rest.

Soft tissue injuries: shin splints
+ Shin splints and medial tibia stress syndrome (MTSS) are terms for chronic shin pain, caused by excessive use of the tendons connecting the muscles to the tibia.
+ The surface of the tibia becomes inflamed, leading to pain in a specific area of the bone.

Chronic injury: a slowly developed injury associated with overuse.

Stress fracture: a tiny crack in the surface of a bone caused by overuse.

Shin splints/medial tibia stress syndrome (MTSS): chronic shin pain due to the inflammation of muscles and stress on the tendon attachments to the surface of the tibia.

- This type of injury is common in distance runners, dancers and football players.
- Being overweight, wearing inadequate footwear or poor leg biomechanics can be a cause.

Soft tissue injuries: tendinosis

- Tendons are tough fibrous connective tissues designed to transmit force.
- Repetitive strain causes small injuries that are not given time to heal.
- This can result in a chronic injury, for example tennis elbow and Achilles tendinosis.

Tendinosis: the deterioration of a tendon in response to chronic overuse and repetitive strain.

Table 1.2.33 Signs and symptoms of tendinosis

Signs	Symptoms
Limited movement/stiffness	Burning/stinging/aching

Now test yourself

TESTED

1. What are the signs and symptoms of concussion? Give a sporting example of when concussion could have occurred.
2. What is the difference between a stress fracture and shin splints?
3. State two acute hard tissue injuries and give sporting examples of how these injuries might have occurred.
4. State two acute soft tissue injuries and give sporting examples of how these injuries might have occurred.
5. What is the difference between an acute and a chronic injury?

Answers on p. 169

Revision activity

Create a revision card for each injury; include injury description, signs, symptoms and treatment.

Injury prevention

REVISED

Risk factors must be identified to try to prevent injuries. Risk factors have two classifications: intrinsic risk factors and extrinsic risk factors.

Intrinsic risk factor: an injury risk or force from inside the body.

Extrinsic risk factor: an injury risk or force from outside the body.

Table 1.2.34 Intrinsic and extrinsic risk factors

Intrinsic risk factors	Extrinsic risk factors
- Previous injury - Posture and alignment issues - Age - Nutrition - Poor preparation - Inadequate fitness level - Inappropriate flexibility level	- Poor technique and training - Incorrect equipment and clothing - Inappropriate intensity, duration or frequency of activity - Warm-up and cool-down effectiveness

Warm-up and cool-down effectiveness

Warm-up

Warm-ups are used for:

- raising body temperature – a rise of 2–3 degrees increases enzyme activity, diffusion gradients and metabolic activity, improving the efficiency of muscular contraction
- preparing the body physiologically – the elasticity of muscles, tendons and ligaments improves, and antagonistic co-ordination improves
- preparing the body psychologically – mentally, performers are ready for the task ahead
- minimising the risk of injury – for example, performers are less likely to suffer strains or sprains.

Quick quizzes at www.hoddereducation.co.uk/myrevisionnotesdownloads

Key features

+ A warm-up has three stages:
  1. pulse raising
  2. stretching and mobility
  3. sport-specific drills (e.g. a passing drill in hockey).
+ It gradually increases in intensity.
+ It lasts 20–45 minutes.
+ Stretching and mobility should be dynamic in sport-specific patterns. Static stretching should be avoided.

Cool-down

Cool downs are used for:

+ maintaining heart rate – to maintain blood flow and metabolic activity, flushing muscle tissue with oxygenated blood
+ aiding the removal of lactic acid – enhancing future performances and delaying fatigue and injuries
+ aiding the healing process.

Key features

+ A cool-down has two stages:
  1. moderate-intensity activity, to maintain HR, aid venous return and remove waste
  2. stretching exercise to reduce muscle tension and lower temperature.
+ It gradually decreases in intensity.
+ It lasts approximately 20–30 minutes.

Debates about warm-up and cool-down

+ Research suggests that static stretching within a warm-up:
  + has no effect on injury prevention
  + may reduce the peak force produced in the Achilles tendon by 8%
  + causes antagonistic co-ordination to deteriorate, hampering explosive movements
  + reduces eccentric strength by 9%, decreasing the ability to change direction at speed
  + reduces the muscles' ability to consume O_2 by 50%.
+ As a result, static stretching should be avoided in a warm-up routine unless advised by a physiotherapist.
+ Injury prevention researchers believe that dynamic stretching exercise such as high knee skips and walking lunges should be used as part of a warm-up.
+ Historically, an active cool-down has been thought to benefit all athletes. However, during low-intensity activity, such as jogging for an aerobically fit athlete, a passive recovery period (such as sitting on a bench) has been shown to be more beneficial.
+ Equally, there is little evidence to suggest that an active cool-down can prevent or limit delayed onset muscle soreness (DOMS; see p. 19 for definition).

> **Now test yourself**
> 6. Identify two internal risk factors of injury.
> 7. Identify two external risk factors of injury.
> 8. Give three reasons why is it important to warm up.
> 9. Give three reasons why is it important to cool down.
>
> **Answers on p. 169**

Responding to injuries and medical conditions in sport

Assessment using SALTAPS

In the event of a sporting accident, a sport-specific assessment such as SALTAPS should take place to consider whether a player should continue.

Table 1.2.35 SALTAPS

Stop	Stop the game and observe the injury.
Ask	Ask questions of the player/participant: How did the injury happen? Where does it hurt?
Look	At the injury site, check for swelling, bruising, deformity or discoloration.
Touch	At the injury site, check for swelling, deformity, lumps and bumps, or heat.
Active movement	Ask for active movements from the participant.
Passive movement	Assessor moves the injured limb/body part.
Strength testing	Ask the player to stand, lift and put pressure on the injured area. Ask them if they can continue.

SALTAPS: protocol for the assessment of a sporting injury: stop, ask, look, touch, active movement, passive movement and strength testing.

Acute management using PRICE

Soft tissue injuries can be treated by using PRICE.

Most minor soft tissue injuries can be managed at home. For the first two to three days after your injury, you should follow the **PRICE** procedure.

PRICE: protocol for the treatment of acute injuries: protect, rest, ice, compress and elevate.

Protect
Protect your injury from further damage, for example, by using a support or splint.

Rest
Rest your injury for the first two to three days. You may need to use crutches if you've injured your leg and you want to remain mobile. Then reintroduce movement gradually so you don't delay your recovery by losing muscle strength.

Ice
Ice the painful area with a cold compress such as ice or a bag of frozen peas wrapped in a towel. This will help reduce swelling and bruising. Do this for 15 to 20 minutes every two to three hours. Don't apply ice directly to your skin as it can damage it.

Compress
Compress the injured area with an elastic bandage or elasticated tubular bandage to help limit swelling and movement. But don't leave the bandage on while you sleep.

Elevate
Elevate your injury by resting it above the level of your heart and keep it supported. This could mean lying on the sofa with your foot on some cushions if you've injured your leg.

Figure 1.2.18 Bupa's guide to PRICE

Recognising concussion using the six Rs

Concussion is a brain injury and is very serious. World Rugby has launched a 'recognise and remove' campaign involving six Rs, shown in Table 1.2.36.

Six Rs: protocol for recognition of concussion: recognise, remove, refer, rest, recover and return.

Table 1.2.36 The six Rs

Recognise	Learn the signs and symptoms of a concussion to help identify when an athlete might have a suspected concussion.
Remove	Any athlete who has a concussion or a suspected concussion must be removed from play immediately.
Refer	Once removed, the athlete should be referred immediately to a qualified healthcare professional who is trained in evaluating and treating concussion.
Rest	Athletes must rest from exercise until symptom-free and must not be left alone in the first 24 hours.
Recover	Athletes must be fully recovered and be symptom-free from the concussion before returning to play. Adults must take a minimum of 1 week and under-18s a minimum of 2 weeks before seeking an authorised return from a healthcare professional.
Return	For safe return to play, the athlete must be symptom-free and cleared in writing by a qualified healthcare professional who is trained in evaluating and treating concussion. The athlete completes the GRTP (graduated return to play) protocol.

Now test yourself

10 When would you use SALTAPS?

11 With what type of injury would you use PRICE?

Answers on p. 169

Rehabilitation of injury

Rehabilitation depends on an accurate diagnosis and specialist treatment. There are three recognised stages of rehabilitation:
1 Early stage: gentle exercise encouraging damaged tissue to heal.
2 Mid stage: progressive loading of connective tissues and bones to develop strength.
3 Late stage: functional exercises and drills to ensure the body is ready to return to training.

Rehabilitation: the process of restoring full function after an injury has occurred.

Non-steroid anti-inflammatory drugs (NSAIDs): medication taken to reduce inflammation, temperature and pain following injury.

Physiotherapy: physical treatment of injuries and disease using methods such as mobilisation, massage, exercise therapy and postural training.

Treatment of common sporting injuries

Simple fracture (depending on site and severity)

Treat as follows:
+ medical attention as soon as possible
+ PRICE
+ immobilisation (plaster cast, sling, crutches)
+ anti-inflammatory and pain medication (NSAIDs)
+ severe fractures may require surgery to realign bones or fix pins and wires
+ physiotherapy may be needed.

Stress fracture
Treat as follows:
- medical attention required for diagnosis and advice
- PRICE
- rest for 2 weeks, avoid activity for 8 weeks
- immobilisation may be needed
- gentle return to exercise
- strengthening exercises for surrounding connective tissue.

Dislocation (depending on site and severity)
Treat as follows:
- medical attention as soon as possible
- immobilisation; no attempt to reposition bones unless a medical professional
- PRICE
- anti-inflammatory and pain medication
- severe dislocations may require surgery to realign bones and pin them into their original position
- physiotherapy will strengthen surrounding connective tissue and improve mobility.

Sprain (depending on site and severity)
Treat as follows:
- medical attention may be required in severe cases
- PRICE
- immobilisation or support using strapping, a brace, crutches
- anti-inflammatory and pain medication
- exercise to strengthen surrounding connective tissue and improve mobility and balance
- severe sprains may need reconstructive surgery
- heat therapy and contrast therapy can be used for pain relief.

Torn cartilage (depending on site and severity)
Treat as follows:
- medical attention
- PRICE
- support using strapping, a brace (e.g. knee brace)
- anti-inflammatory and pain medication
- physiotherapy to strengthen surrounding connective tissue and restore range of motion
- hydrotherapy to maintain fitness without weight bearing
- arthroscopy surgery can be used to reshape and resurface torn cartilage.

Exercise-induced muscle damage
Treat as follows:
- in most cases medical attention is **not** required and symptoms should improve in 5 days
- cold therapy such as ice pack, ice baths post-exercise
- massage therapy and stretching techniques
- anti-inflammatory and pain medication
- medical attention may be needed if heavy swelling or dark urine.

> **Heat therapy**: applying heat to an area before training for a therapeutic effect, such as increased blood flow.
>
> **Contrast therapy**: the use of alternate cold and heat for a therapeutic effect, such as increased blood flow.
>
> **Arthroscopy**: a minimally invasive procedure to examine and repair damage within a joint.
>
> **Cold therapy or cryotherapy**: applying ice or cold to an injury or after exercise for therapeutic effect, such as reduced swelling.
>
> **Massage therapy**: a physical therapy used for injury prevention and soft tissue injury treatment.

> **Making links**
>
> A lack of warm-up or cool-down can impact on a performer and could cause injury (Chapter 1.2b, Preparation and training methods).

Exam practice

1. Explain how a cool-down works and why it is useful for an athlete. [6]
2. Define rehabilitation and describe the three stages of rehabilitation after injury. [4]
3. Explain why a compound fracture is an example of an acute, hard tissue injury. [2]
4. Describe how you might treat a simple torn cartilage. [4]

Answers on pp. 177–178

Knowledge and skills summary

By the end of this chapter, you should have the following knowledge (AO1):

- Acute injuries resulting from a sudden stress to the body: hard tissue injuries, soft tissue injuries, concussion.
- Chronic injuries resulting from continuous stress to the body: soft tissue injuries, hard tissue injuries.
- Injury prevention:
  - intrinsic risk factors: individual variables, training effects
  - extrinsic risk factors: poor technique/training; incorrect equipment/clothing; inappropriate intensity, duration or frequency of activity.
- The debate surrounding effective warm-up and cool-down.
- Assessing sporting injuries using SALTAPS: stop, ask, look, touch, active movement, passive movement, strength testing.
- Acute management of soft tissue injuries using PRICE: protect, rest, ice, compress, elevate.
- Recognising concussion – World Rugby's six Rs: recognise, remove, refer, rest, recover, return.
- Treatment of common sporting injuries: fractures (simple, stress), joint injuries (dislocation, sprain, torn cartilage), exercise-induced muscle damage.
- Treatments: stretching; massage; heat, cold and contrast therapies; anti-inflammatory drugs; physiotherapy; surgery.

AO2 and AO3

- For AO2 marks, you may be asked to apply an example, or give a practical description of a warm-up or cool-down.
- For AO3 marks, you may be asked to analyse the effectiveness of a warm-up in preventing injury.

1.3a Biomechanical principles, levers and the use of technology

Biomechanical principles

Biomechanics is the study of human movement and the effects of force and motion on sport performance.

Newton's laws of motion

Using the laws and principles of physics, we can understand why bodies move or do not move.

Table 1.3.1 Newton's laws of motion

Law of motion	Definition	Application
First law: law of inertia	A body continues in a state of rest or uniform velocity unless acted upon by an external or unbalanced force.	A golf ball will remain still unless the force applied by a golf club makes it move; or that same golf ball will continue to move at a constant velocity (speed in a straight line) unless a force acts on it to slow it down (e.g. wind resistance) or change its direction (e.g. gravity).
Second law: law of acceleration	A body's rate of change of momentum is proportional to the size of the force applied and acts in the same direction as the force applied.	When a golf ball is struck by a golf club, the rate of change of momentum (or velocity) of the ball is proportional to the size of the force applied to it by the club. The bigger the force, the greater the acceleration. A popular way of describing Newton's second law of motion, particularly when doing calculations, is F = ma or force = mass × acceleration.
Third law: law of reaction	For every action there is an equal and opposite reaction.	If a tennis player hits a ball, the racquet exerts a force on the ball and the ball exerts an equal and opposite force on the racquet. The racquet exerts what is known as the action force and the ball exerts the reaction force. If the tennis ball then hits the ground, it exerts a force on the ground and the ground exerts an equal and opposite force on the ball.

Key formulae for calculations

Table 1.3.2 summarises the definitions and equations needed for calculations.

Table 1.3.2 Formulae and how to calculate them

Term	Definition	Equation
Velocity (m/s)	Rate of change of displacement (the shortest straight-line route between start and finish points)	Velocity = displacement/time taken
Momentum (kgm/s)	Quantity of motion possessed by a moving body	Momentum = mass × velocity
Acceleration (m/s/s)	Rate of change of velocity	Acceleration = (final velocity − initial velocity)/time taken
Force (N)	A push or a pull that alters the state of motion of a body	Force = mass × acceleration

Quick quizzes at www.hoddereducation.co.uk/myrevisionnotesdownloads

Worked example

1. Calculate the velocity of a sprinter who completes a 100 m race in 14.1 s.

   $v = d/t$

   $100/14.1 = 7.09\,m/s$

2. If the velocity of a swimmer is 1.75 m/s in a 100 m breaststroke race, how long does it take the swimmer to complete the race?

   $v = d/t$

   $t = d/v$

   $100/1.75 = 57.14\,s$

3. Calculate the momentum of a 4 kg shot put travelling at 5.75 m/s.

   momentum = mass × velocity

   $4 \times 5.75 = 23\,kgm/s$

4. What is the average acceleration of a sprinter who completes a 100 m race in 12.24 s?

   acceleration = (fv − iv)/t

   $fv = 100/12.24 = 8.17\,m/s$

   $iv = 0\,m/s$

   $(8.17 − 0)/12.24 = 0.67\,m/s/s$

5. A discus weighing 1.5 kg accelerates at 9.86 m/s. What is the force of the discus?

   $F = ma$

   $1.5 \times 9.68 = 14.79\,N$

> **Exam tip**
>
> Learn all definitions, equations and correct units.

Force

There are two types of force: external force (comes from outside the body) and internal force (generated by skeletal muscle). Force can have five effects. It can:

+ create motion
+ accelerate a body
+ decelerate a body
+ change the direction of a body
+ change the shape of a body.

Net force

If net force = 0, there is no change in motion as the forces are balanced.

If a net force is present, there is a change in motion as the forces are unbalanced. This occurs when two forces are unequal in size and opposite in direction.

External forces

The external forces acting on a performer in contact with the ground can be divided into:

+ vertical forces: weight and reaction
+ horizontal forces: friction and air resistance.

Vertical forces

+ **Weight** is the gravitational pull that the earth exerts on a body. Weight is measured in newtons (N) and is calculated by multiplying mass (kg) and acceleration due to gravity (m/s/s).
+ **Reaction** is the equal and opposite force exerted by a body in response to the action force placed upon it. It is measured in newtons (N). It is a result of Newton's third law of motion and is always present when two bodies are in contact.

> **Revision activity**
>
> Add a sporting example to each of the effects of force.

> **Net force**: the sum of all forces acting on a body; also termed resultant force. It is the overall force acting on a body when all individual forces have been considered.
>
> **Weight**: the gravitational pull that the earth exerts on a body. Weight (N) = mass × acceleration due to gravity (g).
>
> **Reaction**: the equal and opposite force exerted by a body in response to the action force placed upon it.

Horizontal forces

+ **Friction** is the force that opposes the motion of two surfaces in contact. It is measured in newtons (N). Friction is affected by several factors, as outlined in Table 1.3.3.

Table 1.3.3 Factors that affect friction

Factor affecting friction	Example
Roughness of the ground surface	Athletes run on rough, rubberised tracks.
Roughness of the contact surface	Athletes wear spiked shoes.
Temperature	F1 drivers have a warm-up lap, as friction is increased with higher temperatures.
Size of normal reaction	Shot putters have a high mass; due to Newton's third law, this creates an equal and opposite high reaction force, allowing greater friction in the throwing circle and preventing over-rotation.

+ **Air resistance** is the force that opposes motion through the air. It is a form of fluid friction, measured in newtons (N). It is affected by several factors, outlined in Table 1.3.4.

Table 1.3.4 Factors that affect air resistance

Factor affecting air resistance	Example
Velocity	The greater the velocity of a cyclist, the greater the force of air resistance opposing their motion.
Shape	Most cyclists wear a helmet with a tear-drop or aerofoil shape to minimise air resistance – known as **streamlining**.
Frontal cross-sectional area	The low crouched position of a downhill skier reduces air resistance.
Smoothness of surface	Increased smoothness from lycra suits reduces air resistance.

> **Friction**: the force that opposes the motion of two surfaces in contact.
>
> **Air resistance**: the force that opposes the direction of motion of a body through air.
>
> **Streamlining**: the creation of smooth air flow around an aerodynamic shape to minimise air resistance.

Now test yourself
TESTED

1. Define Newton's laws of motion.
2. What is net force?
3. Name and describe the two vertical and two horizontal forces.
4. A shot put weighs 5 kg and accelerates at 2.54 m/s. What is the force of the shot put?
5. Calculate the velocity of a javelin that travels 65 m in 4 s.
6. Name four factors that affect friction.
7. Name four factors that affect air resistance.
8. For each factor that affects air resistance, identify a different practical example from those given in Table 1.3.4 above.

Answers on p. 169

> **Exam tip**
>
> Biomechanics questions always require a practical example to explain each point. No example = no marks.

Free body diagrams

A **free body diagram** is a clearly labelled sketch showing all the forces acting on a body at a particular instant in time.

> **Exam tip**
>
> Keep free body diagrams simple. Draw a stick person to represent the athlete and identify all the forces acting on them at that moment.

> **Free body diagram**: a clearly labelled sketch showing all the forces acting on a body at a particular instant in time.

Table 1.3.5 Vertical forces

Force (label)	Vertical forces	
	Weight (W)	Reaction (R)
Origin and direction of arrow	From the centre of mass extending vertically downwards	From the point of contact extending vertically upwards
Size of arrow and relationship between forces	If weight is equal in size to reaction (W = R), net force is zero. Forces are balanced (equal in size but opposite in direction). Therefore, the body will remain at rest, for example a basketballer preparing to take a free throw or travelling in constant vertical velocity. If reaction force is greater than weight (R > W), net force is positive. Forces are unbalanced and acceleration in an upward direction will occur, for example a basketballer leaving the ground in the take-off phase of a lay-up shot.	

Table 1.3.6 Horizontal forces

Force (label)	Horizontal forces	
	Friction (F)	Air resistance (AR)
Origin and direction of arrow	From the point of contact and usually extending horizontally in the same direction as motion (parallel to the surfaces)	From the centre of mass and extending horizontally against the direction of motion
Size of arrow and relationship between forces	If friction is equal in size to air resistance (F = AR), net force is zero. Forces are balanced (equal in size but opposite in direction). Therefore, the body will continue to travel in constant velocity, for example a sprint cyclist who has reached maximum velocity on the track. If friction is greater than air resistance (F > AR), net force is positive. Forces are unbalanced and acceleration in a forward direction will occur, for example a sprint cyclist accelerating away from the starting line. If air resistance is greater than friction (AR > F), net force is negative. Forces are unbalanced and horizontal deceleration will occur, for example a sprint cyclist crossing the finish line, sitting up and decelerating.	

Examples of free body diagrams

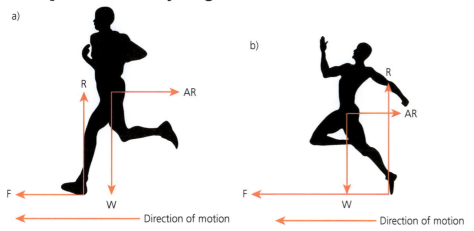

Figure 1.3.1 Free body diagrams: a) marathon runner travelling at a constant velocity: W = R, F = AR, balanced forces, net force = 0; b) long jumper accelerating forwards and upwards at take-off: R > W, F > AR, unbalanced forces, positive net force, long jumper experiences forward and vertical acceleration

Centre of mass

- The centre of mass is the point at which an object or a body is balanced in all directions.
- It is the point where the weight of the body tends to be concentrated.
- For a round object, this is generally in the middle.
- It can be more complex for the human body, especially when moving.

If an athlete raises their arms, their centre of mass will move up. The centre of mass can also be outside the body and act as a point of rotation.

> **Centre of mass**: the point at which an object or a body is balanced in all directions; the point at which weight appears to act.

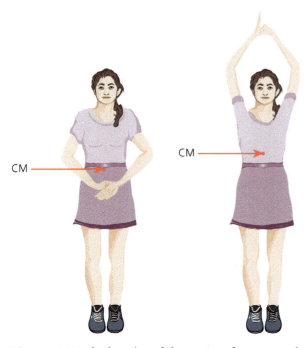

Figure 1.3.2 The location of the centre of mass on a body

Stability

Stability is the ability of a body to resist motion and remain at rest. It is also the ability to withstand a force applied and return to the original position without damage (remain in a balanced position).

The factors that affect stability are outlined in Table 1.3.7.

Table 1.3.7 Factors that affect stability

Factor	Effect on stability
Mass of the body	The greater the mass, the greater the inertia (e.g. a sumo wrestler)
Height of the centre of mass	The lower the centre of mass, the greater the stability
Base of support	The greater the size of the base of support, the greater the stability; this can be increased by more points of contact
Line of gravity	The more central the line of gravity to the base of support, the greater the stability

Maximising and minimising stability: application

- In a sprint start, a sprinter preparing in the blocks has maximum stability.
- When 'set' is called, the sprinter lifts their hips, raising their centre of mass; lifts one knee, reducing the points of contact; and leans forward, thus minimising stability to be ready for movement.
- When the gun is fired, instability is maximised to aid performance. The chest lifts, raising the centre of mass; the hands come off the track; and the line of gravity falls in front of the base of support, causing the body to fall forwards.
- This must be prevented by driving one leg forward with great speed. This minimises movement time and gives the perfect start from which to drive forwards.

Quick quizzes at www.hoddereducation.co.uk/myrevisionnotesdownloads

> **Now test yourself** TESTED
>
> 9 What is centre of mass?
> 10 Name the factors that affect stability.
> 11 Give an example of an activity other than sprinting where it is important to have maximum stability and minimum stability in different aspects of the activity.
>
> **Answers on p. 169**

Levers

REVISED

Lever systems enable the co-ordination of our bones and muscles, primarily to create human movement. They have two main functions:
+ to generate muscular effort to overcome a given load
+ to increase the speed of a given movement.

Components of a lever system

Table 1.3.8 Lever system components applied to a biceps curl

Component	Location in the body	Diagram notation	Example: upward phase of a biceps curl
Lever	Bone	Line	Radius and ulna
Fulcrum	Joint	Triangle	Elbow joint
Effort	Muscular force	Arrow (E)	Force created by biceps brachii
Load	Weight or resistance	Arrow (L)	Weight of the forearm and free weight held

Classification of levers

Most levers in the human body are third-class ones, where the muscle crosses but attaches close to the joint and the load acts at the other end of the lever, such as flexion of the elbow and extension at the knee.

Class	Order of components	Example in the body
First	Fulcrum is in the middle E – F – L or L – F – E	Extension of the neck when preparing to head a football
Second	Load is in the middle E – L – F or F – L – E	Ball of the foot in the take-off phase of a high jump

Class	Order of components	Example in the body
Third	Effort is in the middle L – E – F or F – E – L 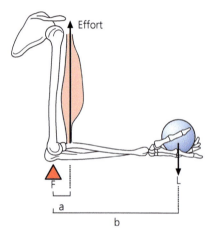	Flexion of the elbow during a biceps curl 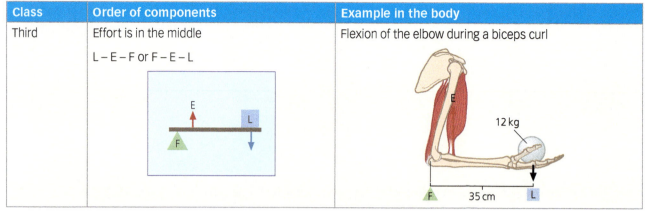

Figure 1.3.3 Classification of lever systems with examples in the human body

Efficiency of the lever system

The order and distance of the lever system components from the fulcrum is important to their function:
1 The distance from the fulcrum to the effort is known as the 'effort arm'.
2 The distance from the load to the fulcrum is known as the 'load arm'.

Figure 1.3.4 Third-class lever system at the elbow: a = effort arm, b = load arm

+ The greater the distance of the effort or load from the fulcrum, the more significant the effort or load becomes.
+ Longer levers generate greater forces as the load arm becomes longer and therefore can give greater acceleration to projectiles.
+ The length of the effort arm and the load arm gives a lever system either the mechanical advantage or the mechanical disadvantage.
+ A second-class lever has the mechanical advantage to move a large load with a small effort, such as at the ball of the foot to vertically accelerate an athlete's whole weight easily.
+ A third-class lever has the mechanical disadvantage, requiring a large effort to move a relatively small load, for example flexion of the elbow in an upward phase of a biceps curl.

Mechanical advantage: second-class lever systems where the effort arm is greater than the load arm. A large load can be moved with a relatively small effort.

Mechanical disadvantage: third-class lever systems where the load arm is greater than the effort arm. A large effort is required to move a relatively small load.

> **Now test yourself** TESTED
>
> 12 Name the components of a lever system.
> 13 What are the mechanical advantage and the mechanical disadvantage?
>
> **Answers on p. 169**

Analysis of movement using technology

Table 1.3.9 details different technologies that can be used to analyse movement.

Table 1.3.9 How technologies can be used to analyse movement

Technology	Definition	Use	Optimising performance
Limb kinematics	Study of movement in relation to time and space	3D or optical motion analysis records an athlete performing a sporting action, allowing the evaluation of the efficiency of movement.	Data produced can be used by coaches to improve performance/specific techniques of athletes.
Force plates	Ground reaction forces are measured in laboratory conditions using force plates	Athletes balance, run and jump on a force plate, which assesses the size and direction of forces acting on the athlete, acceleration rates, work and power output.	Used for sports biomechanics assessment, gait analysis, balance rehabilitation and physical therapy.
Wind tunnels	Steel frame building containing wide fans, where artificial wind is produced	Technology is used to develop the drag reduction system. Objects such as cycle helmets and F1 cars can be tested for aerodynamic efficiency.	Engineers study the flow of air around the object. The aim is to improve the flow of air around an object, streamlining its path through the oncoming air and potentially increasing lift or decreasing drag.

Exam practice

1. Explain how Newton's laws of motion and the application of force can be applied to a tennis serve. [6]
2. Using examples from PE or sport, explain how changes in the position of a performer's centre of mass can affect performance. [5]
3. A rugby player has a mass of 98 kg and takes 2.6 seconds to accelerate from a standing start to 8 m/s. Calculate the weight of the player, their acceleration between 0s and 2.6s and their momentum at maximum velocity. Assume $g = 10$ m/s/s. [6]

Answers on p. 178

Knowledge and skills summary

By the end of this chapter, you should have the following knowledge (AO1):

- Newton's laws of motion.
- Net force.
- Balanced and unbalanced force.
- Weight.
- Reaction.
- Friction.
- Air resistance.
- Factors affecting friction and air resistance and their manipulation in sporting performance.
- Free body diagrams showing vertical and horizontal forces acting on a body at an instant in time and the resulting motion.
- Calculations of force, momentum, acceleration and weight.
- The definition of centre of mass.
- Factors affecting the position of the centre of mass.
- The relationship between centre of mass and stability.
- The components of a lever system.
- First-class, second-class and third-class levers; mechanical advantage of a second-class lever.
- Limb kinematics, force plates, wind tunnels; how each type of technology may be used to optimise performance in sport.

AO2 and AO3

- For AO2 marks, you may be asked to apply Newton's laws to a specific sporting activity (e.g. kicking a football).
- For AO3 marks, you may be asked to analyse why an athlete may wish to move their centre of mass or may value the use of technology within sport biomechanics.
- Quantitative skills may be tested in this chapter, for example biomechanical calculations or interpreting a free body diagram.

1.3b Linear motion, angular motion, fluid mechanics and projectile motion

Linear motion

REVISED

Linear motion results from a direct force being applied to a body, i.e. where force is applied directly to the centre of a body's mass (centre force), for example a skeleton bob at top speed.

Descriptions of linear motion

There are five key descriptors that can be calculated to build data and create a picture of performance.

Table 1.3.10 The five performance descriptors

Descriptor	Definition	Calculation	Unit of measurement
Distance	Total length of the path covered from start to finish	Measured	Metres (m)
Displacement	The shortest straight-line route from start to finish	Measured	Metres (m)
Speed	The rate of change in distance	Speed = distance/time taken	Metres per second (m/s)
Velocity	The rate of change of displacement	Velocity = displacement/time taken	Metres per second (m/s)
Acceleration/deceleration	The rate of change in velocity	Acceleration = (final velocity − initial velocity)/time taken	Metres per second per second (m/s/s)

Graphs of linear motion

Distance/time graphs

A distance/time graph shows the distance a body travels over a period of time. The gradient of the curve indicates the speed of a body at a particular instant.

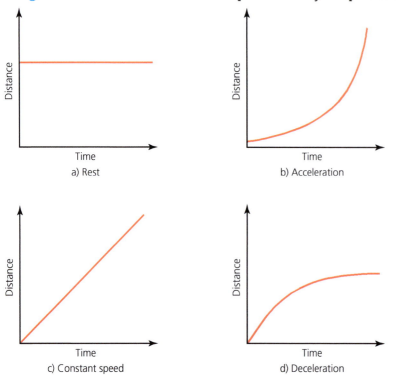

Figure 1.3.5 Stages of motion represented with distance/time graphs: a) rest, b) acceleration, c) constant speed and d) deceleration

> **Linear motion**: movement of a body in a straight or curved line where all parts move the same distance in the same direction over the same time.
>
> **Direct force**: a force applied through the centre of mass resulting in linear motion.
>
> **Distance/time graph**: a visual representation of the distance travelled plotted against the time taken.
>
> **Gradient**: the slope of a graph at a particular moment in time. Gradient = change in y axis/change in x axis.

Quick quizzes at www.hoddereducation.co.uk/myrevisionnotesdownloads

Speed/time graphs

A speed/time graph shows the speed of a body over a particular time. The gradient of the curve indicates the acceleration/deceleration of the body at a particular instant.

Speed/time graph: a visual representation of the speed of motion plotted against the time taken.

Acceleration/deceleration: the rate of change in velocity (m/s/s) calculated as (final velocity – initial velocity)/time taken.

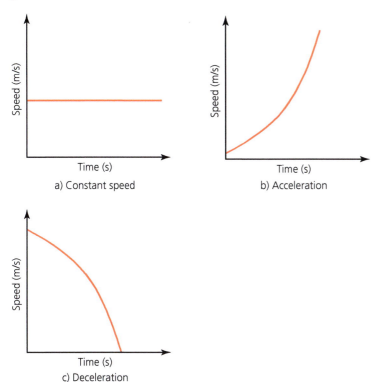

Figure 1.3.6 Stages of motion represented with speed/time graphs: a) constant speed, b) acceleration and c) deceleration

Velocity/time graphs

A velocity/time graph shows the velocity of a body over a period of time. The gradient of the curve indicates the acceleration or deceleration of the body at a particular instant.

Velocity/time graph: a visual representation of the velocity of motion plotted against the time taken.

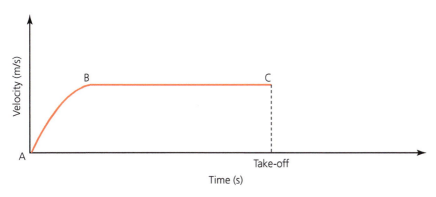

Figure 1.3.7 A velocity/time graph showing the descent of a ski jumper down the ramp prior to take-off

A velocity/time graph can also show any change in direction the body makes. A negative curve below the horizontal axis represents a change in the body's direction.

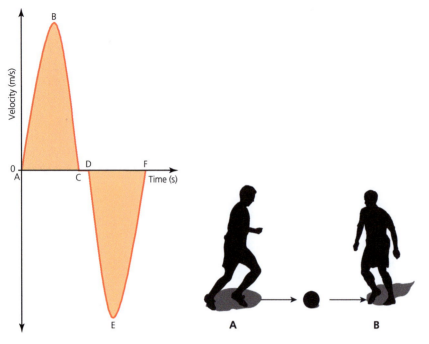

Figure 1.3.8 A velocity/time graph showing the motion of a ball being passed between two players

> **Exam tip**
>
> For graphs of linear motion, always plot time on the horizontal axis, label the axes (including units) and use a curved line of best fit.

> **Now test yourself** TESTED
>
> 1 Define linear motion.
> 2 How is linear motion created?
> 3 What is the difference between distance and displacement?
> 4 Plot a distance/time graph for a body that is accelerating.
> 5 Plot a speed/time graph for a body that is travelling at a constant speed.
>
> Answers on pp. 169–170

Angular motion   REVISED

Angular motion results from an eccentric force being applied to a body, i.e. where the force is applied outside the centre of a body's mass.

An eccentric force is also known as torque – a turning or rotational force, for example a gymnastic somersault.

Principal axes of rotation

If an eccentric force is applied to a body, it will rotate around one (or more) of the three principal axes of rotation.

> **Angular motion**: movement of a body or part of a body in a circular path about an axis of rotation.
>
> **Eccentric force**: a force applied outside the centre of mass, resulting in angular motion.
>
> **Torque**: a measure of the turning (rotational or eccentric) force applied to a body.

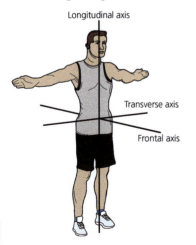

Figure 1.3.9 The principal axes of rotation

Quick quizzes at www.hoddereducation.co.uk/myrevisionnotesdownloads

Table 1.3.11 details the principal axes of rotation with practical sporting examples.

Table 1.3.11 Axes of rotation with sporting examples

Axis	Location	Example
Longitudinal	Runs from the top to the bottom of the body	A trampolinist performs a full twist turn
Transverse	Runs from side to side of the body	A front somersault
Frontal	Runs from the front to the back of the body	A gymnast performs a cartwheel

Descriptions of angular motion

Table 1.3.12 details definitions and equations relating to angular motion.

Table 1.3.12 Angular motion

Descriptor	Definition	Calculation	Unit of measurement
Moment of inertia (MI)	The resistance of a body to change its angular motion or rotation	Moment of inertia = sum (mass × distribution of the mass from the axis of rotation²) $MI = \sum m \times r^2$	Kilogram metres² (kg m²)
Angular velocity	The rate of change in angular displacement or rate of rotation	Angular velocity = angular displacement/time taken	Radians per second (rad/s)
Angular momentum	The quantity of angular motion possessed by a body	Angular momentum = moment of inertia × angular velocity	Kilogram metres² per second (kgm²/s)

Factors affecting the size of the moment of inertia of a rotating body

The two factors that affect moment of inertia (MI) are mass and the distribution of mass from the axis of rotation:

1 **Mass:**
   + The greater the mass, the greater the MI; the lower the mass, the easier it is to change the rate of rotation.
   + Sports with a high degree of rotation (e.g. high board diving) are typically performed by athletes with a low mass.
2 **Distribution of the mass from the axis of rotation:**
   + The further the mass moves from the axis of rotation, the greater the MI.
   + The more closely mass is tucked in around the axis of rotation, the lower the MI, for example a tucked somersault.
   + When performing a tucked front somersault, the body will face less resistance to rotation and therefore will rotate more quickly compared with a straight front somersault.

MI has a direct effect on angular velocity:
+ If MI is high, resistance to rotation is also high, therefore angular velocity is low; the rate of spin is slow.
+ If MI is low, resistance to rotation is also low, therefore angular velocity is high; the rate of spin is fast.

Figure 1.3.10 An ice skater manipulating his body position to alter moment of inertia and angular velocity: a) low MI = fast rate of spin and b) high MI = slow rate of spin

Conservation of angular momentum

+ Angular momentum, once generated, does not change throughout a movement.
+ It remains constant and therefore is termed a 'conserved' quantity.
+ The conservation of angular momentum is a concept associated with the angular analogue of Newton's first law of motion.
+ As angular momentum cannot be changed once in flight, it is important to generate as much angular momentum as possible at take-off.
+ Performers can then manipulate MI and angular velocity to maximise performance.
+ The following should be considered:
  + axis of rotation
  + phases of motion.

> **Conservation of angular momentum**: angular momentum is a conserved quantity that remains constant unless an external eccentric force or torque is applied.
>
> **Angular analogue of Newton's first law of motion**: the angular equivalent of Newton's first law of motion: a rotating body will continue to turn about an axis of rotation with constant angular momentum unless acted upon by an eccentric force or external torque.

Practical example

Figure 1.3.11 Angular momentum remains constant about the longitudinal axis throughout flight when performing a triple axel jump in ice skating

+ At take-off (a) angular momentum is generated by the ice skater applying an eccentric force from the ice to the body.
+ Rotation starts about the longitudinal axis.
+ Distribution of mass is away from the longitudinal axis. MI is high, angular velocity low. The ice skater goes into the jump rotating slowly with control.
+ During flight (b), mass is distributed close to the longitudinal axis. MI is decreased, angular velocity increases. The ice skater spins quickly, allowing several rotations in the air.

Quick quizzes at www.hoddereducation.co.uk/myrevisionnotesdownloads

- In preparation for landing (c), mass is distributed away from the longitudinal axis. MI is raised, angular velocity reduced. The ice skater decreases their rate of spin, increasing control, for landing.
- As the ice skater is landing, the ice applies an external torque to remove the conserved quantity of angular momentum.

Graph of angular velocity, moment of inertia and angular momentum

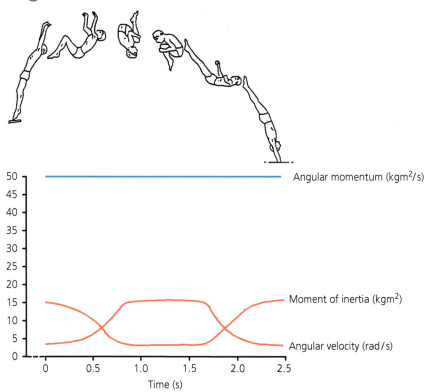

Figure 1.3.12 The relationship between moment of inertia, angular velocity and angular momentum of a diver performing a one-and-a-half backward rotation into the water

- At take-off, angular momentum is generated by an eccentric force from the springboard acting on the body.
- Rotation starts about the transverse axis.
- The straight body position distributes mass away from the transverse axis. MI is high, angular velocity low. The diver rotates slowly with control.
- During flight, the tucked body position distributes mass close to the transverse axis. MI is decreased, angular velocity is increased. The diver rotates quickly.
- Preparing to enter the water, the straightened body distributes mass way from the transverse axis. MI is increased, angular velocity is decreased. The rate of spin decreases, so the diver gains control on entry.
- Angular momentum is conserved throughout the movement.

> **Exam tip**
>
> Use subject-specific vocabulary to fully explain your answers. For example, 'In the flight phase, the gymnast has a tucked position to distribute the mass close to the transverse axis of rotation. This will decrease the moment of inertia and increase the rate of spin, allowing more rotations' – rather than 'the gymnast tucks to spin faster in the air'.

Now test yourself   TESTED

6. What is angular motion?
7. How is angular motion created?
8. What are the three principal axes of rotation?
9. Define moment of inertia, angular velocity and angular momentum, stating the units they are measured in.
10. Calculate the moment of inertia for a 50 kg ice skater who is spinning with their arms out wide, measuring 1.5 m.

Answers on p. 170

Fluid mechanics

REVISED

Fluid mechanics is the study of the forces acting on a body travelling through the air or water.

There are four main factors that affect air resistance and drag on the body, as outlined in Table 1.3.13.

Drag: the force that opposes the direction of motion of a body through water or air.

Table 1.3.13 Factors that affect air resistance and drag

Factor	Explanation and example
Velocity	The greater the velocity, the greater the force of air resistance or drag opposing motion. Track cyclists and freestyle swimmers are greatly affected by this, due to their high velocity.
Frontal cross-sectional area	The greater the frontal cross-sectional area, the greater the air resistance or drag. The low crouched position of a downhill skier reduces air resistance and drag.
Streamlining and shape	The more aerodynamic the shape of a body or equipment, the lower the air resistance or drag. Streamlined body shape out of a tumble turn in swimming reduces drag.
Surface characteristics	The smoother the surface, the lower the air resistance or drag. Lycra suits reduce air resistance. Swimmers wear specially designed suits to minimise drag.

> **Revision activity**
>
> Apply the principles above to downhill mountain biking, track cycling and backstroke.

Projectile motion

REVISED

Factors affecting the horizontal distance travelled by a projectile

Table 1.3.14 identifies the factors affecting the horizontal distance travelled by a projectile.

Projectile motion: movement of a body through the air following a curved flight path under the force of gravity.

Projectile: a body that is launched into the air, losing contact with the ground surface, such as a discus or a long jumper.

Table 1.3.14 Factors affecting the horizontal distance travelled by a projectile

Factor	Explanation
Speed of release	Due to Newton's second law, the greater the outgoing speed of the projectile, the further it will travel.
Angle of release	45 degrees is the optimal angle to maximise horizontal distance.
Height of release	45 degrees is the optimal angle if the release height and landing height are equal. Where release height is higher than landing height, the optimal angle is less than 45 degrees (e.g. javelin). Where release height is lower than landing height, the optimal angle is greater than 45 degrees (e.g. bunker shot in golf).
Aerodynamic factors	Bernoulli and Magnus (see pp. 98 and 100).

Projectiles in flight

Once released, a projectile follows a flight path determined by the relative size of the forces acting on it. Depending on the dominant force, the flight path will be more or less parabolic (parabola-like) in nature.

Parabola: a uniform curve symmetrical about its highest point.

If weight is the dominant force and air resistance is very small, a parabolic flight path occurs.
+ For example, a shot put has a high mass and travels through the air with a low velocity, with a small front cross-sectional area and smooth surface, making air resistance minimal.
+ The flight path has a parabolic shape, symmetrical about its highest point.

Parabolic flight path: a flight path symmetrical about its highest point caused by the dominant weight force of a projectile.

Quick quizzes at www.hoddereducation.co.uk/myrevisionnotesdownloads

If air resistance is the dominant force and weight is very small, a non-parabolic flight path occurs.
+ For example, a badminton shuttle has a very low mass and travels at high velocities with a relatively uneven surface, which all increase air resistance.
+ The flight path has a non-parabolic shape, asymmetrical (unequal) about its highest point.

> **Non-parabolic flight path**: a flight path asymmetrical about its highest point caused by the dominant force of air resistance on a projectile.

Figure 1.3.13 The parabolic flight path of a shot compared with the non-parabolic flight paths of a shuttle and a discus

Free body diagrams

The forces acting on a projectile can be represented with a free body diagram.
+ There are three phases of motion within a flight path to the highest point, after which gravity will accelerate the projectile's mass to the ground.
+ These can be described as start of flight, mid-flight and end of flight.
+ Weight does not change over the three phases. Air resistance will be greater at the start.

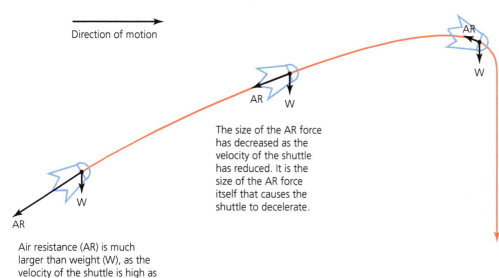

Figure 1.3.14 Free body diagram of a shuttle in the start of flight, mid-flight and end of flight phases

	Free body diagram	Dominant force	Resulting flight path
Shot	Direction of motion; Air resistance ← ○ ↓ Weight	Weight > air resistance	Parabolic
Shuttle	Direction of motion; Air resistance ← 🏸 ↓ Weight	Air resistance < weight	Non-parabolic

Figure 1.3.15 Free body diagrams, dominant forces and flight paths compared for a shot in athletics and a hard-hit badminton shuttle

Parallelogram of forces

A parallelogram of forces can be drawn to consider the result of all the forces acting on a projectile in flight.

How to draw a parallelogram of forces
1. Draw a free body diagram showing weight and air resistance.
2. Add broken parallel lines to weight and air resistance arrows to create a parallelogram.
3. Draw a diagonal line from the origin of the weight and air resistance (centre of mass of the projectile) to the opposite corner of the parallelogram with a double arrow labelled 'resultant force'.

The resultant force shows the acceleration of a projectile and the direction in which the acceleration occurs. It will also indicate flight path.
+ If the resultant force is closer to the weight arrow, weight is dominant, so the flight path will be more parabolic.
+ If the resultant force is closer to the air resistance arrow, air resistance is dominant, so the flight path will be non-parabolic.

Parallelogram of forces: a parallelogram illustrating the theory that a diagonal drawn from the point where forces are represented in size and direction shows the resultant force acting.

Resultant force: the sum of all forces acting on a body or the net force acting on a projectile.

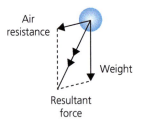

The resultant force shows deceleration to be occurring and weight to be dominant, leading to a parabolic flight path

Figure 1.3.16 Parallelogram of forces for a shot mid-flight showing the resultant force

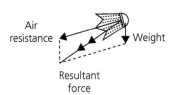

The resultant force shows deceleration to be occurring and air resistance to be dominant, leading to a non-parabolic flight path

Figure 1.3.17 Parallelogram of forces for a badminton shuttle mid-flight showing the resultant force

> **Exam tip**
>
> Do not create the parallelogram on the same free body diagram. Draw a second diagram, to ensure you can gain maximum marks.

Lift and the Bernoulli principle

The Bernoulli principle explains how an additional lift force can be created during flight based on a projectile's shape.

An aerofoil shape has:
+ a curved upper surface, forcing air flow to travel further distance and therefore move at a higher velocity
+ a flat underneath surface that allows air to travel a shorter distance at a lower velocity.

Therefore:
+ As velocity increases, pressure decreases.
+ As all fluids move from an area of high to low pressure, a pressure gradient forms, creating an additional lift force (following the Bernoulli principle).
+ Additional lift force can increase the time that a projectile hangs in the air, extending the flight path and horizontal distance covered, and leading to better results. Examples include discus, ski jumping and javelin.
+ Angle of attack must be considered for each projectile to maximise lift force.

Bernoulli principle: creation of an additional lift force on a projectile in flight resulting from Bernoulli's conclusion that the higher the velocity of air flow, the lower the surrounding pressure.

Lift force: an additional force created by a pressure gradient forming on opposing surfaces of an aerofoil moving through a fluid.

Aerofoil: a streamlined shape with a curved upper surface and flat lower surface designed to give an additional lift force to a body.

Angle of attack: the most favourable angle of release for a projectile to optimise lift force due to the Bernoulli principle.

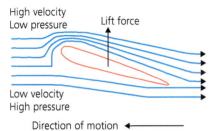

Figure 1.3.18 Air flow diagram of a discus in flight

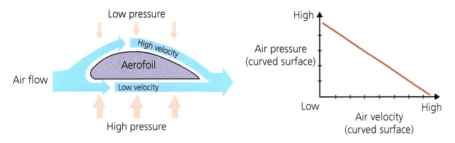

Figure 1.3.19 Air flow, velocity and pressure around an aerofoil in flight

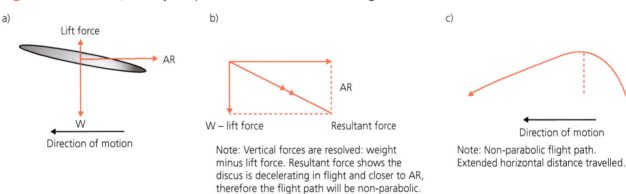

Figure 1.3.20 The effects of Bernoulli's lift force on a discus in flight: a) free body diagram, b) resultant force diagram and c) flight path diagram

Downward lift force

Bernoulli's lift force also works in the downward direction if the aerofoil shape is inverted. This is important in sports such as Formula 1 and track cycling to increase the downward force that holds the car or bike to the track at high speeds around corners.

> **Revision activity**
>
> Complete air flow diagrams, as in Figure 1.3.18, applied to the javelin throw and a ski jumper.

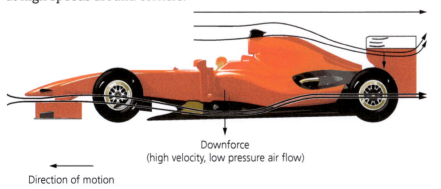

Figure 1.3.21 The downward lift force created by a Formula 1 car design: air flow diagram with high velocity air flow and low pressure underneath the car and spoiler

+ The front wing funnels air down through the narrow space underneath the car's chassis.
+ The spoiler acts as an inverted aerofoil, forcing air underneath to travel a further distance.
+ Air velocity underneath the car is increased, creating areas of low pressure.
+ A pressure gradient is formed; additional downward lift force is created.
+ The result is increased grip and friction around corners at high speeds.

> **Revision activity**
>
> Apply the downward lift force principles to a track cyclist. Consider the high seat position and helmet design (creating a flat upper body surface).

> **Now test yourself** TESTED
>
> 11 What is air resistance?
> 12 What is drag?
> 13 What are four main factors that affect air resistance and drag on a body?
> 14 What are the factors that affect the horizontal distance travelled by a projectile?
> 15 Which force is most dominant in a parabolic flight path of a projectile?
> 16 Which force is most dominant in a non-parabolic flight path of a projectile?
> 17 What is the Bernoulli principle?
> 18 Sketch a parallelogram of forces diagram for a cricket ball mid-flight and explain what the resultant force is and why.
>
> **Answers on p. 170**

Spin and the Magnus force

Spin is created by applying an external force outside the centre of mass. There are four types of spin, outlined in Table 1.3.15.

Table 1.3.15 The four types of spin

Type of spin	Where eccentric force is applied	How projectile spins
Topspin	Above the centre of mass	Downwards around the transverse axis
Backspin	Below the centre of mass	Upwards around the transverse axis
Sidespin hook	Right of the centre of mass	Left around the longitudinal axis
Sidespin slice	Left of the centre of mass	Right around the longitudinal axis

The way a projectile spins determines the direction, velocity and pressure of the air flow around it. A force called the Magnus force is created from a pressure gradient on either side of the spinning projectile, and an additional Magnus effect is created which deviates the flight path.
+ A topspin rotation creates a downward Magnus force, shortening the flight path.
+ A backspin rotation creates an upwards Magnus force, lengthening the flight path.
+ A sidespin rotation creates a Magnus force to the left or right, swerving the projectile left (hook) or right (slice).

Magnus force: a force created from a pressure gradient on opposing surfaces of a spinning body moving through the air.

Magnus effect: creation of an additional Magnus force on a spinning projectile which deviates the flight path.

Hook: a type of sidespin used to deviate a projectile's flight path to the left.

Slice: a type of sidespin used to deviate a projectile's flight path to the right.

Topspin: tennis example

For a ball with topspin, the additional Magnus force is created by:
1. the upper surface of the ball rotating towards the oncoming air flow, opposing motion, decreasing velocity of air flow and creating a high-pressure zone
2. the lower surface of the ball rotating in the same direction as the air flow, increasing velocity of air flow and creating a zone of low pressure
3. a pressure gradient forming and an additional Magnus force being created downwards.

The downward Magnus force adds to the weight of the projectile, the effect of gravity is increased and the projectile 'dips' in flight, giving less time in the air as the flight path shortens.

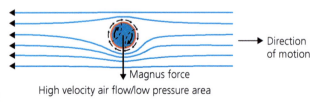

Figure 1.3.22 Air flow diagram illustrating the downward Magnus force created by topspin

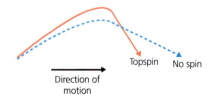

Figure 1.3.23 Flight path diagram showing the effect of topspin

Quick quizzes at www.hoddereducation.co.uk/myrevisionnotesdownloads

Benefits of spin in tennis and table tennis

+ It gives the ball stability in flight.
+ The use of topspin shortens the flight path, allowing ball to be hit harder but still land in court/on the table.
+ It can confuse the opposition.

Use of spin in golf and football

In golf and football, sidespin will allow the ball to swerve in flight, moving around obstacles (e.g. trees, or defensive walls in a free kick).

> **Exam tip**
>
> Always include the direction of travel or direction of motion in an air flow or flight path diagram.

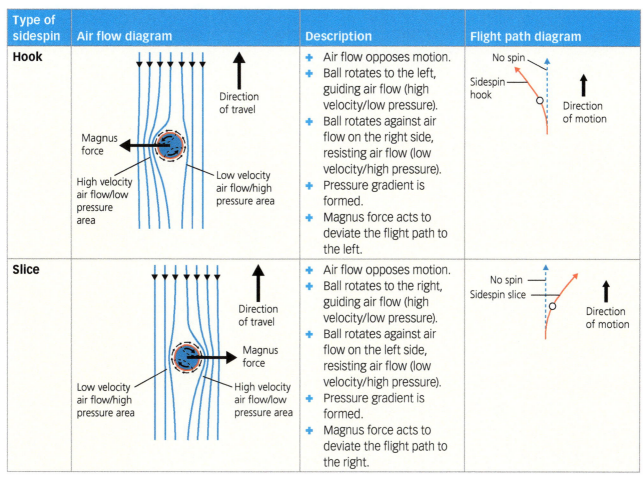

Figure 1.3.24 An overview of a golfball/football struck with sidespin (hook or slice)

> **Exam tip**
>
> When drawing an air flow diagram for a ball with topspin/backspin, it is viewed from the side, whereas sidespin is viewed from above. Air flow diagrams must show a) direction of air flow opposing direction of motion, b) direction of rotation of ball, c) velocity and pressure labels, d) tighter air flow lines with the direction of rotation side of the ball, e) Magnus force in the direction of the flight path deviation from the centre of mass.

> **Making links**
>
> + Consider the many links between topics within this chapter. Newton's laws are foundation knowledge for all principles of biomechanics.
> + The distance travelled by projectiles is linked to the factors at take-off.
> + Consider horizontal and vertical forces in all elements of human and projectile movement.

Now test yourself TESTED

19 What are the four types of spin?
20 What is a Magnus force?
21 Sketch the flight path of a tennis ball with topspin compared to a tennis ball with no spin.

Answers on p. 170

Exam practice

1. An athlete performs with rotation prior to the release of a discus. Identify the axis of rotation through which the discus thrower rotates and explain how the thrower uses the law of conservation of angular momentum to enhance performance. [6]
2. A player is kicking a football. Sketch and label a free body diagram showing the forces acting on the ball at the moment of contact. [2]
3. A rugby player is kicking a stationary ball. Using Newton's laws of motion, explain the effect of the resultant force acting on the ball. [4]
4. Identify the three main axes of rotation and give a sporting example for each. [3]
5. What is meant by the term 'centre of mass' and how does this help to explain why the Fosbury Flop is the preferred technique for the high jump? [4]
6. Explain how a lift force affects a discus during flight. [4]
7. Explain the methods used to reduce the forces acting on a swimmer while racing. [5]
8. Describe a cyclist's use of the Bernoulli principle to increase speed. [6]
9. Use a diagram to work out the resultant force acting on a hard-hit badminton shuttle during the early stages of the flight path of a long serve. Explain the effect of the resultant force acting on the flight path of the shuttle. [5]
10. Explain how a performer generates spin on a ball and describe the effects of spin on the bounce of a ball. [5]

Answers on pp. 178–179

Knowledge and skills summary

By the end of this chapter, you should have the following knowledge (AO1) and be able to apply all of it to sporting examples (AO2):

+ The definition of linear motion.
+ The creation of linear motion by the application of a direct force through the centre of mass.
+ Definitions, calculations and units of measurement for each of the following quantities of linear motion: distance, displacement, speed, velocity, acceleration/deceleration.
+ How to plot and interpret graphs of linear motion: distance/time graphs, speed/time graphs, velocity/time graphs.
+ The definition of angular motion.
+ The creation of angular motion through the application of an eccentric force about one (or more) of the three axes of rotation: longitudinal, frontal, transverse.
+ Definitions, calculations and units of measurement for each quantity of angular motion: moment of inertia, angular velocity, angular momentum.
+ Factors affecting the size of the moment of inertia of a rotating body: mass of the body (or body part), distribution of the mass from the axis of rotation.
+ The relationship between moment of inertia and angular velocity.
+ The conservation of angular momentum during flight in relation to the angular analogue of Newton's first law of motion.
+ How to interpret graphs of angular velocity, moment of inertia and angular momentum.
+ Factors that impact the magnitude of air resistance (on land) or drag (in water) on a body or object.
+ Factors affecting the horizontal distance travelled by a projectile.
+ Free body diagrams showing the forces acting on a projectile once in flight: weight, air resistance.
+ Resolution of forces acting on a projectile in flight using the parallelogram of forces.
+ Patterns of flight paths as a consequence of the relative size of air resistance and weight.
+ Parabolic (symmetrical) flight paths – shot put.
+ Non-parabolic (asymmetric) flight paths – badminton shuttle.
+ The addition of lift to a projectile through the application of the Bernoulli principle:
    + the angle of attack to create an upwards lift force on a projectile: discus, javelin, ski jumper
    + the design of equipment to create a downwards lift force: F1 racing cars, track cycling.
+ The use of spin in sport to create a Magnus force, causing deviations to expected flight paths.
+ Imparting spin to a projectile through the application of an eccentric force; types of spin: topspin, sidespin and backspin in tennis and table tennis, sidespin in football, hook and slice in golf.

AO3 and quantitative skills

+ Evaluation and analysing (AO3) are widely examined in this chapter. A possible example is analysing why a performer may wish to impart spin and the impact that this has.
+ Quantitative skills may be tested in this chapter, for example performing biomechanical calculations, sketching graphs and parallelograms of forces, and interpreting data.

2.1 Skill acquisition

Classification of skills

REVISED

Skills are classified using continua, as sometimes skills have more or less of each element depending on the situation.

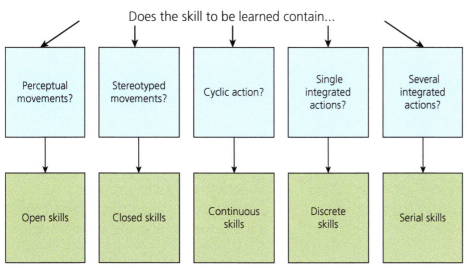

Figure 2.1.1 Identifying the type of skill

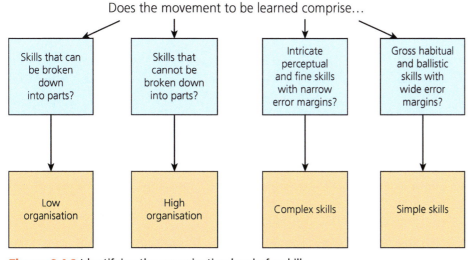

Figure 2.1.2 Identifying the organisation level of a skill

Table 2.1.1 identifies, describes and gives sporting examples of the skill classification continuum.

> **Sub-routines**: the elements or separate movements that make up a particular skill. For example, striking a ball in hockey involves grip, stance, back lift, forward swing, strike and follow-through.

Exam tip

Always refer to a sporting example when classifying skills on a continuum. It is often helpful to use the same skill, e.g. a tennis serve, throughout your response.

Table 2.1.1 The skill classification continuum

Continuum	Description	Sporting example
Muscular movement Gross/fine	Gross skills are large muscle movements using large muscle groups which are not very precise. Movement patterns include walking, running and jumping.	The shot put
	Fine skills are intricate movements using small muscle groups. They tend to be precise and generally involve high levels of hand–eye co-ordination.	A snooker shot or playing darts
Environmental influence Open/closed	Open skills are affected by the environment (e.g. team games). The environment is constantly changing and so movements have to be continually adapted. Therefore, skills are predominantly perceptual.	Skills in netball, football, hockey, etc., e.g. pass in the game
	Closed skills are not affected by the environment. The environment is predictable and the performer knows exactly what to do and when. Movements follow set patterns and have a clear beginning and end. The skills tend to be self-paced.	A free throw in basketball, serving in squash or tennis
Continuity Discrete, serial and continuous	Discrete skills are brief, well-defined actions that have a clear beginning and end. They are single, specific skills.	A penalty flick in hockey
	Serial skills are a group of discrete skills strung together to make a new and complex movement.	The sequence of skills for the triple jump
	Continuous skills have no obvious beginning or end. The end of one cycle of movements is the beginning of the next, and the skill is repeated.	Swimming, running, cycling
Pacing Externally and internally paced	Internally paced or self-paced skills: the performer controls the rate at which the skill is executed. These skills are usually closed skills.	Javelin throw, discus
	Externally paced skills: the environment controls the rate of performing the skill. The performer must pay attention to external events in order to control their rate of movement. These skills involve reaction and are usually open skills.	In ball games, the performer must time their actions with the actions of other players and the ball
Difficulty Simple and complex	Simple skills are straightforward, involving very few judgements and decisions. They also require little concentration and cognitive ability of the performer.	Swimming, sprinting
	Complex skills involve many decisions and judgements. They are complicated and are practised in training repeatedly to make it easier to perform in competition.	Somersault, tennis serve
Organisation Low and high	A low-organisation skill is very easy and uncomplicated. The phases that make up the skill are usually discrete and might be practised separately to improve technique. **Sub-routines** are easy to separate.	Swimming strokes, trampolining sequence
	Many sub-routines are closely linked together to make a high-organisation skill. They cannot be broken down and practised separately.	Cartwheel, golf swing

> **Revision activity**
>
> Classify the following skills on all six continua and then draw the continua:
> + netball pass
> + forward roll
> + triple jump.

Types and methods of practice

REVISED

Practice conditions are the type and style of practice administered by the coach. The appropriate type of practice will ensure the opportunity for the performer to make improvements. The conditions in which a skill is learned or practised, as far as possible, replicate the circumstances of the real performance.

Quick quizzes at www.hoddereducation.co.uk/myrevisionnotesdownloads

Part practice

What is it?	When is it used?	Why is it used?	Practical example
Working on an isolated sub-routine with the aim of perfecting it	+ With skills that are low in organisation – easily broken down into separate sub-routines + If the task is complex and dangerous	+ Allows performers to make sense of a skill, gaining confidence as they learn each element + Reduces the possibility of overload	Practising the backswing only in the tennis serve

Whole practice

What is it?	When is it used?	Why is it used?	Practical examples
Skills being taught without breaking down into sub-routines or parts	With skills that are high in organisation and need to be taught as a whole	Allows the learner to experience the feel of the skill – kinaesthesis	+ Sprinting and dribbling, because of their cyclic or continuous nature, will not break down into sub-routines + Golf swing

Whole–part–whole practice

What is it?	When is it used?	Why is it used?	Practical example
Practising the whole skill, then practising a sub-routine in isolation, then practising the whole skill again	With serial skills or skills with low organisation when sub-routines have distinct features	+ To recognise strengths and weaknesses, then correct specific skill errors + Allows some feel of the skill	1 Practise whole swimming stoke. 2 Practise leg kick in isolation (using a float). 3 Practise whole stroke again.

Progressive-part practice

What is it?	When is it used?	Why is it used?	Practical examples
Skills are broken down into sub-routines; performer learns one link, then a second link, and practises these; then further links are added on (known as chaining)	+ With complex skills as it reduces information load + With low-organisation skills + Good for serial skills	Helpful to allow performer to learn links between sub-routines and transfer these into the whole skill	Gymnastic floor routine, triple jump, lay-up shot in basketball, trampoline routine

> **Chaining**: this has the same meaning as the progressive-part method of practice. A serial skill is often broken down into its sub-routines, which can be seen as links of a chain.

Massed practice

What is it?	When is it used?	Why is it used?	Practical examples
Practice sessions with very short or no rest intervals	+ Good for discrete skills of short duration + With highly motivated performers with good fitness levels	+ To groove skills + Long sessions used when coach wants to simulate elements of fatigue	Basketball players practise their shooting skills by doing drills that involve many shots from different positions around the 'key'

Distributed practice

What is it?	When is it used?	Why is it used?	Practical examples
Practice sessions with rest intervals included	+ With continuous skills + With beginners or those with low levels of fitness and motivation + Good for dangerous or complex skills	+ Rest intervals allow learner to receive feedback + Helps maintain motivation	+ A swimmer swims a width and then has a rest while the teacher gives feedback + A beginner trampolinist performs a single somersault, then waits for the coach to give feedback before attempting again

Fixed practice

What is it?	When is it used?	Why is it used?	Practical example
A specific movement pattern is practised repeatedly in a stable environment; sometimes called a drill	+ With closed skills that require specific movement patterns to become overlearned + In preparation for events where conditions never change	To allow skills to become habitual and automatic	Discus thrower practises in the discus circle – the discus is always the same weight and the circle is always the same area

Varied practice

What is it?	When is it used?	Why is it used?	Practical examples
When a skill is practised in many environments	+ With open skills + Practice conditions must be as realistic as possible	+ Allows the storing of experiences in long-term memory, which performer can draw on + Develops performer's perceptual and decision-making skills	Small-sided game in football, where performer can work on passing, positional play and strategy

> **Exam tip**
>
> Always give a relevant practical example to support your answer. No sporting example = no marks. Learn the practical examples stated above alongside the other material.

> **Making links**
>
> Types and methods of practice (e.g. distributed practice) can be linked to preparation and training methods (e.g. circuit training).

Transfer of skills

REVISED

Learning or regularly performing a skill can affect the learning of a second skill. Different types of transfer of skill are outlined in Table 2.1.2 and then further discussed below.

Table 2.1.2 Types of transfer of skill

Type of transfer	Description
Proactive transfer	When a skill learned previously affects a skill yet to be learned or performed
Retroactive transfer	When learning a new skill affects a skill learned previously
Positive transfer	When the learning and performance of one skill help the learning and performance of another skill
Negative transfer	When the learning and performance of one skill hinder the learning and performance of another skill
Bilateral transfer	The transfer of learning from one limb to another

Positive transfer

+ This occurs when the two skills in question are similar in some way.
+ If one of the skills has already been mastered, this makes learning the second skill easier.
+ Coaches can aid this positive transfer by:
  + making sure the athlete understands the similarities between the two skills
  + making sure that the basics of the first skill are well learned so that they transfer more easily into the second skill.

For example, the skill of throwing can be transferred to the arm action of the tennis serve.

Negative transfer

+ This occurs when learning one skill then makes it more difficult to learn the second skill.
+ It happens when a stimulus common to both skills requires a different response.
+ Negative transfer can be avoided by:
  + making sure the athlete is aware of the differences
  + making practice sessions similar to match situations, to ensure a larger, generalised motor programme.

For example, a squash player who takes up tennis may find it difficult to learn not to use their wrist during shots.

Figure 2.1.3 A player of both squash and tennis may experience negative transfer

Bilateral transfer

+ This involves the transfer of learning from one limb to another.
+ It refers to the capacity of a performer who can perform a skill with their dominant or preferred side to learn to perform this skill with the other, non-dominant side of the body.

Bilateral transfer takes place in two ways:
1. through the cognitive aspects, i.e. understanding what is required (e.g. 'I swing my left foot in the same way as I swing my right foot')
2. through transfer of the motor programme so that the pattern of movement learned by one limb is used subconsciously by the other limb.

Such transfer can be very valuable. For example, a footballer who can shoot with the right and left foot with matching power and accuracy is a considerable asset to the team.

Optimising positive transfer and limiting negative transfer

+ Allow positive transfer by offering variable practices that imitate game situations.
+ Make performers aware of transferable elements (e.g. by highlighting that throwing a javelin is like throwing a rounders ball – the arm position is the same).
+ Give clear and concise demonstrations.
+ Diverse childhood experiences enhance probability of transfer; the performer must learn a wide range of fundamental motor (or movement) skills.

> **Motor (or movement) skill:** an action or task that has a goal and requires voluntary body and/or limb movement to achieve that goal; it is learned rather than being innate.

Now test yourself

TESTED

1. For each of the following types of practice method, identify the classes of skill for which it is most suitable and give a practical example for each:
   + part
   + whole
   + progressive-part
   + whole–part–whole.
2. What are the five types of transfer?
3. As a coach, how would you optimise positive transfer?
4. For the practical examples below, identify the types of transfer taking place:
   a) A former basketball player continues to dribble the ball when playing netball.
   b) A baseball player fields the ball using both right and left hands.
5. What is the difference between proactive and retroactive transfer?

Answers on p. 170

Learning theories

REVISED

A good understanding of how learning occurs will ensure effective teaching and coaching can take place. The following learning theories are important:
+ operant conditioning
+ Thorndike's laws
+ cognitive theory of learning
+ Bandura's observational learning/social learning theory (SLT).

Table 2.1.3 Overview of learning theories

Learning theory	Description	Sporting example
Operant conditioning	**Associationist view** + Trial and error learning + A correct response is rewarded + This reinforces the correct response + This behaviour is shaped (changed)	During football shooting practice, the coach may direct the players to strike the ball into the right of the goal. If this is done, they are rewarded. The area is then reduced to the top half of the right side, and then maybe the top right-hand corner only. Rewarding this behaviour strengthens the link.
Thorndike's laws	**Based on strengthening S–R bonds** + Law of exercise: rehearsing or repeating actions strengthens reinforcement + Law of effect: if followed by a pleasant reaction, then the S–R bond is strengthened; if the following reaction is negative, then the S–R bond is weakened + Law of readiness: the athlete must be both mentally and physically capable of performing the skill efficiently	During hockey: + exercise: repeated dribbling practice strengthens the S–R bond + effect: positive comments about dribbling technique strengthen the S–R bond, negative comments weaken the S–R bond + readiness: if a performer is injured, they may not be able to dribble effectively.
Cognitive theory of learning	**Intervening variables and insight learning** + Learning is best achieved by practising the whole skill + The learner must understand and think about the problem as a whole + Thought processes are dependent on perception + The learner will use intelligence, current knowledge and previous experience to plan or predict a solution	A cricketer learns to swing the ball when bowling by understanding the basic mechanics of movement.
Observational learning/SLT	**Copying behaviour of others** + Behaviour will be copied if the role model is a significant other and of high status + Role models are more likely to be copied if they are the same gender as the learner + It is a form of visual guidance + A demonstration is presented for the learner to copy + The process involves attention, retention, motor reproduction and motivation	A young rugby player may copy the behaviour of a professional player they have seen on television. This behaviour could be positive fair play or negative aggressive behaviour.

> **Associationist**: a group of theories related to connecting stimulus and response, often referred to as S–R theories. An individual is conditioned by stimuli that are 'connected' or 'bonded' to appropriate responses.

Stages of learning

REVISED

Fitts and Posner identified three stages of learning:
+ Stage 1: cognitive stage (initial)
+ Stage 2: associative stage (intermediate)
+ Stage 3: autonomous stage (final).

Table 2.1.4 indicates the key features of these stages, with sporting examples.

Table 2.1.4 Overview of stages of learning

Stage of learning	Description	Sporting example
Cognitive	+ The learner is trying to create a mental picture of the skill. + Demonstrations are vital. + Teachers should not give too much information. + Give guidance to focus on important cues (selective attention). + Practise the skill with trial and error. + Reinforce success with positive feedback. + Performances will be inconsistent and full of errors, and will lack co-ordination and flow. + Specific feedback is needed to correct errors.	A teacher demonstrates a serve to a beginner badminton player. The performer has a mental picture, plus key cues, and practises.
Associative	+ This is the practice stage. + The learner attends to relevant cues. + Errors are fewer and smaller. + Big improvements are made in performance. + Motor programmes are developed. Sub-routines become more co-ordinated, resulting in the skill becoming smoother. + The learner develops the ability to use internal/kinaesthetic feedback to detect their own errors. + Detailed verbal feedback is given.	The badminton player is becoming more consistent with their serve, and is now concentrating on height over the net. The performer can detect errors and make adjustments without the teacher's help.
Autonomous	+ The learner can execute the skill with little conscious thought (automatically). + Thus they can concentrate on other factors. + Motor programmes are established and stored in long-term memory and are put into action in response to appropriate stimuli. + There is less need for external feedback. + If practice is not maintained, the learner may drop back into the associative stage.	+ The badminton player can focus on where to place the shuttle in relation to their opponent, rather than on their grip, stance and so on. + Team players can focus on tactics and strategies rather than on executing skills.

Guidance

REVISED

There are four types of guidance that can be used by the teacher or coach to help the learning process:
+ verbal
+ visual
+ manual
+ mechanical.

Verbal guidance

+ Verbal feedback can be provided by a coach or significant other.
+ It is used to describe and explain how to perform an activity.
+ It is often used alongside visual guidance.

Table 2.1.5 Advantages and disadvantages of verbal guidance

Advantages	Disadvantages
+ Can reinforce good movements and identify errors to be corrected + Can hold the attention of the performer and be used to motivate	+ Can lead to 'information overload' + If guidance is inaccurate, skills will be hindered

Visual guidance

+ Images or demonstrations can be used to help a learner, such as still images (pictures/posters) or moving images (videos or animations, particularly the use of slow motion).
+ A coach should highlight key points of the movements. Reinforcing these key points is known as 'cueing'.
+ The image or demonstration shown should be accurate.

Table 2.1.6 Advantages and disadvantages of visual guidance

Advantages	Disadvantages
+ Easy to create a mental picture	+ If demonstration incorrect, bad habits could form
+ Skill can be seen at different stages	+ Coach may not be able to show accurate demonstration
+ Encourages observational learning	+ Visual representation may be unclear or too quick

Manual and mechanical guidance

+ This involves physical support by another person or mechanical device, for example a twisting belt in trampolining.
+ It may involve another person physically directing a performer, for example holding the arms of a performer and forcing their arms through a pattern of movement in a golf swing.

Table 2.1.7 Advantages and disadvantages of manual and mechanical guidance

Advantages	Disadvantages
+ Helps with confidence and a sense of safety	+ Can be over-restrictive – performer may feel they lack control
+ Can reduce fear in dangerous situations	
+ Can give kinaesthetic feel	+ Can lead to a false kinaesthesis
+ Can be used to isolate a skill action, e.g. holding a float to only practise leg kick in swimming – can then concentrate on this aspect	+ Could negatively affect motivation and cause negative transfer

> **Now test yourself** TESTED
>
> 6 What are the four learning theories?
> 7 Identify the learning theory illustrated in each of the following examples:
>   a) A child attempts to score a penalty in football in the top right-hand corner after seeing a professional on television do the same.
>   b) A high jumper performs the whole skill to enable them to decide the best technique for them, for example which foot to take off from.
> 8 Outline the characteristics of the three stages of learning.
> 9 What are the four types of guidance?
>
> **Answers on pp. 170–171**

Feedback

REVISED

There are a number of types of feedback, summarised below.

Intrinsic feedback

+ **Intrinsic feedback** is feedback from internal proprioceptors about the feel of the movement. Kinaesthesis is also involved.
+ An example would be the feel of whether or not you have hit the ball in the middle of the bat in a cricket shot.

> **Intrinsic feedback**: a type of continuous feedback that comes from the proprioceptors – nerve receptors found in muscles, ligaments and joints that pick up movement information.

Extrinsic feedback
+ Extrinsic feedback is feedback from external sources such as the teacher/coach or teammates. It is received by the visual and auditory systems and is used to augment intrinsic feedback.
+ An example would be a coach saying 'you need to point your toes in the pike jump'.

Positive feedback
+ Positive feedback is received when the movement is successful and this reinforces learning.
+ For example, in badminton a coach praises the learner when they perform the short serve correctly.
+ Positive feedback can be intrinsic or extrinsic.

Negative feedback
+ Negative feedback is received when the movement is incorrect. It is then used to correct the movement to make it successful the next time.
+ Negative feedback can be intrinsic or extrinsic.

Knowledge of results (KR)
+ Knowledge of results is feedback about the outcome of our movements. It is extrinsic.
+ For example, a learner observes whether their shot went in the basket or watches their movement on a video recording.
+ KR can be positive or negative.
+ It is important in improving the next performance of the movement.

Knowledge of performance (KP)
+ Knowledge of performance is feedback about the movement itself and its quality.
+ It normally comes from external sources but it can be internal, arising from kinaesthetic awareness.
+ It can come from a teacher/coach, explaining what went well and not so well.
+ It can also come from a video recording or the feeling of the movement.
+ It can be positive or negative.

> **Extrinsic feedback**: feedback that comes from external sources, for example a teacher or coach.
>
> **Positive feedback**: feedback that reinforces skill learning and gives information about a successful outcome.
>
> **Negative feedback**: information about an unsuccessful outcome, which can be used to build more successful strategies.
>
> **Knowledge of results**: a type of terminal feedback that gives the performer information about the end result of the response.
>
> **Knowledge of performance**: information about how well the movement is being executed, rather than about the end result.

Table 2.1.8 Overview of different types of feedback

Type of feedback	Advantages	Disadvantages
Intrinsic	+ Occurs as movement happens – so movements can be corrected immediately + Performer does not have to rely on anyone	+ If in the cognitive stage, performer may not be able to interpret information correctly and performance will deteriorate
Extrinsic	+ Coaching points can lead to improvements, if information is accurate	+ Inaccurate feedback can negatively affect performance + If source is unreliable, motivation can drop + Does not encourage kinaesthetic awareness
Positive	+ Can lead to positive reinforcement, correct S–R bond is formed + Extremely motivating + Helps build self-esteem and confidence	+ If undeserved, can lead to inappropriate S–R bonds and performance will deteriorate + Some performers do not respond to praise and may ignore it
Negative	+ Some are motivated by negative feedback – resulting in a more determined performer + Allows performer to be clear which aspect needs improvement + Best suited to autonomous learners who require skill refinement	+ Can be demotivating + Can be detrimental to learning

Quick quizzes at www.hoddereducation.co.uk/myrevisionnotesdownloads

Table 2.1.8 continued

Type of feedback	Advantages	Disadvantages
Knowledge of results	+ Allows performer to see the outcome of their action + Can motivate performer	+ May demotivate if performers are unsuccessful
Knowledge of performance	+ Allows performer to know what good performance feels like + Can motivate performer	+ May demotivate if performers are unsuccessful

Effective feedback

The type, amount and timing of feedback are crucial. The following should be considered to ensure feedback is effective:
+ Feedback should correspond to the skill level of the performer (cognitive/associative/autonomous).
+ Limit the amount of information given.
+ Feedback should be given immediately or as soon as possible.
+ Feedback should relate to the individual.
+ Try to facilitate internal feedback/kinaesthesis.

> **Revision activity**
>
> Draw a table to include all the different types of feedback. Give a practical example from your own sport of each type of feedback.

> **Now test yourself** — TESTED
>
> 10 What are the six types of feedback?
> 11 What is the difference between knowledge of results and knowledge of performance?
>
> **Answers on p. 171**

Memory models   REVISED

Atkinson and Shiffrin's multi-store memory model

Memory is so important for sports performers. It is used when learning new skills, developing skills already acquired and remembering tactics and strategies. There are three stages of remembering information:
+ short-term sensory store (STSS)
+ short-term memory (STM)
+ long-term memory (LTM).

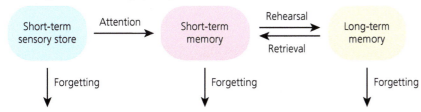

Figure 2.1.4 Adapted from Atkinson and Shiffrin's multi-store memory model

Short-term sensory store (STSS)
+ The STSS is a limitless memory store for holding information for about 1 second.
+ It is viewed as a subdivided part of short-term memory (STM).
+ Streams of sensory stimuli/information are passed into and stored very briefly in the STSS and processed simultaneously before the next streams enter and are processed.
+ Selective attention selects the relevant stimuli in the STSS and directs them into STM for further processing. Irrelevant stimuli are lost.

> **Selective attention**: relevant information is filtered through into short-term memory and irrelevant information is lost or forgotten.

Short-term memory (STM)
+ STM represents a 'working memory space' where information from the STSS and LTM is received and brought together.
+ STM has a limited capacity to store information – around seven items. The information is held for as long is attention is held.
+ STM is limited in the amount of time that information can be stored – less than 1 minute.

- Information can also be held in STM through a process called chunking.
  - For example, instead of trying to remember each separate move made by each player in a lineout in rugby or penalty corner in hockey, a player might remember the whole drill as a single number.

Long-term memory (LTM)

- LTM contains well-learned, retained and permanent coded information collected over past experiences.
- LTM is limitless in capacity and length or retention, for example learning to ride a bike.
- Well learned and rehearsed movement skills (or motor skills; see p. 108 for definition) from STM will eventually be stored in LTM as motor programmes for future use.
- Relevant information from LTM can be retrieved into STM workspace to be used for comparison, to identify stimuli (perception), for decision making or to select an appropriate motor programme.

> **Chunking**: different pieces of information can be grouped (or chunked) together and then remembered as one piece of information.

Critical evaluation of multi-store memory model approach

Table 2.1.9 Advantages and disadvantages of the multi-store memory model

Advantages	Disadvantages
+ Simplifies the memory process + Explains how those with brain damage may have a dysfunctional memory or amnesia	+ Too simplified – does not explain why we remember different sorts of information + Does not prove the distinction between STM and LTM and does not explain the interaction between STM and LTM

Craik and Lockhart's levels of processing model

This approach is used to explain how memory works; it opposes the view that there are set memory stores. It seeks to explain what we do with the information rather than how it is stored. According to this approach, the meaning of the information is more relevant than repetition.

Information received by the brain will be transferred to long-term memory (and remembered) if the information is:
+ considered
+ understood
+ meaningful (related to past memories).

How much this information is considered is called the depth of processing. The more deeply the information is processed, the longer the memory trace will last. There are three levels related to the processing of verbal information:
1. Structural level: paying attention to what words look like (shallow processing level).
2. Phonetic level: processing words and sounds.
3. Semantic level: considering the actual meaning of words (deepest level of processing).

> **Memory trace**: when the brain cells retain or store information.

Practical example: a gymnastics coach explains why it is important to tuck in a somersault to ensure there is greater rotation, for instance by explaining biomechanical principles. The performer is then more likely to understand why the tuck is important and therefore more likely to remember it.

Critical evaluation of levels of processing model approach

Table 2.1.10 Advantages and disadvantages of levels of processing model

Advantages	Disadvantages
+ Explains that if we understand information, we are likely to remember it + Explains that the longer we consider and analyse information, the more we remember it	+ Longer time taken to process information does not always lead to better recall + It is difficult to know what 'deep' processing involves + It does not take into account individual differences

Quick quizzes at www.hoddereducation.co.uk/myrevisionnotesdownloads

Relating both memory models to learning and performance of physical activity skills

To make our memory processes more effective to learn and perform skills, there are a number of ways in which our memory can be improved:

+ rehearsal – a tennis player will rehearse the serve physically and mentally
+ meaningfulness – a tennis coach will show that coaching information being given will raise the player's performance levels
+ association – a tennis coach will show the player that new information regarding the serve technique is simply an adaptation of the old serve, so learning a whole new skill is not required
+ avoiding overload – a tennis coach will only give the player a few points to remember before the match
+ organising information – a trampolinist will remember a complex sequence by mentally putting together the small moves to make bigger ones
+ mental imagery – a trampoline coach will demonstrate the move or show a video of the sequence so that the performer can remember it more effectively.

> **Making links**
>
> Many parts of this chapter are linked, for example:
>
> + Types of practice used can be linked with the type of skill.
> + The type of feedback links with the stage of learning of a performer and with the classification of a skill.

> **Now test yourself** TESTED
>
> 12 Outline the three key parts of the multi-store memory model.
> 13 What is a memory trace?
> 14 How can you make memory processes more effective when learning and performing skills?
>
> **Answers on p. 171**

> **Exam practice**
>
> 1 The classification of skills can help us to understand and learn new movement skills. Using a practical example for each, describe what is meant by a simple skill and a complex skill. [4]
>
> 2 For the three phases of learning, describe the use of different types of guidance to improve the performance of movement skills. [6]
>
> 3 Describe each part of the multi-store memory model and give a practical example to show how each part contributes to the performance of physical activities. [6]
>
> 4 Apply your knowledge of the stages of learning to complete the passage below, choosing from the words in the box. Each word can only be used once. [4]
>
> | cognitive | external | autonomous | intrinsic |
> |---|---|---|---|
> | neutral | demonstration | associative | kinaesthesis |
> | negative | terrible | inconsistent | anxious |
> | positive | correct | first | arousal |
>
> The initial phase of learning is termed the _____ stage. A _____ is vital because it allows the learner to create a mental picture of a skill. A coach should be aware that performances will be _____ and that lots of _____ reinforcement is required.
>
> 5 Feedback is important in the learning of motor skills.
>   a) Define intrinsic feedback. [1]
>   b) Describe the main functions of feedback in the learning of motor skills. [3]
>
> 6 Using practical examples, explain how a teacher or coach can ensure that transfer of learning helps the learning of motor skills. [4]
>
> **Answers on pp. 179–180**

2.1 Skill acquisition

Knowledge and skills summary

By the end of this chapter, you should have the following knowledge (AO1) and be able to apply all of it to sporting examples (AO2):

- Classification of skills.
- Types and methods of practice.
- Transfer of skills.
- How to optimise positive transfer.
- How to limit negative transfer.
- Theories of learning.
- Stages of learning.
- Types and uses of guidance.
- Types and uses of feedback.
- Advantages and disadvantages of using each type of feedback.
- Atkinson and Shiffrin's multi-store memory model.
- Uses of selective attention.
- Craik and Lockhart's levels of processing model.
- How to relate both memory models to learning and performing physical activity skills.

AO3 skills

- AO3 skills may be examined for this chapter, for example in evaluating which type of feedback is suitable for a specific stage of learning.

Quick quizzes at www.hoddereducation.co.uk/myrevisionnotesdownloads

2.2 Sports psychology

Individual differences

Personality

Trait theories of personality

Personality traits are innate characteristics and are thought to be relatively stable. They are highly consistent attributes that exert a widely generalised causal effect on behaviour, for example outgoing, aggressive, tense, shy, relaxed or sensitive.
+ According to trait theories, the situation or environment does not have any bearing on a person's behaviour.
+ Behaviour is said to be consistent.
+ Trait theory attempts to predict behaviour.

> **Personality**: the patterns of thoughts and feelings and the ways in which we interact with our environment and other people that make us a unique person.
>
> **Anxiety**: a negative emotional state that is closely associated with arousal. It is experiencing apprehension and being aware of high arousal linked to our fears and worries.

Type A and B personalities (narrow band approach)

This approach recognises two distinct personality types, each with its own characteristics. By recognising these, a coach may become more aware of a performer's anxiety levels and therefore be able to suggest intervention strategies.

Table 2.2.1 Type A and Type B characteristics

Type A characteristics	Type B characteristics
+ Highly competitive	+ Non-competitive
+ Strong desire to succeed	+ Unambitious
+ Works fast	+ Works more slowly
+ Likes to be in control	+ Does not enjoy being in control
+ Prone to suffer stress	+ Less prone to stress

Stable and unstable personality traits, extroversion and introversion

Table 2.2.2 Personality traits

Trait	Description of person with trait
Stable personality trait	Someone who does not swing from one emotion to another but is usually constant in emotional behaviour
Unstable (neurotic) personality trait	Someone who is highly anxious and has unpredictable emotions
Extroversion	A person who seeks social situations and likes excitement but lacks concentration
Introversion	A person who does not seek social situations but likes peace and quiet, and is good at concentrating

Social learning and personality

Social learning theory suggests that rather than being born with characteristics, we learn them from other people, especially from those we hold in high esteem, such as parents, coaches, role models, friends and other people of significance to us.
+ Behaviour changes depending on the situation and is therefore a product of our interaction with the environment.

+ Personality is learned by observational learning, modelling and imitating behaviour, and through experience. Psychological functioning occurs because of environmental determinants affecting behaviour.

Interactionist approach
+ This combines trait theory and social learning theory. It recognises that both traits and social learning have a role in determining behaviour and personality.
+ It offers a more realistic explanation of personality, explaining how different behaviours are produced for different situations.
+ It suggests that we base behaviour on inherent traits that we then adapt to the situation we are in.

Attitudes
Attitudes are used to explain a pattern of behaviour or a response in a given situation.

Attitude is an enduring emotional and behavioural response, and although it can be established firmly, an attitude is unstable and can be changed and controlled. Attitudes are directed towards attitude objects, which can be places, situations and the behaviour of other people.

> **Attitude**: a predisposition to act in a particular way towards something or someone in a person's environment.

Factors affecting attitude formation
Table 2.2.3 Formation of positive and negative attitudes

Positive attitudes are formed by:	Negative attitudes are formed by:
+ belief in the benefits of exercise	+ not believing in the benefits of exercise
+ enjoyable experiences in sport	+ a bad past experience, e.g. injury
+ being good at a particular sport	+ a lack of ability
+ being excited by the challenge of sport	+ fear of taking part in sport
+ using sport as a stress release	+ suffering stress when taking part
+ the influence of others where participation is the norm	+ the influence of others when non-participation is the norm

Components of attitudes
According to the triadic model, attitudes have three elements (components):
+ a cognitive component – what we know and believe about the attitude object (beliefs)
+ an affective component – how we feel about the attitude object (emotions)
+ a behavioural component – how we behave towards, respond to or intend to respond to the attitude object (behaviour).

> **Revision activity**
> Use practical examples to explain how positive and negative attitudes are formed.

> **Revision activity**
> Give a sporting example for each component of the triadic model.

Methods of changing attitudes
There are two ways of changing attitudes used particularly in sport:
1 persuasive communication
2 cognitive dissonance.

Persuasive communication
This is an active, non-coercive attempt to reinforce, modify or change the attitude of others. The effectiveness of the persuasion depends on:
+ the persuader: the person attempting the change (coach, team manager, teacher, captain)
+ the message: the quality of the message the persuader is giving
+ the receiver: the person whose attitude the persuader is trying to change.

Cognitive dissonance
+ According to this theory, individuals like to be consistent in what they do, feel and believe (triadic model).
+ Therefore it can be uncomfortable for an individual to have contradictory thoughts about something or someone, and this may lead them to change their attitude.

Quick quizzes at www.hoddereducation.co.uk/myrevisionnotesdownloads

+ For example, a male rugby player might believe that aerobics is too 'unmanly', so the coach tells him that some of the fittest people do it to improve stamina. This attack on the player's beliefs causes a change in attitude and the player now does aerobics to keep fit.

> **Now test yourself** TESTED
>
> 1 Define personality.
> 2 Name and briefly explain the three personality theories.
> 3 Define attitude.
> 4 Name three factors that affect attitude formation.
> 5 What are the three components of attitude? Give an example of each.
>
> **Answers on p. 171**

Motivation

Motivation is the psychological drive to succeed. Without it there is no reason for anyone to want to acquire and develop motor skills in sport. Motivation has three key aspects:
1 our inner drive towards achieving a goal
2 external pressures and rewards we perceive
3 the intensity (arousal level) and the direction of our behaviour.

There are two types of motivation:
1 **Intrinsic motivation** is the drive from within, for example wanting to achieve mastery for its own sake. This includes feelings of fun, enjoyment and satisfaction.
2 **Extrinsic motivation** comes from an outside source, for example a trophy or rewards. It is a valuable motivator for the beginner but will eventually undermine intrinsic motivation.

Motivation: 'the internal mechanisms and external stimuli that arouse and direct our behaviour' (Sage 1974).

Drive: directed, motivated or 'energised' behaviour that an individual has towards achieving a certain goal.

Arousal: the 'energised state' or the 'readiness for action' that motivates us to behave in a particular way.

Arousal

Motivation is related to the intensity and direction of behaviour. Arousal represents the intensity aspect of motivation. Arousal can be somatic or cognitive and can be a positive or negative influence on performance.

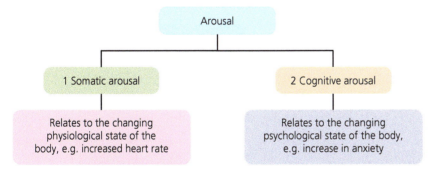

Figure 2.2.1 Diagram of arousal

As a performer's arousal increases, the state of readiness and expectation increases, but if the arousal gets too high, a performer can lose concentration and feel over-aroused. It is essential to understand the three theories of arousal:
1 drive theory
2 inverted U theory
3 catastrophe theory.

Drive theory

This demonstrates a linear relationship between performance and arousal. This means that at low levels of arousal, performance is low; performance increases in line with an increase in arousal.

> **Making links**
>
> Arousal level can be linked closely to anxiety. Anxiety is a negative experience of arousal and stress (see the 'Anxiety' section later in this chapter on p. 122).

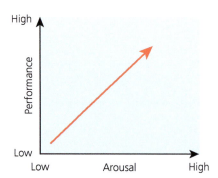

Figure 2.2.2 Drive theory

Key points of drive theory
+ Quality of performance depends on how well the skill has been learned.
+ Motor programmes that have already been learned are said to be the dominant response.
+ A dominant response or behaviour is most likely to emerge when a performer experiences an increase in arousal.
+ Hull (1943) predicted that as arousal increases in a competitive situation or when a learner feels the pressure of assessment, there is a greater likelihood of the dominant response occurring.
+ Behaviour = habit × drive (arousal).

Practical application
+ High arousal is beneficial to expert performers (autonomous learning stage) because their dominant behaviour would tend to produce a response that is fluent and technically correct. For example, an elite taekwondo performer will benefit from being psyched up – their technique is well learned, so high arousal will benefit them.
+ The opposite would be true for a novice learner.
+ High arousal also helps the performance of gross and simple skills.

Inverted U theory
This theory states that arousal improves performance up to an optimal point. Past this point, performance begins to decrease. The conditions of both under- and over-arousal severely limit the capacity to learn skills and perform them up to potential.

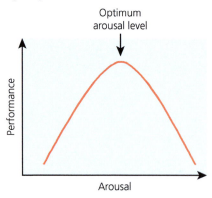

Figure 2.2.3 Inverted U theory

Key points of inverted U theory
It is important to consider:
+ personality: extroverts learn best under conditions of high arousal, introverts under conditions of low arousal
+ type of task: gross/simple/ballistic/closed – high arousal; fine/complex/open – low arousal
+ stage of learning: cognitive/associative – low arousal; autonomous – high arousal
+ level of experience: experienced – high arousal; novice – low arousal.

> **Making links**
>
> Arousal is linked to the type of skill being performed (classification of skills) and to the stage of learning of performers (see Chapter 2.1, Skill acquisition).

Arousal levels can impact performance, as outlined in Table 2.2.4.

Table 2.2.4 Impact of arousal levels on performance

Under-arousal	Optimum arousal	Over-arousal
+ Difficult to direct and focus attention and concentration onto relevant environmental cues + Concentration is lost because attentional field is too wide + There are many unwanted cues in the environment – learner may be daydreaming + Selective attention, cannot operate + Information overload prevents decision making	+ Perfect state + Attentional field is ideal width + Performer is able to learn or concentrate fully + Increased capacity to concentrate means the most important cues can be absorbed from the environment – accurate decision making + Cue utilisation theory predicts that the detection of the most important information occurs at the optimum point of arousal	+ Causes attentional field to narrow + Relevant environmental cues are lost + Performer is often in a state of panic + Also known as hypervigilance + Selective attention, cannot operate + Concentration is seriously impeded

Catastrophe theory

+ Like the inverted U theory, catastrophe theory claims that as somatic arousal increases, the quality of performance improves.
+ However, a third dimension is added to this prediction by stating that performance will reach maximum potential at the optimum level only if cognitive arousal anxiety is kept low.
+ If high cognitive anxiety coincides with high somatic anxiety, the athlete will go beyond the optimum level of arousal and is thought to have 'gone over the edge'. Under these conditions, performance drops.

Cognitive anxiety: anxiety experienced by the mind, for example worry about failing.

Somatic anxiety: anxiety experienced physiologically, for example sweating.

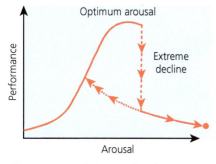

Figure 2.2.4 Catastrophe theory

Key points of catastrophe theory

+ The drop is not on a smooth curve as predicted in inverted U theory but plummets vertically.
+ The vertical descent depicts a performance 'disaster' or catastrophe.
+ After a catastrophe, the performer can rejoin the upward curve of arousal and once again attain the optimum threshold.
+ This return requires the athlete to reduce cognitive anxiety.
+ When somatic arousal is low, skill learning and performance can be enhanced if cognitive arousal is increased.
+ Serious debilitation in learning performance will arise when low levels of physiological and psychological arousal converge.

Revision activity

Create three revision cards highlighting the key points of the drive, inverted U and catastrophe theories. Include practical examples and diagrams on your cards.

Exam tip

Drawing a diagram is an excellent way to help you explain. Diagrams such as one for inverted U theory can help you gain marks. Ensure they are accurate and fully labelled.

Now test yourself  TESTED

6 What are intrinsic and extrinsic motivation? Give an example of each.
7 What are somatic and cognitive arousal? Give an example of each.
8 What are the three theories of arousal?

Answers on p. 171

Anxiety

Anxiety is the negative aspect of experiencing stress and can be caused by worry, apprehension or fear of failure.

+ Trait anxiety relates to personality. A performer with high trait anxiety is likely to feel anxious in any stressful situation, such as an exam or interview.
+ Competitive trait anxiety is the worry or apprehension experienced during or about competition.
+ The sport competitive anxiety test (SCAT) is used to help predict how anxious a performer will be in future competitions – their state anxiety.

> **Trait anxiety**: a trait that is enduring in an individual. A performer with high trait anxiety has the predisposition or the potential to react to situations with apprehension.
>
> **Competitive trait anxiety**: a tendency to perceive competitive situations as threatening and to respond to these situations with feelings of apprehension or tension.
>
> **State anxiety**: an athlete's emotional state at any given time, variable from situation to situation.

Somatic and cognitive anxiety

Two types of anxiety have been identified: somatic and cognitive anxiety. Both can be experienced at different levels before, during and after sports performance. The control of both types of anxiety is very important to ensure optimal performance.

Table 2.2.5 Types of anxiety and their symptoms

Anxiety type	Possible symptoms
Somatic	Increased BP, sweating, adrenaline boost, need to urinate, muscle tension, pacing, yawning, nausea, vomiting, diarrhoea, loss of appetite
Cognitive	Indecision, confusion, negative thoughts, poor concentration, irritability, loss of confidence, images of failure

Zone of optimal functioning

The zone of optimal functioning is thought of as an important state of wellbeing. This zone is an emotional response that facilitates top performance and is often referred to as the peak flow experience.

When 'in the zone', top performers can be described as:
+ relaxed
+ confident
+ completely focused, concentrating on cues that are relevant (cue utilisation)
+ finding activity is effortless
+ finding movements are automatic
+ having fun
+ being in control.

Aggression in sport

Aggression, according to Baron (1977), is 'any form of behaviour directed toward the goal of harming or injuring another living being who is motivated to avoid such treatment'. Aggressive behaviour that is controlled within the laws of the game is seen as assertion.

> **Aggression**: intent to harm or injure outside the rules of the event.
>
> **Assertion**: forceful behaviour within the laws of the event.

Theories of aggression

Table 2.2.6 Overview of theories of aggression

Instinct theory of aggression	Frustration–aggression hypothesis	Social learning theory	Aggressive cue hypothesis
+ Views aggression as being a natural response, innate and instinctive + Animalistic + Humans developed aggression as survival instinct + For example, a boxer channels their aggression to win in a boxing match	+ Frustration will always lead to aggression + Any blocking of goals that an individual is trying to reach increases an individual's drive, thus increasing aggression and frustration + If success follows, then aggression leads to catharsis + For example, a hockey player is fouled and then becomes frustrated; this frustration is channelled and they become determined to score; they score later in the game, and feel a sense of catharsis	+ Aggression is learned by observation of others' behaviour + Imitation of this aggressive behaviour is then reinforced by social acceptance + For example, if a player sees a teammate fouling an opponent and this stops the opponent from playing well, it is reinforced and copied	+ For aggression to occur, certain stimuli must be present + These stimuli are cues for the performer that are subconsciously linked to aggression, for example baseball bats or ice hockey sticks + Frustration causes anger and arousal and this creates a readiness for aggression + For example, a player sees a colleague fouled, then decides to join in

Social facilitation and social inhibition

The effect of having others present during performances can be either positive or negative:

+ positive = social facilitation
+ negative = social inhibition.

Other performers are known as co-actors; the spectators are known as the audience.

Zajonc (1965) identified the following factors as affecting performance:
1. The presence of an audience increases arousal.
2. Increases in arousal will trigger the dominant response.
3. If a skill is well-learned, the response will be correct.
4. If the skill is new or poorly learned, the response will be incorrect.

> **Social facilitation**: the positive influence on sports performance of others who may be watching or competing.
>
> **Social inhibition**: the negative influence on sports performance of others who may be watching or competing.

Evaluative apprehension

Performers can suffer from evaluative apprehension. This increases arousal levels, which in turn increases heart rate and causes other detrimental effects.

+ For example, a person who is trying out for cheerleading may feel a heightened sense of arousal leading to incompetence, not just because others are around but because of the fear that others are observing and ridiculing them.

Effects of social facilitation and social inhibition on performance

The presence of an audience will spur some athletes on to great performances while others may 'choke', with an adverse effect on their performance.

Table 2.2.7 How performance can be affected

Factor	Effects
Home vs away	+ Teams more often win at home, maybe due to the nature of the audience. + Some research suggests it is harder to win at home due to increased pressure.
Personality (Type A vs Type B, introverts vs extroverts)	+ Type A (high anxiety) personalities perform less well in front of an audience than Type B (low anxiety) personalities. + Extroverts tend to perform better in front of a crowd than introverts.

Table 2.2.7 continued

Factor	Effects
Level of experience (beginners vs experts)	+ Previous experiences in front of an audience can help alleviate nerves and improve performance. However, if a performer has failed in front of an audience, they may expect to fail again. + Elite/higher-skilled individuals perform better than beginners/novices, due to the dominant response being correct. + Performing in front of peers can aid experts but increase anxiety of novices.
Types of skills/activities	+ Gross skills are helped by high arousal, therefore an audience can facilitate performance. + Fine or complex skills are helped by lower levels of arousal, so an audience could inhibit performance.
Other influences	+ The nature of the crowd – if they are hostile or noisy, a performer may feel more anxious. + The proximity of the audience, e.g. a close audience could make a performer feel threatened and increase arousal.

Strategies to minimise social inhibition

The following strategies may be used by athletes to cope with the negative effects of an audience:

+ imagery techniques to 'shut out' the audience
+ relaxation techniques
+ training with an audience present
+ preparing to deal with negative reactions of co-actors
+ decreasing the importance of an event
+ remaining calm and focused.

> **Now test yourself** TESTED
>
> 9 What are cognitive and somatic anxiety? State two symptoms of each.
> 10 Why is it important to control cognitive and somatic anxiety?
> 11 What performance characteristics would a performer who was 'in the zone' display?
> 12 Outline the four theories of aggression.
> 13 What is the difference between social facilitation and social inhibition?
>
> Answers on pp. 171–172

Group and team dynamics in sport   REVISED

Group or sports team formation

Tuckman (1965) identified group development in the model 'Forming-Storming-Norming-Performing', as shown in Table 2.2.8.

> **Group**: a collection of people who share similar goals and interact with one another.

Table 2.2.8 Overview of Forming-Storming-Norming-Performing

Forming	+ High dependence on leader for guidance + Group members are getting to know each other + Very little agreement on the aims of the team + Individual roles are unclear + Team leader needs to give strong direction
Storming	+ Group decisions are difficult + Team members are establishing themselves in the group + Focus is clearer + Cliques form; there may be power struggles + Need for environmental compromise + Leader has a more advisory role
Norming	+ Much more agreement and consensus of opinion + Roles and responsibilities are accepted + Decisions made through group agreement

Table 2.2.8 continued

	+ Strong sense of commitment and unity + Team members are social and friendly with each other + Respect for the leader and leadership is shared
Performing	+ More strategies, a clear vision and aim + No interference or participation from the leader + Focus on achieving goals + Team is trusted to get on with job in hand + Disagreements occur but are resolved within the team + Team is able to work and be personable + Team does not need to be instructed or assisted + Team members may ask for assistance from the leader with personal and interpersonal issues

Team cohesion

Cohesion is a term used when describing group dynamics. Festinger (1963) states that cohesiveness is 'the total field of forces that act on members to remain in the group'.

According to Carron (1980), cohesion has two dimensions:
+ group integration – how the individual members of the group feel about the group as a whole
+ individual attraction to the group – how attracted the individuals are to the group.

Group or sports team performance

Steiner (1972) proposed the following model of group effectiveness, which is helpful when looking at the relationship between individuals and group performance:

Actual productivity = potential productivity – losses due to faulty processes

Potential productivity refers to the best possible performance of the group, taking into account resources available and the ability of the players. For example, a non-league team losing 4–0 to Chelsea might well be reaching their full potential but are not winning due to their limited resources.

Losses due to faulty processes are caused by two factors:
1. Co-ordination problems: if co-ordination and timing of team members do not match, team strategies that depend on them will suffer. Examples would include positional errors or ill-timed moves.
2. Motivational problems: if individual members of a team are not motivated to the same extent, they will be 'pulling in different directions' and players will withdraw effort.

The Ringelmann effect

This occurs when individual performances decrease as group size increases.

Research on co-ordination and motivational losses was based on studies into tug of war, where it was found that a team of eight did not pull eight times as hard as solo performers.

Latane (1979) found that group performance suffered as a group got larger; he termed the motivational losses social loafing.
+ For example, a water polo team may not be playing very well because one particular player is not trying very hard.

Social loafing is undesirable in teams and should be eliminated as far as possible. Strategies to eliminate social loafing include:
+ highlighting individual performances
+ support from others in the team – social support
+ feedback
+ peer pressure to reinforce individual effort.

> **Social loafing**: some individuals in a group seem to lose motivation. It is apparently caused by the individual losing identity when placed in a group. Individual efforts may not be recognised by those who are spectating or taking part.

Goal setting

Goal setting can develop positive self-perception and reduce the anxiety that may arise prior to and during performance. The correct use of goal setting can help improve the confidence and motivation levels of the athlete.

Goal setting influences performance in several ways:
1. It directs the attention of the performer onto the required task or strategy.
2. It increases the effort applied by the performer and allows performance to be monitored.
3. It improves persistence when a task becomes difficult or when failure is experienced.
4. The performer becomes increasingly motivated to learn and to apply different approaches to learning in order to complete a task successfully.
5. Successful completion of a goal will help raise confidence and self-efficacy.
6. Goals can help break down performance into manageable tasks, helping to control arousal and anxiety.

SMART goal setting

+ **S**pecific – goals must be clear and specific.
+ **M**easurable – goals must be assessed and therefore need to be measurable.
+ **A**chievable – goals that performers and coaches have shared are more likely to be achievable as all interested parties have a common purpose and the goals set are realistic in relation to the ability of the performers.
+ **R**ecorded – goals should be recorded so progress can be monitored.
+ **T**ime-phased – goals should be split into short-term goals leading to long-term goals.

Different types of goal

+ Performance goals – for example to achieve a certain time, such as 100m in under 10 seconds.
+ Process-oriented goals – for example to ensure front crawl arm technique is correct.
+ Outcome goals – for example to win the race.

> **Now test yourself**   TESTED
>
> 14 What is a group? Outline the stages in the formation of a group.
> 15 Outline Steiner's model of group effectiveness and give a practical example of the model.
> 16 Explain the Ringelmann effect and social loafing.
> 17 Give three reasons why a coach might use goal setting with an athlete.
> 18 What does SMART stand for?
>
> **Answers on p. 172**

Attribution in sport

Attribution is the perceived cause of a particular outcome.
+ It comprises the reasons, justifications and excuses we give for winning, losing and drawing in sport.

> **Making links**
>
> Attribution theory is linked to motivation, as our attributions will directly affect future efforts and performances (see the earlier section on individual differences for discussion of motivation, p.119).

The model in Figure 2.2.5 is a well-known representation of the process of attribution.

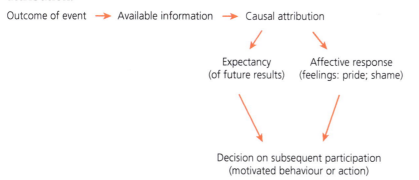

Figure 2.2.5 The process of attribution

+ Often attributions are inappropriate or unreal; it is important to change these to have a positive effect on future performance. This is known as **attribution retraining** (see p. 128).

Weiner's model of attribution

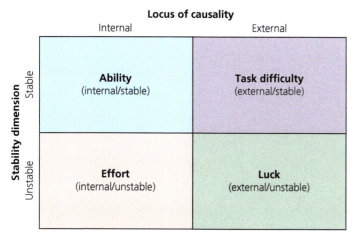

Figure 2.2.6 Weiner's model of attribution

Weiner's model is not sports-specific.
+ The locus of causality refers to whether attributions come from within the person (internal) or from the environment (external).
+ Stability refers to whether the attribution is changeable or unchangeable.
+ If reasons for winning are stable, the individual is motivated to achieve again.
+ If failure is attributed to an unstable factor, the individual is more likely to try again because there is a good chance the outcome will change.
+ Sports performers who lose tend to attribute their failure to external causes while those who succeed attribute their success to internal causes. This is known as the self-serving bias.

Controllability
+ Weiner added a third dimension to his attribution model – the dimension of controllability.
+ This dimension takes into consideration whether a cause for a sports outcome is controllable or uncontrollable.

> **Self-serving bias**: a person's tendency to attribute their failure to external causes (e.g. 'I lost the badminton match because the floor was too slippery') and their success to internal causes.
>
> **Controllability**: whether attributions are under the control of the performer or under the control of others, or whether they are uncontrollable, i.e. nothing can be done by anyone (e.g. luck, weather).

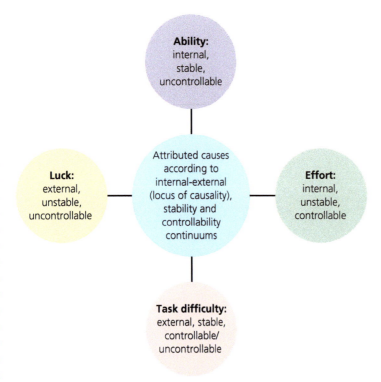

Figure 2.2.7 Attribution theory: how each attributed cause links to controllability

Learned helplessness and mastery orientation

+ Learned helplessness is the belief that failure is inevitable and that the individual has no control over the factors that cause failure.
+ Learned helplessness is a barrier to sports performance.
+ Low achievers often attribute their failures to uncontrollable factors, which can lead to learned helplessness.
+ Mastery orientation is the view that an individual will be motivated by becoming an expert (master) in skill development.
+ Mastery orientation can optimise performance.
+ An athlete who is mastery oriented will often attribute failure to internal, controllable and unstable factors.

Attribution retraining

Performers should be encouraged to make attributions to **controllable, unstable factors**.

+ For example, a hockey team that has just lost narrowly should be encouraged to think in terms of 'trying harder next week'. This is more likely to result in **mastery orientation**.

> **Revision activity**
>
> Sketch Weiner's model of attribution diagram (Figure 2.2.6). Add a sporting example from your own experience to each box.

> **Now test yourself** — TESTED
>
> 19 What is an attribution?
> 20 What are the three dimensions of Weiner's model of attribution?
> 21 A netball player states, 'We won our game today as the umpire gave a few calls our way and we were more experienced than the opposition.' With reference to Weiner's model, describe these two attributions.
> 22 What is learned helplessness and how can this be a barrier to sports performance?
> 23 What is mastery orientation and how can this optimise sports performance?
>
> **Answers on p. 172**

Confidence and self-efficacy in sports performance

REVISED

Levels of sports confidence affect:

+ performance – with high levels of sports confidence, you will be more motivated to achieve and will take firm decisions that are more likely to have positive outcomes
+ participation – low levels of sports confidence may mean you shy away from activities; high levels enable you to participate and not feel inhibited
+ self-esteem – high levels of sports confidence will mean high self-esteem; those with low levels may experience low self-esteem and feel they are not good enough.

> **Sports confidence**: the belief or degree of certainty individuals possess about their ability to be successful in sport.
>
> **Self-esteem**: the feeling of self-worth that determines how valuable and competent we feel.

Vealey's sport confidence model

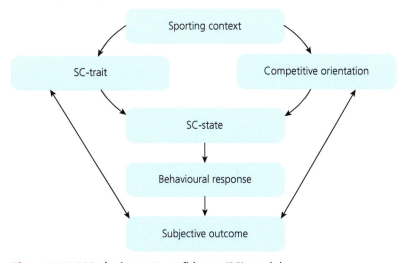

Figure 2.2.8 Vealey's sport confidence (SC) model

Table 2.2.9 explains the key points of Vealey's model.

Table 2.2.9 Overview of Vealey's model

Component	Explanation	Sporting example
Sporting context	The sporting situation a performer is in	Penalty kick in football
SC-trait	Everyone has an existing level of sport confidence (SC)	High levels of confidence in football (high levels of SC-trait)
Competitive orientation	Everyone has an existing level of competitiveness	Player who enjoys highly competitive situations
SC-state	+ The confidence that can be shown in a specific situation in sport + SC-state = (SC-trait) + (competitive orientation)	+ Experienced penalty taker has been successful in same situation many times – high levels of SC-state so likely to be successful + If SC-state was low, an inexperienced, nervous penalty taker would be unlikely to be successful
Behavioural response	Response to the situation	Penalty is scored or not scored
Subjective outcome	+ The emotion felt towards the behavioural response + These perceived feelings affect future SC-trait and competitive orientation: positive perceived feelings may increase confidence while negative perceived feelings may decrease confidence	+ Satisfaction if penalty is scored + Disappointment if penalty is not scored + Increased future confidence if outcome is successful, possible decreased confidence if outcome is poor

Bandura's theory of self-efficacy

According to Bandura (1977), our expectations of self-efficacy depend on four types of information:
+ performance accomplishments: a reminder of previous successes in the related skill or situation
+ vicarious experiences: watching others perform the skill in question
+ verbal persuasion: convincing the athlete of their ability to perform the skill
+ emotional arousal: the evaluation the performer makes of a physiological state.

> **Self-efficacy**: the confidence we have in specific situations.

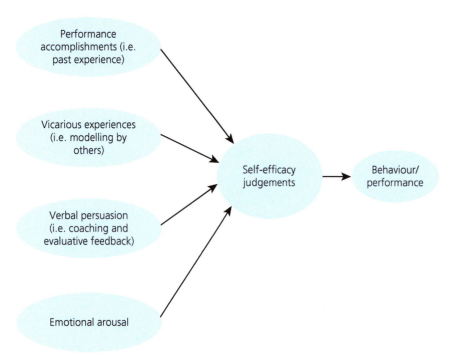

Figure 2.2.9 Bandura's model of self-efficacy

> **Exam tip**
>
> When explaining a model or theory, use the same practical example throughout, showing the examiner you can apply theory to practice consistently.

Now test yourself TESTED

24 On what three things can sports confidence have an effect?
25 What are the six components of Vealey's model of sport confidence? Apply your knowledge of this model to a novice gymnast performing a vault.
26 According to Bandura, what four things can affect self-efficacy?

Answers on p. 172

Leadership in sport REVISED

There are many leadership positions in sport, for example captain, manager, director, coach, physiotherapist and team sport psychologist.

Characteristics of effective leaders

Qualities of effective leaders include:
+ good communication skills
+ high motivation
+ enthusiasm
+ a clear goal or vison of what needs to be achieved
+ empathy
+ comprehensive knowledge of the sport/being good at the sport
+ charisma.

Emergent and prescribed leaders

+ An emergent leader becomes a leader through their hard work and determination. People who look up to and respect them help them to become a leader. They may be skilful in their sport and become a leader to show others how well they can do and inspire teammates. An example might be a committed rugby player who joins a team and eventually becomes the captain.
+ A prescribed leader is someone appointed by people of a higher authority. For example, Gareth Southgate was appointed manager of the England men's football team by the Football Association in 2016.

Leadership styles

Table 2.2.10 Overview of leadership styles

Leadership style	Description	Explanation of when used
Autocratic	+ Task-oriented and dictator style + Makes all the decisions and is very direct in their approach	+ Used when discipline or control are needed + Used with hostile groups or if there is a lack of time + Novice performers and males tend to like this style* + If the situation is dangerous/not favourable or the task is clear
Democratic	Person-oriented: considers team members' ideas and feelings, shows interest in others	+ When group members want to be involved in decision making + Advanced performers and females tend to like this style* + If the situation is not dangerous or is favourable and the task requires greater interpersonal communication + With small teams or individuals
Laissez-faire	Provides little support or input and lets team members do as they wish	+ With high-level performers or elite athletes + To develop creativity in team members + When leader has full trust in members' capabilities + When group is being assessed + If leader is incompetent

*Results of research by sports psychologists led by Crust (2006)

Theories of leadership

Table 2.2.11 Overview of theories of leadership

Leadership theory	Explanation	Evaluation
Trait theory	+ Leaders are born with their leadership qualities. + These traits are stable and enduring and can be generalised across different situations.	+ Popular belief that 'great leaders are born not made'. Leaders have characteristics that make them effective. + People in sport tend to be quite specific in their leadership skills, which works against the generalised trait approach.
Social learning theory	+ Leadership characteristics can be learned from others. + Behaviour of others is watched and copied – **vicarious learning**.	+ High-status models are more likely to be copied. This theory shows the importance of the social environment for adopting leadership qualities, unlike the trait approach which does not take the environment into account.
Interactionist theory	An individual may have certain in-born traits, such as assertiveness, but they are not evident unless a situation (state) demands the leadership behaviour.	This theory accounts for the fact that people may not be leaders in everyday life but show leadership qualities in sports situations.

> **Vicarious learning**: this happens when one person observes that a reward is given to another person for certain behaviours and learns to emulate that same behaviour.

Chelladurai's multi-dimensional model of sports leadership

> **Exam tip**
>
> Do not confuse the leadership theories with the personality theories.

The most popular view of leadership is that people learn to be leaders through social learning and interactions with the environment.

Chelladurai's multi-dimensional model of leadership (1984), shown in Figure 2.2.10, is a popular approach to the study of leadership in sport.

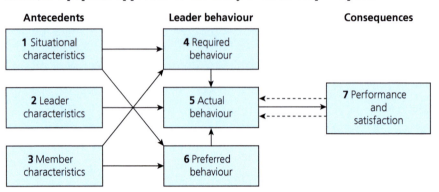

Figure 2.2.10 Chelladurai's multi-dimensional model of leadership

- The more the elements of this model match each other, the more effective the leadership is likely to be.
- If the leadership qualities are what the group want and expect, then they are more likely to follow the leader.
- If the leadership style matches the situation, again leadership is likely to be more effective.

Table 2.2.12 explains the model further.

Table 2.2.12 Overview of Chelladurai's multi-dimensional model of leadership

Number	Part of model	Explanation
1	Situational characteristics	Environmental conditions, e.g. activity (football, rock climbing), number of people in the group, time constraints, strength of opposition.
2	Leader characteristics	The personality/skill level/experience of the leader. The leader may have a preferred style of leadership.
3	Member characteristics	What is the group like? Skill level/attitudes/experience/age/personalities.
4	Required behaviour	What style of leadership is needed for this task? The situation (and member characteristics) dictates the appropriate style of leadership.
5	Actual behaviour	What does the leader actually choose to do? The behaviour the leader displays as a result of the situation and the characteristics of members and leader.
6	Preferred behaviour	What leadership style does the group prefer? Member characteristics (and the situation) dictate the appropriate style of leadership.
7	Performance and satisfaction	The overall performance of the members and leader and the level of satisfaction.

> **Now test yourself** TESTED
>
> 27 What is the difference between a prescribed leader and an emergent leader?
> 28 Which style of leadership do you think would be best suited to each of the following?
>   a) a large team sport
>   b) individual sport
>   c) elite athletes
>
> **Answers on p. 172**

> **Revision activity**
>
> Sketch Chelladurai's multi-dimensional model of leadership.

Stress management to optimise performance

REVISED

- **Stress** causes a release of hormones in the body.
- In the short term, adrenaline is released, which increases heart rate, raises blood pressure and gives extra energy that is beneficial.
- Stress that is long term, or too intense, can increase the risk of health problems and have a negative effect on a performer's readiness to perform.

> **Stress**: often linked to negative feelings; a psychological state produced and perceived by physiological and psychological forces acting on our sense of wellbeing.

Causes of stress

A number of things may cause stress; these are termed stressors. Stressors are environmental changes that induce a stress response. A stressor generally arises when there is an imbalance between the person's perception of the demand being made on them by the situation and their ability to meet the demand. In sport there are many stressors:
- competition (a powerful stressor)
- conflict (with other players or the opposition)
- frustration (with your own or team members' performances)
- climate (excessively hot or cold).

Stress/anxiety management techniques

Two types of state anxiety have been recognised:
- cognitive anxiety (stress response of the mind)
- somatic anxiety (stress response of the body).

The ways in which performers control the amount of stress can be cognitive or somatic, or in many cases a mixture of both.

Cognitive stress management techniques

Table 2.2.13 Overview of cognitive stress management techniques

Technique	Description	Evaluation
Mental rehearsal	Recalling movement experiences from memory or creating a mental picture of new experiences. Forming a mental image of the skill they are about to perform, for example seeing themself score the goal.	+ For a novice, it may help improve confidence and control arousal levels. + Research has shown that it can create optimism in performance.
Positive thinking/ positive self-talk	Used to motivate and 'psych up'. Being positive about their past performance by talking to themself can help confidence and performance, for example saying to themself 'I am going to score today'.	It is only of value if performers are experienced and of a high standard.
Goal setting	Setting SMART goals can break tasks down and reduce levels of anxiety. Setting short-term goals that lead to long-term goals will make a performer feel in control and reduce their stress.	+ Goals need to be clearly defined and decisions shared. + Performers should be aware of outcome, performance and process goals.
Negative thought stopping	Instructions aimed at halting negativity, for example stopping feelings of 'I can't score'.	Individuals prone to learned helplessness may find stopping negative thoughts difficult.
Rational thinking	Challenging any negative thoughts by looking at logical and real aspects of a situation, for example thinking about an extensive training programme and how this will have prepared them.	Perception is the key because it is the interpretation of the situation that dictates the level of stress the performer experiences.
Mindfulness	A therapeutic technique, often involving meditation, with the individual taking into account the present. It concerns our environmental awareness and our relationships with others at a particular point in time. For example, if a golfer is worrying about their next hole, they should concentrate on their peaceful surroundings and the 'flow' of their golf swing.	Can lead to the 'peak flow experience' of the zone of optimum functioning.

Table 2.2.13 continued

Technique	Description	Evaluation
Imagery + External (seeing yourself from outside your body) + Internal (seeing yourself from within)	Can help improve concentration and develop confidence. Imagery involves the formation of mental pictures that are often unrelated to the actual activity. Imagery can be visual, auditory, kinaesthetic or emotional. For example, images of escape, such as lying on a beach and hearing the sea, may help control stress.	Internal imagery is more effective than external imagery. For imagery to be effective the individual should: practise in a relaxed environment, keep exercises short but frequent, set goals for each session and evaluate their programme at regular intervals.

Somatic stress management techniques

Table 2.2.14 Overview of somatic stress management techniques

Technique	Description	Evaluation
Centring	Combines somatic and cognitive responses. Similar to mindfulness in that the individual focuses on the here and now. Concentration is shifted to the centre of the body. The mind recognises that the body is responding to a stressful event. Through centring, the athlete will redirect energy to the centre of the body and then achieve a calm steady state.	Skill needs to be mastered, focusing on breathing. It requires regular practice so it can be used automatically.
Progressive muscular relaxation	Developed by Jacobson (1932) and sometimes called the Jacobson technique. Athletes have to learn to be 'aware' of tension in muscles and then 'let it go'. Gradually, muscle groups should be combined until the whole body can be relaxed on one command.	Takes longer to learn than self-directed relaxation but is thought to be more effective.
Biofeedback	Performers are taught to control muscular tension by relaxing (by any chosen method) the specific muscles showing tension on a machine. The degree of tension is noted by the sound the machine makes. By linking the feeling with the noise, the performer eventually can identify the tension without assistance.	The machine provides objective biological feedback about muscle activity, skin temperature, heart rate and electromyography, which informs about the performer's success at relieving the tension.
Breathing control	Slow deep breaths ensure the individual gets enough oxygen and feels more relaxed and in control. Focusing on breathing can help take the mind off things.	It can be helpful as part of a routine, for example between serves in tennis.

> **Revision activity**
>
> Create a spider diagram of the stress management techniques. Include pictures to help you revise and remember.

> **Now test yourself**   TESTED
>
> 29 What is stress? Name possible causes of stress in sport.
> 30 Name the four somatic techniques used to reduce stress.
>
> **Answers on p. 172**

Exam practice

1. Identify two characteristics of an extroverted performer and two characteristics of an introverted performer and explain why a coach may take personality type into account during training. [6]
2. Identify what is meant by an attitude and describe the components of attitudes that young people might have towards sport and PE. [4]
3. Use practical examples from sport to describe Type A and Type B trait personalities. [2]
4. Briefly describe the difference between aggression and assertion. Use an example from sport in your answer. [4]
5. Anxiety is a negative aspect of stress. What is meant by the terms 'trait anxiety' and 'state anxiety'? Use examples from a practical activity to illustrate your answer. [4]
6. The audience or crowd at a sports event may help or hinder performance. Using psychological theories and practical examples from sport, explain how an audience can affect performance. [10]
7. Why is goal setting relevant to managing anxiety in sport? [4]
8. With reference to Chelladurai's multi-dimensional model of leadership, explain how effective leadership can encourage participation in sport. [6]
9. Describe the methods that might be used to raise self-efficacy in sports performance. [4]
10. Outline the characteristics of a favourable situation and name the style of leadership that should be used when this occurs. [4]
11. Outline how a captain could use knowledge of self-serving bias to motivate their team. [4]

Answers on pp. 180–182

Knowledge and skills summary

By the end of this chapter, you should have the following knowledge (AO1) and be able to apply all of it to sporting examples where appropriate (AO2):

+ Definition of personality.
+ Theories of personality: trait, social learning, interactionist.
+ Definition of attitude.
+ Factors affecting attitude formation/components of attitude: cognitive, affective, behavioural.
+ Methods of attitude change: persuasive communication, cognitive dissonance.
+ Definitions of intrinsic motivation and extrinsic motivation.
+ Uses and effects of intrinsic motivation and extrinsic motivation.
+ Definition of arousal.
+ Effects of arousal: drive theory, inverted U theory, catastrophe theory.
+ Definition of anxiety.
+ Types of anxiety: state and trait.
+ Response to anxiety: somatic and cognitive.
+ The zone of optimal functioning.
+ Definition of aggression.
+ Theories of aggression: instinct theory, social learning theory, frustration–aggression hypothesis, aggressive cue hypothesis.
+ Definitions of social facilitation and social inhibition.
+ The effect of an audience on: introverts/extroverts, beginners/experts, simple/complex skills, gross/fine skills.
+ Evaluative apprehension.
+ Strategies to minimise social inhibition.
+ Definition of a group.
+ The formation of groups and sports teams in terms of stages of group development: forming, storming, norming and performing.
+ Steiner's model of group effectiveness.
+ The Ringelmann effect and social loafing.
+ The importance and effectiveness of goal setting: the SMART principle (specific, measurable, achievable, recorded, time-phased).
+ Weiner's model of attribution.
+ Learned helplessness as a barrier to sports performance; mastery orientation to optimise sports performance.
+ Definitions of sports confidence and self-efficacy and the impact of sports confidence on: performance, participation, self-esteem.
+ Vealey's model of sport confidence.
+ Characteristics of effective leaders.
+ Emergent and prescribed leaders.
+ Leadership styles: autocratic, democratic, laissez-faire.
+ Theories of leadership: trait perspective, social learning, interactionist.
+ Chelladurai's multi-dimensional model of leadership.
+ Definition and causes of stress.
+ Use of cognitive stress management techniques.
+ Use of somatic stress management techniques.

AO3 skills

+ AO3 skills may be examined, for example when analysing and evaluating the use of stress management techniques.

3.1 Sport and society

Emergence and evolution of modern sport

REVISED

How social and cultural factors shaped sports and pastimes in pre-industrial Britain

The following factors, discussed below, had a major influence on sports and pastimes in pre-industrial Britain: social class, gender, law and order, education and literacy, availability of time, availability of money, and type of transport available.

Social class

Table 3.1.1 The influence of social class on the sports and pastimes undertaken

Class	Description	Examples of sports and pastimes
Upper class	Aristocracy or gentry who were hereditary landowners	+ Real tennis and fox hunting: sophisticated activities with complex rules and requiring money to participate + Pedestrianism: as patrons (sponsors) of lower-class competitors; derived from putting wagers on footmen + Cricket: played as 'gentleman' amateurs
Lower/peasant class	Peasants who worked manually, mainly on the land	+ Mob football, dog fighting, prize fighting: simple activities, often violent, with few rules + Pedestrianism: as competitors, racing (walking or running); derived from footmen racing and beating others. + Cricket: played as 'player' lower-class professionals

> **Revision activity**
>
> Outline the main characteristics of a) mob football, b) real tennis and c) prize fighting.

Gender

Table 3.1.2 The influence of gender on participation

Class	Gender – influence on participation
Upper and lower	+ Women participated in very different activities from men + Women were seen as the 'weaker' sex + Activities women participated in were not 'too strenuous' or 'dangerous'
Upper	Women could take part in archery
Lower	During country fairs, women were allowed to take part in 'smock races'

Law and order

Table 3.1.3 The influence of law and order on participation

Class	Law and order – influence on participation
Upper and lower	There was little law and order, reflected in the activities undertaken
Lower	+ Involved in bare-knuckle fighting or animal baiting, reflecting lack of order and animal cruelty + Games like mob football had few rules, showing lack of law and order in society at this time

Education and literacy

Table 3.1.4 The influence of education and literacy on participation

Class	Education and literacy – influence on participation
Upper	+ Educated and literate + Could read and write, and understand written rules of sophisticated activities like real tennis
Lower	+ Uneducated and illiterate + Could understand simple activities with few rules, like mob football

Availability of time

Table 3.1.5 The influence of time on participation

Class	Availability of time – influence on participation
Upper	Had more time and could be involved in longer-lasting activities, e.g. fox hunting
Lower	+ Worked long exhausting hours, so had little time or energy for physical activities + The few activities they participated in were confined to festivals or holy day fairs, based around pubs, e.g. drinking contests, bare-knuckle fighting

Availability of money

Table 3.1.6 The influence of money on participation

Class	Availability of money – influence on participation
Upper	+ Had more money and therefore more opportunities to be involved in physical activity of their choice + Could afford horses, clothing and equipment, e.g. for hunting, real tennis + Had access to specialist facilities, e.g. real tennis courts
Lower	Had no spare money to spend on physical activities

Type of transport available

Table 3.1.7 The influence of transport on participation

Class	Type of transport available – influence on participation
Upper and lower	Activities were local; transport was generally by horse and cart or walking
Upper	+ Had more opportunity to travel further by horse and carriage, but this was often limited by the state of the roads + Could get to facilities such as real tennis courts; some gentry would even build the facility within their stately homes
Lower	Roads were in a poor state, preventing people from leaving their villages; this influenced the simple, local and unwritten rules, varying from village to village

How social and cultural factors shaped sports and pastimes in post-1850 industrial Britain

The industrialisation of Britain changed the way people lived and worked, as there was much more distinction between work and leisure. The following factors enable us to analyse how sports and pastimes were shaped.

Social class
+ The upper and lower (working) classes were now accompanied by a middle class.
+ The middle class included professionals, factory owners and managers, who did not own big estates and were not born into aristocracy.
+ Many members of the middle class went to public schools, which were influential in the development of sports such as rugby and football.

Amateurism and professionalism
+ Amateurs were not paid; this status suited the upper and middle classes.
+ **Cricket:** amateurs and professionals played in the same team.
    + Social distinction was preserved through different changing rooms.
    + The lower-class professionals bowled and cleaned the kit.
+ **Soccer and rugby:** professionalism was the most controversial here.
    + The growth of socially mixed northern teams led to broken-time payments, where lower-class players were paid to miss a day's work to play.
    + These payments were against the amateur principles of the upper classes.
    + Tensions led to the splitting of rugby into two codes, league and union, in 1895.
+ **Golf:** before 1861 there were separate Open Championships for amateurs and professionals.
    + The professionals did not fit in with the image of the gentlemanly game.

Gender and the changing status of women
+ In the early nineteenth century, women were expected to marry, have children and be financially dependent on their husbands. Many people regarded education for women as pointless.
+ Schooling for girls was initially limited, compared to boys. Women were allowed to become teachers, but this was a low-status, poorly paid job.
+ During the late nineteenth century, the status of women began to change; a shortage of men, due to high mortality rates and a large number serving in the armed forces, suppressed the assumption that women had to marry.
+ Limitations on schooling for women were identified by the Taunton Royal Commission Report in 1868. Efforts formed part of a wider movement of campaigns that fought for equal rights to study, work, own property and eventually vote.
+ This had an encouraging effect on women to be more involved in sport and physical education in schools.

Law and order
+ The development of laws affected the types of activity undertaken, especially for the lower (working) class.
+ Laws led to a decline in blood sports, for example animal baiting and cock fighting.
+ Upper classes held on to their sports, such as fox hunting.
+ Lawmakers were from the upper and middle classes, so it was in their interest to support the sports these classes enjoyed.

Education and literacy
+ The majority of the working classes had little interest in education because it was perceived to be of little relevance.
+ Child labour was still common practice; working-class families were reluctant to give up the earnings of their children for the benefits of education.
+ The employment of children continued to increase even after 1850.
+ The 1870 'Forster Act' modernised education in England. Elementary education became free with the passing of the 1891 Elementary Education Act.

Public school: a place of education of old standing that the sons of gentlemen traditionally attended in large numbers from 8 to 18 years old.

Amateurs: people who compete in sporting activities but do not receive monetary reward for participating.

Professionals: people who compete in sporting activities and earn an income by participating.

Quick quizzes at www.hoddereducation.co.uk/myrevisionnotesdownloads

- Education then became more accessible to the working classes, allowing them to understand more sophisticated rules in sport. Sport became widespread.

Availability of time and money
- An increase in leisure time after the mid-nineteenth century allowed sport to develop quickly.
- However, working-class people still found participation difficult due to lack of disposable income.
- The growth of factories meant that for many, working hours were long and pay was poor.
- 72-hour weeks were common, leaving little energy and time for sport.
- Introduction of the Saturday half-day, initially for skilled workers and then for labourers, allowed more time for sport and leisure.
- Living conditions remained poor, and deprivation and poverty were high, but some sports clubs developed.
- Factory owners recognised a happy, healthy workforce as being more productive, so some organised annual excursions to the seaside.
- By 1965, the working week was 40–45 hours, reducing by the end of the twentieth century to 37–40 hours; this increased the amount of time available for sport.
- The law today states that workers must have four weeks' holiday a year, allowing time for playing and watching sport.

Type of transport available
- The railways were important in the development of seaside resorts and, in sport, allowed fixtures to be played and spectators to visit venues around the country.
- Cars were mass-produced in the twentieth century, and most households have a car nowadays; compared to 50 years ago, it is much easier to both follow and participate in sport.

Influence of public schools

The promotion and organisation of sports and games
- Public schools were influential in the development of modern sports, both at home and abroad.
- At the beginning of the nineteenth century, sport was unorganised, reflecting society. Bullying and exploitation of younger boys was common in public schools. Headteachers were not in favour of sport.
- In the middle of the nineteenth century, with the changing ethos of public schools, sport became an important element of the education of upper- and middle-class boys in these schools.

The promotion of ethics through sports and games
- Thomas Arnold, headteacher at Rugby School, wanted pupils to grow up as Christian gentlemen. He revised the fagging system (whereby younger boys were required to act as personal servants to older boys) and promoted more regulated sports, which provided exercise and encouraged healthy competition.
- Arnold developed the house system, influencing the formation of competitive teams.
- Arnold instigated prefects, who organised sports.

The 'cult' of athleticism
- The ideas of muscular Christianity linked sport with being a Christian gentleman, establishing a link between sports and games and a moral and ethical character.
- The development of character through sport is referred to as the cult of athleticism.

> **Athleticism**: a combination of physical endeavour (trying hard) and moral integrity (being honourable and truthful and showing fair play).

The spread and export of games and the games ethic
+ By 1845, pupils at Rugby wrote down the rules of football at their school to ensure fair play.
+ Pupils took the games with them to university but played many different versions.
+ In 1863, a common set of rules was decided for football. At the end of that year, players from around the country came together to form the Football Association (FA).
+ Other sports followed suit: the Amateur Athletic Club (AAC) formed in 1866, Rugby Football Union (RFU) in 1871 and the Lawn Tennis Association (LTA) in 1888.

How social factors shaped sport in twentieth-century Britain

There was a massive development of scientific and technological innovation throughout the twentieth century. Sport in Britain had taken the shape it would keep, more or less, until the television boom of the 1960s and 1970s.

The following social factors, outlined in the sections below, enable us to analyse how sport was shaped in the twentieth century: class; gender; law and order; education; the availability of time, money and space for sport; and transport.

Class, gender, and law and order

Table 3.1.8 How class, gender, and law and order shaped sport in the twentieth century

Class	+ The pub was the centre of (amateur) sporting activity for working-class men. + In horse racing and boxing, the middle class and upper class put up the money and the lower class took part. + In team sports such as cricket, the working class and middle class would compete side by side. + Working-class men and women had less free time for sport than the upper and middle classes. + Sport played an important part in troop morale during the First World War. In the aftermath of the war, spectator sport reached new heights of popularity. + Crowds were mostly well behaved, leading to the view that sport was a symbol of the orderliness and good nature of the British working class. + Unemployed and unskilled workers could not afford to spectate.
Gender	+ Participation of women in physical recreation had dropped dramatically in 1900. + Crowds at professional football and rugby league games became male-dominated, showing a shared sense of community and class. + Professional sport was mainly watched by male skilled workers, with only a few women and middle-class spectators. + Working-class women were excluded from professional sport by the constraints of time and money.
Law and order	+ Fields of play were enclosed, formal games were timetabled, there were written codes of conduct, e.g. in rugby and football, and most cruel sports had disappeared. + Spectators had to pay to watch; in boxing, gloves were worn, and numbered kit to assist spectators appeared in football. There was a fixed number of players per side in most sports. + Teams and spectators were able to travel widely. Sports events were held on Saturdays rather than on festival days. + Professional teams formed in football, rugby and cricket. + Growing crowds demanded purpose-built grounds and stadia. Spectatorism emerged, with more watching than participating. + Gambling was still an essential part of sport. + A sports press developed.

Education

The Education Act of 1944 (Butler Act) stated: 'It shall be the duty of the local education authority for every area, so far as their powers extend, to continue the spiritual, mental and physical developments of the community.'

Before the introduction of comprehensive schools, the state education system was made up of grammar schools, secondary modern schools and secondary technical schools.
+ All schools' curricula included physical education and some elements of sport.
+ Grammar schools often emulated the public school provision of sport and ran competitive sports teams in major sports.
+ Secondary modern schools ran a range of sports teams.
+ Sport was also promoted through extra-curricular provision in schools.

Availability of time, money and space for sport
+ With the gradual increase in leisure time and money, men played as well as watched sport.
+ Towns offered many different sports, from water polo in public baths to pigeon races on allotments and quoits in fields behind pubs.
+ The availability of money enabled darts, dominoes and billiards to flourish inside pubs.
+ Space was a key requirement, but it was at a premium and the land that was available was heavily used.

Transport
+ Public and private transport became much more available to everyone; increased numbers could now participate in and spectate sport.
+ In the late 1940s, radio coverage increased the spectacle of football, rugby and cricket, attracting large crowds.
+ Large crowds were at the 1948 London Olympics, rejuvenating tourism and the economy.
+ International competitions, accessible by international travel, served as a 'shop window' for the host city.

> **Exam tip**
> Learn specific facts and give practical examples – don't be vague.

> **Now test yourself** TESTED
> 1 Outline the differences between the upper and lower classes in pre-industrial Britain. How did the activities they participated in differ?
> 2 When and why did the middle class emerge?
> 3 How did education and literacy and law and order impact the development of sport in Britain post-1850?
> 4 What are the key factors that shaped the development of sport in the twentieth century?
>
> **Answers on pp. 172–173**

How contemporary factors are shaping sport in twenty-first-century Britain

Class
+ Sport is still associated with those who are perceived to be of a certain social class.
+ Traditionally, football was played and watched by working-class people, but it is now much more mixed. Middle-class people are now likely to state they are football fans.
+ Tennis, golf and polo are still associated with the upper and middle classes because of the expense and social elitism associated with joining such clubs.
+ Elite Olympic sport has a disproportionate number of privately educated and, therefore, more middle-class athletes.
+ The sport participation of over-16-year-olds is greater among higher socio-economic groups.
+ Social mobility can be achieved through sports.

Amateurism and professionalism
+ Social class is a factor in whether someone is likely to be an amateur or a professional in sport.
+ Amateurs in cricket and rugby have traditionally been middle-class.
+ Professionals in football have traditionally been working-class.
+ Rugby now consists of a broad range of professionals from all backgrounds.

Gender
+ More men than women still participate in or watch sport.
+ Sport is still regarded by some as 'unfeminine', reinforcing male dominance in sport and sports coverage.
+ Certain activities are traditionally linked to males (team sports) and females (dance).
+ However, more women than ever are now involved in physical exercise and there is more interest in health and fitness activities.
+ Participation rates of women in football and rugby are continuing to grow.
+ There is an increased number of female sports presenters, encouraging interest and providing female role models.

Law and order
+ Legislation that affects sport is sophisticated and specific to sport.
+ The rights of athletes and spectators and their safety are now protected by law.
+ The law has also been used increasingly to protect or to litigate against officials and referees.
+ Banning orders have been used in football to stop disruptive fans from attending matches and from travelling abroad.
+ The law has been involved in the areas of misuse of drugs, misconduct on and off the field and match fixing.
+ Laws to prevent discrimination based on race, gender, disability, age, sexual orientation and religion exist in the UK, and these have impacted sport.

Education
+ Children between the ages of 5 and 16 must receive an education.
+ Young people must remain in education or training until their 18th birthday.
+ Examinations and qualifications in physical education and sport, including sports science, have increased in availability in the twenty-first century.
+ GCE A-level, GCSE, Cambridge National, BTECs and Cambridge Technical qualifications are available in PE/sport.
+ Universities offer a wide range of PE/sport-related degrees.

Availability of time, money and transport
+ Society has become much more technological, increasing the time available.
+ Flexible working conditions (following the Covid-19 pandemic) have increased the time available.
+ Most people are better off, although a substantial number of people struggle to make ends meet; one in six people live in poverty.
+ The global Covid-19 pandemic may have affected disposable income; less money is being spent on sport and exercise, and participation rates among children suffered during the pandemic.
+ The availability of transport has increased; access to cars, buses, trains and cheap airfares has increased sport participation and spectatorship. However, the rising costs of fuel and fares may be a limiting factor.

Globalisation of sport

International sport is a big business, with massive investment involved as well as the reputation of countries and international companies. It has been affected by the following key factors:
+ freedom of movement for performers
+ greater exposure of people to sport
+ media coverage.

Table 3.1.9 The globalisation of sport

Freedom of movement for performers and greater exposure of people to sport	Media coverage (television, press, radio, internet, cinema)
+ Sport is a global marketplace for participants to demand high wages for their skills (e.g. in football). + National and international laws allow freedom of movement (particularly in the EU). + Some performers change nationality (e.g. in athletics). + Many spectators now travel to support teams or watch international competitions (e.g. the Olympics); cheap air travel is available.	+ Increased television coverage due to the commercial boost of the late 1990s (satellite television) led to the **globalisation** of sport. + The media have increased the number of people who watch televised sport – rugby league changed its season to fit in with this. + Very little media attention has been devoted to sporting inequalities based on class, gender and ethnicity. + Rules have been influenced and the timings of games are fixed to suit television. + Olympic Games events are often scheduled at unsuitable times, due to television. + In cricket, the third umpire has come into play due to the influence of television.

Making links

Globalisation of sport links with commercialisation and the media (see the section on that topic in Chapter 3.2, Contemporary issues in physical activity and sport).

Now test yourself — TESTED

5 How has education affected sport in the twenty-first century?
6 What is the globalisation of sport and what are the key factors that facilitate this?

Answers on p. 173

Globalisation: a process that involves sport as a worldwide business and features corporate brands, media coverage and freedom of movement of sport participants, officials and spectators.

Global sporting events — REVISED

The modern Olympic Games

In 1896, Baron Pierre de Coubertin established the first modern Olympic Games, held in Athens.

The aims of the games are to:
+ promote development of the physical and moral qualities of sport
+ spread Olympic principles, creating international goodwill
+ bring together athletes of the world every 4 years
+ educate young people through sports in a spirit of better understanding between each other and of friendship, thereby helping to build a peaceful world.

The Olympic values

1. Encourage effort – striving for **excellence** (determination).
2. Preserve human dignity – demonstrating **respect** (courage, inspiration).
3. Develop harmony – celebrating **friendship** (equality).

The British Olympic Association (BOA) and International Olympic Committee (IOC)

Table 3.1.10 Overview of the BOA and IOC

BOA	IOC
+ Formed in 1905 + Responsible for planning and execution of GB's Olympic Team participation in the winter and summer games + Responsibility for developing the Olympic movement in the UK + Not funded by government, no political interest, dependent on commercial sponsorship and fundraising income	+ Created by the Paris Congress in 1894 + Owns all rights to the Olympic symbol and the Games themselves + Administers the Olympic movement and has headquarters in Lausanne, Switzerland + Members are appointed to the IOC and are responsible for selecting host cities

Political exploitation of the Olympic Games

The Olympic Games have been used as a tool to make political points, due to their extensive global publicity.

Table 3.1.11 Overview of political exploitation of the Olympic Games

Games	Politics
Berlin 1936 – Third Reich ideology	The Games were used by Hitler and the Nazi Party as a stage for political **propaganda** for the Third Reich – an ideology that viewed Germany as a superior 'empire'. German athletes trained full-time, undermining the amateur ideal of the Games. Hitler refused to place the gold medal around the neck of the African-American athlete Jesse Owens after he beat the German athlete Lutz Long in the long jump.
Mexico City 1968 – Black Power demonstration	South Africa's invitation to the Games was withdrawn because of other countries threatening to boycott the Games due to its **apartheid** regime. African-Americans were able to protest to the world when two black athletes used a medal ceremony to protest about the lack of civil rights in the USA. They raised black-gloved fists – a gesture called the Black Power salute.
Munich 1972 – Palestinian terrorism	A day before the Games, Palestinian terrorists entered the Olympic village and seized 11 Israeli athletes. The terrorists made a political request to release 234 Palestinians imprisoned in Israel. The German authorities attempted a rescue, but all hostages and five terrorists were killed.
Moscow 1980 – boycott led by the USA	In December 1979, the Soviet Union invaded Afghanistan, which created a conflict that lasted 10 years and extended the Cold War. The USA boycotted the Games, alongside some British athletes. In all, an estimated 4,000 athletes boycotted the Games.
Los Angeles 1984 – boycott led by the Soviet Union	In response to the events of the 1980 Games, the Soviet Union, East Germany, Poland, Bulgaria, Hungary and Cuba announced they would boycott the 1984 Games. A total of 14 nations refused to take part. The Soviet Union blamed the commercialisation of the Games and the lack of security measures.

> **Propaganda**: a type of communication that seeks to influence people towards a certain cause and, in this case, a political philosophy. The information given as part of this communication is biased towards a certain belief or set of values.
>
> **Apartheid**: a range of policies of racial segregation under a system of legislation. Apartheid existed in South Africa from 1948 to 1994. Under apartheid, non-white South Africans (the vast majority of the population) were forced to live in separate areas from white South Africans and use separate public facilities, and contact between the two groups was limited by law.

Hosting global sporting events

Many cities bid to host global events (e.g. the Olympics and the FIFA World Cup). Hosting an event can bring many advantages and disadvantages.

Quick quizzes at www.hoddereducation.co.uk/myrevisionnotesdownloads

Table 3.1.12 The advantages and disadvantages of hosting major sporting events

Area of impact	Advantages	Disadvantages
Sporting impact	+ Raises the profile of the sport; may lead to increased participation, e.g. BMX, skateboarding from Tokyo 2020. + New or upgraded venues are built, e.g. Sandwell Aquatics Centre, Birmingham 2022. + The event can focus on minority sports, which may inspire participation, e.g. boccia and wheelchair rugby. + There is an increase in funding for the sports involved, e.g. 2020 Netball World Cup. + The event can bring increased sponsorship and commercial income for individuals and the governing body.	+ New facilities can end up not being used after the event, e.g. Olympic Aquatic Centre, Rio 2016; Olympic kayaking course, Beijing 2008. + Lesser-known non-global sports can suffer, e.g. squash is not an Olympic sport and attracts little funding, with participation figures dropping. + Sports deviance is likely to be highlighted by the media at global events, e.g. hooliganism at Euro 2020.
Social impact	+ More money is brought into a city or country, which can be used to benefit the local population. + Events can give pride to the host nation or city and help with 'nation-building'. + There will be improved use of sport facilities by local communities. + It can improve transport systems. + Accommodation built for the event can be used by the community, e.g. the Olympic Village built for Tokyo 2020 has been sold off as private housing.	+ Some areas of the country may not get the same benefits as the host city. + Some areas of the host country do not benefit from improved infrastructure and transport. + Local inhabitants may have to vacate land being used for sport venues, e.g. be rehoused. + Events bring increased numbers of people into cities, which can lead to increased pollution and negative environmental impacts.
Economic impact	+ Increased income leads to positive economic impact. More money is brought to the host city by those who participate or spectate. + More jobs are created through the building of facilities and the creation of transport infrastructure and other support for the event. + There is an increase in tourism and related economic benefits during and after the event. + There are commercial benefits related to goods sold in the area of the event and also in the sale of event-related goods.	+ Bidding to host an event can be expensive, e.g. England's failed 2018 FIFA World Cup bid (estimated cost £21 million). + Events can cause an overall economic loss, e.g. the 1976 Montreal Olympics took 30 years to pay off. + Benefits to employment and long-term jobs are often exaggerated. + If events or participants are linked with failure (e.g. a player exits Wimbledon early), it can lead to loss of revenue in merchandising sales.
Political impact	+ Individual political parties and their leaders can gain credit and therefore more votes if a bid is successful. + Staging an event can bring unity and a sense of purpose to a country. + The country or city can be used as a 'shop window' for its culture and commerce, raising its status in the eyes of the world.	+ If the cost is too high or over budget, it can bring political disadvantage, losing votes and decreasing economic resources. + If something goes wrong, e.g. a terrorist attack, politicians have to shoulder responsibility. + If the host nation does poorly, it can reflect badly on the political party. + Negative environmental impacts can decrease political popularity. + If the legacy of the event is negative, this can be politically damaging. + Protests by athletes or spectators can be politically embarrassing, e.g. Black Power, Mexico 1968.

> **Exam tip**
>
> If a question asks for an evaluation of global sporting events, ensure you mention advantages and disadvantages alongside relevant examples from sport.

Now test yourself

TESTED

7 What are the aims of the Olympic Games?
8 What are the values of the Olympic Games?
9 Give three examples where the Olympic Games have been the subject of political exploitation.

Answers on p. 173

Exam practice

1 How did social class influence the physical activities of people in pre-industrial Britain? [4]
2 With reference to practical examples, outline the difference between amateurism and professionalism in post-1850 industrial Britain. [4]
3 Identify and describe two political incidents that took place at the Olympic Games after 1970. [2]
4 Explain the impact of gender on sport in the twentieth century. [3]
5 Evaluate the various impacts of hosting a global sporting event. Refer to specific sporting examples in your answer. [10]

Answers on pp. 182–183

Knowledge and skills summary

By the end of this chapter, you should have the following knowledge (AO1) and be able to apply all of it to sporting examples where appropriate (AO2):

+ How social and cultural factors shaped the characteristics of, and participation in, sports and pastimes in pre-industrial Britain:
  + social class, gender, law and order, education and literacy, and the availability of time, money and transport.
+ How social and cultural factors shaped the characteristics of, and participation in, sport in post-1850 industrial Britain:
  + social class, amateurism and professionalism, gender/the changing status of women, law and order, education and literacy, availability of time/changing work conditions, availability of money, availability of transport (notably the railways)
  + influence of public schools on: the promotion and organisation of sports and games, the promotion of ethics through sports and games, the 'cult' of athleticism, the spread and export of games and the games ethic.
+ How social factors shaped the characteristics of, and participation in, sport in twentieth-century Britain:
  + class, amateurism and professionalism, gender/the changing role and status of women, law and order, education, and the availability of time, money and transport.

+ How contemporary factors are shaping the characteristics of, and participation in, sport in twenty-first-century Britain:
  + class, amateurism and professionalism, gender/changing role and status of women, law and order, education, and the availability of time, money and transport.
+ The globalisation of sport, media coverage, freedom of movement for performers, greater exposure of people to sport.
+ The modern Olympic Games; background and aims (1896).
+ Political exploitation of the Olympic Games:
  + Berlin 1936, Third Reich ideology; Mexico City 1968, Black Power demonstration; Munich 1972, Palestinian terrorism; Moscow 1980, boycott led by the USA; Los Angeles 1984, boycott led by the Soviet Union.
+ Hosting global sporting events; positive and negative impacts on the host country/city of hosting a global sporting event (such as the Olympic Games or FIFA World Cup): sporting, social, economic, political.

AO3 skills

AO3 skills may be examined for this chapter, for example in questions on the positive and negative impacts of hosting a global sporting event.

3.2 Contemporary issues in physical activity and sport

Ethics and deviance in sport

REVISED

Drugs and doping in sport
Sports activities can be affected by poor ethics and behaviour. Both illegal consumption of performance-enhancing drugs and blood doping have been a feature of many sports and are examples of deviance.

Blood doping
- Blood doping is a process that increases a person's red blood cell (RBC) count.
- More RBCs = higher volumes of haemoglobin.
- Extra O_2 can be transported to working muscles.
- This allows a higher level of performance.
- It involves the removal of approximately 2 pints of blood.
- Blood is then frozen, thawed and re-injected prior to competition.
- Blood doping has been used by some endurance athletes, for example runners and cyclists.

Performance-enhancing drugs
- Anabolic steroids: allow athletes to train harder for longer, and often increase strength and aggression.
- Beta blockers: control heart rate and keep an athlete calm.
- Stimulants: increase alertness, for example amphetamines.

Other prohibited substances are: narcotic analgesics, anabolic agents, diuretics, peptide hormones, mimetics and analogues, substances with anti-oestrogen activity and masking agents.

Prohibited methods are: enhancement of oxygen transfer, blood doping and gene doping.

> **Ethics**: rules that dictate an individual's conduct. They form a system of rules that groups and societies are judged on. An ethic in sport would be that an athlete sticks to the spirit of the rules of the game.
>
> **Blood doping**: defined by the World Anti-Doping Agency (WADA) as the misuse of techniques and/or substances to increase one's red blood cell count.
>
> **Deviance**: unacceptable behaviour within a culture. Any behaviour that differs from the perceived social or legal norm is seen as deviant.

Legal supplements versus illegal drugs and doping
Many sports performers use legal supplements to maximise training and performance. The philosophy of sport is for fair play and the taking of legal supplements is within the bounds of acceptable fair play, whereas taking illegal substances is not deemed to be so.

Table 3.2.1 The advantages and disadvantages of legal supplements

Advantages	Disadvantages
- Dietary supplements are claimed to help to build muscle, increase stamina, control weight, etc. - Ergogenic aids are claimed to increase strength, performance and recovery, e.g. creatine supplements can help performance during high-intensity exercise. - Staying hydrated through the drinking of water or energy drinks can improve and aid performance.	- Some supplements may not be what they seem and could contain banned substances or be contaminated. - Health implications have been suggested for the long-term use of creatine supplements, e.g. effects on the digestive system and increased risk of cancer. - Energy drinks contain high levels of sugar, contributing to obesity and tooth decay. - Philosophical argument – taking supplements is not in the spirit of fair play.

Reasons why elite performers use illegal drugs and doping

Reasons for the use of illegal drugs and doping by elite performers include the following:

+ pressure to succeed – can affect a performer's judgement and decision making
+ pressure from coaches
+ political pressures – for example the Russian doping scandal
+ high monetary rewards for winning and lucrative sponsorship deals
+ thinking that 'everyone else is doing it'.

Consequences of drug taking in sport

Table 3.2.2 The consequences of drug taking in sport

Societal consequences	+ Society seen as corrupt and full of unethical citizens who will do anything to 'win at all costs'
Sporting consequences	+ Concept of fair play is severely challenged + Cheating + Sports become 'tainted', struggling to gain sponsorship, e.g. cycling – loss of public support
Performer consequences	+ Severe dangers to health and wellbeing + Possible death

Strategies to stop the use of illegal drugs and doping

+ WADA draws up a list of banned substances. It provides assistance to countries' own anti-doping programmes and funds research.
+ Drug testing can be performed in and out of competitions.
+ Drug education can be provided for athletes and coaches.
+ A culture of keeping sport free from drugs cheats should be created and reinforced.
+ Punishments for drug use are to be more rigorous and longer. WADA doubled the length of the ban for doping offences in 2015.

> **Exam tip**
>
> Focus on the societal impact of drugs and doping, rather than the physiological impact on a performer, when answering a question from this area. Try to be clear and not confuse elements of other chapters with the relevant content.

Violence in sport

Causes of violence in sport (players and spectators)

Causes of violence in sport include the following:

+ a desire to win so overwhelming it leads to violence – importance of result
+ the nature of the activity – with physical sports like ice hockey being more prone to violence
+ the frustration of events
+ alcohol and social drugs or performance-enhancing drugs
+ rivalries
+ the media increasing tensions
+ the perception of unfairness or poor officiating
+ deindividuation.

> **Violence**: intense physical force that is directed towards harming another individual or group of individuals and can cause injury and death.
>
> **Deindividuation**: when you lose your sense of being an individual; this can cause violent behaviour.

Implications of violence in sport

Table 3.2.3 The implications of violence in sport

Societal implications	+ If violence is to be tackled in sport, then violent behaviour in society should also be tackled. Sport is often a reflection of society. + Spectators relish violence in sports such as boxing. Should a sporting action on the field of play be treated in the same way as a violent act on our streets?
Sporting implications	+ Governing bodies have their own disciplinary processes to ensure standards and maintain non-violent behaviour. + Playing strategies that promote violence should be punished. + Rule changes should be adopted to make violence less likely.
Performer implications	+ Education of performers is important; performers are responsible for their individual actions and fair play at all times. + Performers need to be aware that they are role models and their behaviour is likely to be copied.

Quick quizzes at www.hoddereducation.co.uk/myrevisionnotesdownloads

Strategies to prevent violence in relation to players and spectators

Strategies for preventing violence include:
+ the education of performers, encouraging awareness of their emotions and stress levels
+ punishments at the time: fines, bans, docking points
+ encouraging coaches to promote assertion rather than aggression in players
+ law enforcement (in spectator violence) – banning orders have been served in football
+ sophisticated policing methods, CCTV, etc.

Gambling in sport

+ Gambling in itself is not an example of deviant behaviour, as it is legal in the UK.
+ Sport lends itself to gambling because the outcomes of events are supposed to be unpredictable and there is an element of chance in most competitions. Gambling is a big business.
+ Match fixing, bribery and illegal sports betting are examples of deviance. They are designed to make individuals and illicit organisations a great deal of money.

> **Match fixing**: when a sports competition is played to a completely or partly predetermined result. This is against the law. Match fixing involves contacts being made between corrupt players, coaches and team officials.

Now test yourself — TESTED

1. What is deviance? Give two examples of deviance in sport.
2. Why might a performer use performance-enhancing drugs?
3. Name three causes of violence in sport.
4. What is match fixing?

Answers on p. 173

Commercialisation and the media — REVISED

Factors leading to the commercialisation of contemporary physical activity and sport

Table 3.2.4 The factors leading to commercialisation of sport

Growing public interest and spectatorship	More people now play sport at least once a week. There has also been a growth in the numbers who spectate. The greater the spectatorship, the more money is attracted to sports.
More media interest	Events are televised, leading to companies wanting to sponsor events and their participants.
Professionalism	Sporting professionals are now likely to attract sponsorship from commercial organisations.
Advertising	Sports present opportunities to sell more goods and use sports as a 'billboard'. The sport used (e.g. tennis, Emma Raducanu) is promoted, which can affect participation rates.
Sponsorship	Sponsorship leads to increased publicity and sales for the sponsor and provides free clothing/equipment or financial support for the performer. For example, Emma Raducanu has a sponsorship deal to wear a particular brand of clothing.

> **Spectatorship**: the act of watching something without taking part; often related to sports spectators.
>
> **Sponsorship** (in sport): to support an event, activity or person related to sport, by providing money or goods.

Positive and negative impacts of commercialisation of physical activity and sport

Table 3.2.5 Overview of the positive and negative impacts of commercialisation of sport

Positive impacts	Negative impacts
Individual sports	
+ Sports can promote themselves, attracting more participants or spectators, which can lead to increased revenue (e.g. BMX). + More money for sports can mean more facilities can be built and development takes place (e.g. skateboarding). + Commercial investment into sports can develop all areas from grassroots to international teams.	+ Less popular sports attract less sponsorship and therefore are unable to develop as much as others (e.g. handball). + Female and disabled events may lose out on commercial investment, as they are less popular and therefore attract less media exposure for a potential sponsor (e.g wheelchair basketball).
Society	
+ In the UK we hold the view that sport is about fair competition and everyone has an equal chance to participate and win. Sponsorship supports this ideal, in that it can help to support training and competition.	+ Attracting sponsorship can depend on a number of factors. Some sportspeople are more 'marketable' than others. This is a reflection of our society in that success can be based on factors other than talent and ability.
Performers	
+ Performers can receive kit and equipment from companies wishing to promote their products. + Commercial organisations can fund athletes' accommodation and travel. + Athletes can spend more time training and competing, rather than having to go to work.	+ There is pressure to perform well to secure and keep sponsorship deals. + Pressure to win could lead to deviant behaviour. + Companies can demand a great deal of a performer's time to promote their products. + Performers may find they have little control over their careers, with sponsors demanding they enter specific tournaments.
Spectators	
+ A commercially supported event can provide a more exciting spectacle and additional entertainment. + Giant video screens and play-back technology provide more information. + Due to commercial investment, there are more competitions in some sports, increasing accessibility for a greater range of spectators.	+ Actual sporting action can take second place to advertisements for goods. + At live events, advertising can be overwhelming and may spoil enjoyment. + Spectators may not agree with a particular company's ethics (e.g. should alcohol advertising have a place in sport?). + Spectators may not want their team to be associated with particular brands (e.g unhealthy foods). + The cost to watch sport is high; commercialism can be seen as doing little to make spectatorship more affordable.

Coverage of sport by the media today

Coverage of sport today is extensive and different types of media make it accessible to many people. Types of media include:
+ television – terrestrial, satellite, pay-per-view
+ printed press – newspapers, magazines
+ radio – local and national stations, dedicated sports stations
+ the internet
+ social media
+ cinema.

Reasons for changes since the 1980s
+ In the 1980s, media coverage was different from how it is today. Sports presenters were generally male and very little attention was paid to female sport.

+ Football hooliganism was rife and often the media were dominated by reports of the negative behaviour of sports spectators.
+ Changes occurred with the introduction of satellite television in the 1990s. Sky spent money on securing the rights to prominent football events. Other companies now have followed suit to show other sporting events.
+ Now, different types of media are available to most people. Media coverage is more global; events are recorded or streamed online.
+ Many different sports are now accessible, although minority, female and disability sports are still underrepresented.

Positive and negative effects of the media on sport

Table 3.2.6 Overview of the positive and negative effects of the media on sport

Positive effects	Negative effects
Performers	
+ Can raise the profile of a performer, e.g. Marcus Rashford + Can help develop performers' careers, e.g. GB Olympic boxers	+ Can highlight and promote sensational news, which can increase pressure to perform
Individual sports	
+ Can raise the profile of a sport + Can boost participation numbers, e.g. Wimbledon + Can increase financial revenues, in terms of sponsorship and funding for sports events and facilities + Can attract more funds for international teams + Can give more coverage to minority sports and disability sports, e.g. the Paralympics	+ Can highlight negative aspects of sport, e.g. hooliganism in football
Spectators	
+ Increases number of people watching + Rules have been influenced to make sports more accessible to a wider audience + Different types of media are available 24/7 and sport is broadcast live all over the world	+ Can provide negative coverage – possibly promoting hooliganism and unrest among some countries, e.g. England vs Germany (football) + Cost of subscriptions to satellite television can be prohibitive

Relationship between sport and the media

Sport is viewed as a commodity by commercial organisations, and the media help to promote both sport and its commercial partners.

The relationship between sport, sponsorship and the media is often referred to as the 'golden triangle'. For example, Sky Sports (media) show the Sky Bet (sponsor) Championship (football/sport).

Commodity: an article that can be traded. In this case, sport is the article that can be sold to different media outlets or companies that wish to associate their brand with a particular sport.

Golden triangle: the interdependence and influences of the three factors of sport, sponsorship and the media – each one influences the others.

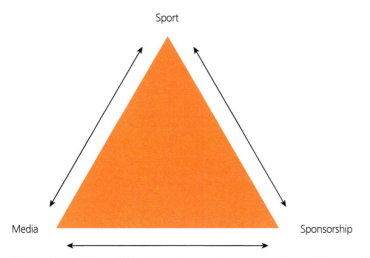

Figure 3.2.1 The golden triangle: sport, sponsorship and the media

Making links

The relationship between sport and the media links to the globalisation of sport (see that section in Chapter 3.1, Sport and society).

> **Now test yourself** TESTED
>
> 5 Name the different types of media that cover sport.
> 6 What is a commodity?
> 7 Outline an example of the golden triangle from contemporary sport, different from the one given above.
>
> **Answers on p. 173**

Routes to sporting excellence in the UK

REVISED

From talent identification to elite performance

The identification of potential elite athletes in sports has been formalised and organised by UK Sport. This organisation develops elite athletes by:

1 identifying potential talent in sport:
   + testing phases 1, 2 and 3
     – phase 1: a range of generic physical and skill-based tests; also includes an in-depth analysis of each athlete's training and competition history
     – phases 2–3: tests in functional movement screening, medical screening, performance lifestyle workshops and psychology and behavioural assessments
     – confirmation phase: selected athletes will embark on a 6–12-month confirmation phase during which they are immersed in the sport's training environment; unsuccessful athletes are provided with opportunities to continue the sport through the club system
   + #DiscoverYourGold: a partnership between UK Sport and other bodies, targeting 15–24-year-olds to be fast-tracked into the world of high-performance sport.
2 supporting an athlete's lifestyle
3 supporting an athlete's coaching
4 supporting through research, sports science and sports medicine, via the English Institute of Sport
5 providing a World Class Programme or pathway to success, with two levels:
   + podium: supporting athletes with realistic medal-winning capabilities at the next Olympic or Paralympic Games (i.e. maximum 4 years from podium)
   + podium potential: supporting athletes whose performance suggests that they have realistic medal-winning capabilities at the subsequent Olympic and Paralympic Games (i.e. maximum 8 years from podium).

> **UK Sport**: an organisation whose aim is the development of the country's sportspeople. It is funded jointly by the government and the National Lottery.

Some sports also have their own campaigns to identify talent, for example:
+ British Gymnastics with #Bounce4Gold, seeking talented young gymnasts to aim for Olympic qualification in 2028
+ British Cycling with #Power2Paris, aiming to identify potential Paralympians for the 2024 Games and beyond.

The role of schools, clubs and universities in contributing to elite sport success

Schools, colleges and clubs

+ These provide PE for all young people and often extra-curricular activities and clubs for those who are keen to participate or might excel in a particular sport.
+ The government supplies schools with funds to support school sport and the development of elite sports performers.

Quick quizzes at www.hoddereducation.co.uk/myrevisionnotesdownloads

- The FA, ECB (England and Wales Cricket Board), RFU, LTA and Premier League send coaches to primary schools to improve sports provision.
- Sport England encourages schools and colleges to link with community sport to increase sports participation and the likelihood of students realising their potential and becoming elite performers.
- Schools and colleges offer qualifications in sports at GCSE and A-level. All these have sports performance as part of the qualification.
- Schools and colleges often run sport teams, playing fixtures. This helps to develop sports talent in the UK.
- Advanced Level Apprenticeships in Sporting Excellence (AASE) and the Diploma in Sporting Excellence (DiSE) offer a structured training and development route across a number of sports for talented young athletes (16–19 years).
- Sports clubs are in often in leagues or national competitions, which enable those with talent to gain competitive experience.
- Sports clubs nurture and encourage talent, often giving financial concessions and providing coaching and guidance to develop sports performers.

Universities
- Most higher education (HE) institutions offer university sports scholarships or bursaries. This enables access to special support services.
- Many top sports facilities are located at universities, so HE is increasingly involved in the development of sporting excellence in the UK.
- The Talented Athletes Scholarship Scheme (TASS) and, in Scotland, the Winning Students Scheme are both government-funded sport programmes, delivered through a partnership between universities and national governing bodies (NGBs).
- Some universities host centres of sporting excellence, which can be linked to a National Sports Institute.

The role of UK Sport in developing elite sport

The main role of UK Sport is to invest National Lottery funds and income from central government to maximise the performance of UK athletes in the Olympic and Paralympic Games and global sporting events. Success is measured by medals won and the number of medallists developed.

UK Sport invests about 70% of its income in two ways:
1 to NGBs, enabling them to operate a World Class Programme
2 funding athletes directly through the Athlete Performance Award.

The role of National Institutes of Sport in developing elite sport

Each country that makes up the UK has a National Institute of Sport. Their role is to:
- provide sports science and technological help to elite sportspeople
- work with coaches and sports administrators to help improve the performance of their athletes
- give technical support that enables athletes and coaches to optimise their training programmes, maximise competition and improve their health and availability to train

The EIS (English Institute of Sport) has a dedicated team of sports scientists who support coaches and their athletes.

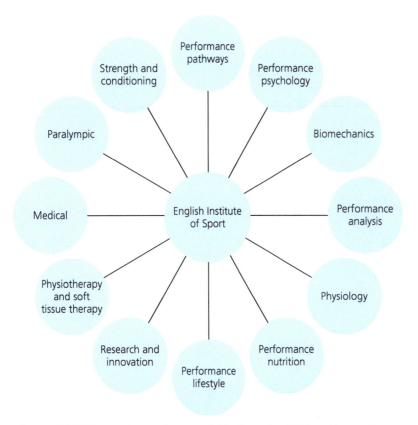

Figure 3.2.2 The main services available from the EIS for elite performers

Strategies to address drop-out or failure rates from elite development programmes and at elite-level sport

Drop-out and failure in elite sport can be a result of:
+ poor performances
+ injury
+ pressures from outside sport, such as family commitments
+ pressure from the media
+ stress relating to the financial impact of training, travelling, competing and fulfilling commitments outside of sport.

The programmes run by UK Sport include a lifestyle component that attempts to help athletes cope with the pressures and demands of elite sport.
+ 'Lifestyle' is available to all athletes on World Class Programmes.
+ Training advisers at the EIS give athletes the necessary skills to cope with the special demands of being an elite performer and to prepare them for life after sport.

> **Now test yourself** TESTED
>
> 8 State the five ways UK Sport identifies and supports elite athletes.
> 9 Give two roles of universities in contributing to elite sport success.
> 10 What is the role of UK Sport in developing elite sport?
>
> **Answers on pp. 174–175**

Modern technology in sport

REVISED

Elite performance and general participation

Table 3.2.7 outlines the extent to which modern technology has increased or improved general participation and elite performance in sport in terms of facilities, access, monitoring of exercise, equipment and safety.

Quick quizzes at www.hoddereducation.co.uk/myrevisionnotesdownloads

Table 3.2.7 Overview of how modern technology has increased or improved general participation and elite performance in sport

Type of technology	Aspect benefited	General or elite
Assessment of whether someone has the potential to be an athlete, e.g. assessing bone density and internal body fat	Equipment	Elite
Health screening devices	Monitoring of exercise, equipment	General and elite
Prosthetic devices for athletes who have lost a lower limb, e.g. Springlite	Equipment	General and elite
Wheelchair devices with slanted back wheels allowing tennis players to move across the court quickly	Equipment, access	General and elite
Improved access to buildings, e.g. specialist hoists at swimming pools	Access	General and elite
Rehabilitation and elite training sites	Facilities	Elite
Various simulated competitive environments, e.g. surf simulators	Facilities	General and elite
Improved sports surfaces and artificial lighting	Facilities, safety	General
Provision of equipment, e.g. most recently engineered ski boots	Equipment	Elite
Use of composite material in racquets and protective gear, making them lighter	Equipment, safety	General and elite
Improvement in the design of trainers	Equipment, safety	General and elite
Development of the **hypoxic chamber**	Facilities	Elite
Precision hydration techniques	Monitoring of exercise	Elite
More effective physiological laboratory testing	Facilities, monitoring of exercise	Elite
Gait analysis in runners to help avoid injury	Facilities, safety	General and elite
Heart rate monitors and GPS watches	Monitoring of exercise, equipment	General and elite

> **Prosthetic**: an artificial device that substitutes for or supplements a defective part of the body.
>
> **Hypoxic chamber**: a sealed room that simulates high altitude.
>
> **Precision hydration**: the monitoring of sodium loss during sweating, leading to more effective replacement of essential salts in the body.

The extent to which modern technology has limited or reduced participation

There are some drawbacks to the increased use of modern technology in sport:
+ Cost of equipment and facilities:
  + Equipment is expensive, which has led to inequality for both elite and recreational performers.
  + In developing countries, the expense of sophisticated equipment and facilities is prohibitive.
+ Range of alternatives to physical activity and sport:
  + Computers, game consoles and so on can make people sedentary and less likely to take part in sport.

> **Revision activity**
>
> Create a spider diagram about the use of modern technology in sport. Include small diagrams; this may help you remember important information in an exam.

Fair outcomes

Modern technology has had an influence on producing fair results or outcomes in important competitions.

The extent to which modern technology has increased fair outcomes
- There is increased accountability of officials.
- Most professional sports use instant replay to help officials make the right decision.
    - Rugby uses video-replay systems to check referees' decisions.
    - Basketball referees use video-replay systems to make sure players are shooting within the allotted time.
- There is improved detection of doping, for example by using biological passports.
- There is improved detection of foul play. For example, officials have access to video footage or replays to detect foul play in the run-up to tries or touchdowns.
- Better timing devices are available, for example laser beam timing and photo-finish camera systems (e.g. Scan'O'Vision) that can measure finish-line times in thousandths of a second and be used in a wide range of sports, including athletics, rowing and speed skating.

The extent to which modern technology has limited or decreased fair outcomes
- Many sports officials report feeling under pressure to use the technology more, rather than making their own decisions.
- It enables the media to highlight an official's mistakes during a sports competition, which can lead to judgements from the public and high levels of anxiety for the official.
- Advances in genetic technology are relevant to doping in sport. Gene therapy is being developed, with the potential to affect athletic performance.
- Performance-enhancing drug testing technology cannot keep up with new drug development.
- Access to modern technology can be limited.

> **Gene therapy**: the use of genes and genetic elements to treat human disease.

Entertainment

Modern technology can enhance or hinder the enjoyment of sport.

The extent to which modern technology has increased entertainment
- Modern technology has increased entertainment for television viewers via action replays and slow-motion playback. Exciting moments can be watched again and nothing need be missed.
- There are often giant screens at live sports events to show the action and also replays (e.g. action replays of goals scored or missed chances during matches in the English Premier League).
- In some sports, officials can access video replays to make key decisions. This increases entertainment for fans, who wait on the edge of their seats until the replay call is announced (e.g. Rugby Union referees making try decisions).
- Multiple camera angles allow spectators to enjoy every aspect of performance and see whether officiating decisions are correct.
- Performance is analysed at intervals by pundits, using motion-capture analysis.
- Mobile phones and 4G/5G mean sport as entertainment is available 24/7.

The extent to which modern technology has reduced or limited entertainment

+ Constant interruptions can interfere with the flow of an event and can irritate viewers.
+ It could potentially reduce the number of people attending live sport events. For example, review by video assistant referees (VARs) can mean long delays for fans, so some may prefer to watch at home.

> **Exam tip**
> Always give a relevant sporting example to improve your answer.

Now test yourself TESTED

11 Give four examples of how modern technology can benefit sport.
12 Give two examples of how modern technology can affect fair outcomes in sport.
13 Give two examples of how modern technology can enhance or hinder the enjoyment of sport.

Answers on p. 174

Exam practice

1 Describe two social implications of violence in sport. [2]
2 Discuss the reasons why new technology has divided opinion among many who participate in sport. [6]
3 Outline the reasons for the growth of commercialisation in contemporary sport. [5]
4 Evaluate the effect that increased media coverage might have on the sport of BMX racing. [5]

Answers on p. 183

> **Making links**
> Throughout this chapter, links can be made to socio-cultural factors and sport in the twenty-first century, e.g. the globalisation of sport and the role played by commercialisation and the media.

Knowledge and skills summary

By the end of this chapter, you should be able to understand (AO1) and give relevant practical examples (AO2) of the following:

+ Drugs and doping in sport.
+ Legal supplements versus illegal drugs and doping.
+ Reasons why elite performers use illegal drugs/doping; consequences/implications to: society, sport and performers.
+ Strategies to stop the use of illegal drugs and doping.
+ Violence in sport: causes in relation to players and spectators; implications for society, sport and performers.
+ Strategies to prevent violence in relation to players and spectators.
+ Gambling in sport, match fixing/bribery, illegal sports betting.
+ Factors leading to the commercialisation of contemporary physical activity and sport.
+ Positive and negative impacts of the commercialisation of physical activity and sport on society, individual sports, performers and spectators.
+ Coverage of sport by the media today and reasons for changes since the 1980s.
+ Positive and negative effects of the media on sport, individual sports, performers and spectators.
+ The relationship between sport and the media.
+ Sport as a commodity; links with advertising and sponsorship (the 'golden triangle').
+ Development routes from talent identification through to elite performance: the role of schools, clubs and universities in contributing to elite sporting success.
+ The role of UK Sport and National Institutes of Sport in developing sporting excellence/high-performance sport.
+ Strategies to address drop-out/failure rates from elite development programmes/at elite level.
+ Modern technology in sport: its impact on elite-level sport, participation, fair outcomes and entertainment.
+ The extent to which modern technology has affected elite-level sport.
+ The extent to which modern technology has increased participation in sport.
+ The extent to which modern technology has limited or reduced participation in sport.
+ The extent to which modern technology has increased fair outcomes.
+ The extent to which modern technology has limited or decreased fair outcomes.
+ The extent to which modern technology has increased entertainment.

AO3

+ Analysis and evaluation of the content above will form AO3 assessment, for example a comparison between the benefits and drawbacks of the use of modern technology in sport.

Glossary

Term	Definition	Page(s)
Abrasion	Superficial damage to the skin caused by scraping against a surface	75
Acceleration/ deceleration	The rate of change in velocity (m/s/s) calculated as (final velocity − initial velocity)/time taken	91
Acclimatisation	A process of gradual adaptation to a change in environment (for example lower pO_2 at altitude)	41
Actin filaments	Proteins that form the contractile units of skeletal muscles	16
Action potential	Positive electrical charge inside the nerve and muscle cells that conducts the nerve impulse down the neuron and into the muscle fibre	17
Acute injury	A sudden injury associated with a traumatic event	73
Adaptation	A physiological change in response to training, e.g. increased RBC production	54
Aerobic capacity	The ability of the body to inspire, transport and utilise oxygen to perform sustained periods of aerobic activity	58
Aerofoil	A streamlined shape with a curved upper surface and flat lower surface designed to give an additional lift force to a body	98
Aggression	Intent to harm or injure outside the rules of the event	122
Agonist	A muscle responsible for creating movement at a joint. Also known as the prime mover	16
Air resistance	The force that opposes the direction of motion of a body through air	84
All-or-none law	Depending on whether the stimulus is above the threshold, all the muscle fibres will give a complete contraction or no contraction at all	17
Altitude	The height or elevation of an area above sea level	41
Alveoli	Clusters of tiny air sacs covered in a dense network of capillaries which together serve as the external site for gaseous exchange	28
Amateurs	People who compete in sporting activities but do not receive monetary reward for participating	138
Angle of attack	The most favourable angle of release for a projectile to optimise lift force due to the Bernoulli principle	98
Angular analogue of Newton's first law of motion	The angular equivalent of Newton's first law of motion: a rotating body will continue to turn about an axis of rotation with constant angular momentum unless acted upon by an eccentric force or external torque	94
Angular motion	Movement of a body or part of a body in a circular path about an axis of rotation	92
Antagonist	A muscle that opposes the agonist, providing a resistance for co-ordinated movement	16
Anxiety	A negative emotional state that is closely associated with arousal. It is experiencing apprehension and being aware of high arousal linked to our fears and worries	117
Apartheid	A range of policies of racial segregation under a system of legislation	144
Arousal	The 'energised state' or the 'readiness for action' that motivates us to behave in a particular way	119
Arterioles	Blood vessels carrying oxygenated blood from the arteries to the capillary beds, which can vasodilate and vasoconstrict to regulate blood flow	27
Arthroscopy	A minimally invasive procedure to examine and repair damage within a joint	80
Assertion	Forceful behaviour within the laws of the event	122
Associationist	A group of theories related to connecting stimulus and response, often referred to as S–R theories. An individual is conditioned by stimuli that are 'connected' or 'bonded' to appropriate responses	109
Athleticism	A combination of physical endeavour (trying hard) and moral integrity (being honourable and truthful and showing fair play)	9

Quick quizzes at www.hoddereducation.co.uk/myrevisionnotesdownloads

Term	Definition	Page(s)
Attitude	A predisposition to act in a particular way towards something or someone in a person's environment	118
Barometric pressure	The pressure exerted by the Earth's atmosphere at any given point	41
Basal metabolic rate (BMR)	The minimum amount of energy required to sustain essential physiological function at rest, which can account for as much as 75% of total energy expenditure	48
Bernoulli principle	Creation of an additional lift force on a projectile in flight resulting from Bernoulli's conclusion that the higher the velocity of air flow, the lower the surrounding pressure	98
Blister	Separation of layers of skin where a pocket of fluid forms, caused by friction	75
Blood doping	Defined by the World Anti-Doping Agency (WADA) as the misuse of techniques and/or substances to increase one's red blood cell count	147
Bohr shift	A move in the oxyhaemoglobin dissociation curve to the right caused by increased acidity in the bloodstream	33
Carbohydrates (CHOs)	Sugars and starches stored in the body as glycogen and converted to glucose to fuel energy production	46
Cardiac control centre (CCC)	A control centre in the medulla oblongata responsible for HR regulation	25
Centre of mass	The point at which an object or a body is balanced in all directions; the point at which weight appears to act	86
Chaining	This has the same meaning as the progressive-part method of practice. A serial skill is often broken down into its sub-routines, which can be seen as links of a chain	105
Chronic injury	A slowly developed injury associated with overuse	75
Chunking	Different pieces of information can be grouped (or chunked) together and then remembered as one piece of information	114
Cognitive anxiety	Anxiety experienced by the mind, for example worry about failing	121
Cold therapy or cryotherapy	Applying ice or cold to an injury or after exercise for therapeutic effect, such as reduced swelling	80
Commodity	An article that can be traded. In this case, sport is the article that can be sold to different media outlets or companies that wish to associate their brand with a particular sport	151
Competitive trait anxiety	A tendency to perceive competitive situations as threatening and to respond to these situations with feelings of apprehension or tension	122
Concussion	A traumatic brain injury resulting in a disturbance of brain function	75
Conduction system	A set of structures in the cardiac muscle that create and transmit an electrical impulse, forcing the atria and ventricles to contract	23
Conservation of angular momentum	Angular momentum is a conserved quantity that remains constant unless an external eccentric force or torque is applied	94
Contrast therapy	The use of alternate cold and heat for a therapeutic effect, such as increased blood flow	80
Controllability	Whether attributions are under the control of the performer or under the control of others, or whether they are uncontrollable, i.e. nothing can be done by anyone (e.g. luck, weather)	127
Coupled reaction	Where products of one reaction are used in another reaction	35
Dehydration	Loss of water from body tissues, largely caused by sweating	42
Deindividuation	When you lose your sense of being an individual; this can cause violent behaviour	148
Delayed onset muscle soreness (DOMS)	Pain and stiffness felt in the muscles, which peaks 24–72 hours after exercise, associated with eccentric muscle contraction	19
Deoxygenated blood	Blood depleted of oxygen, saturated with carbon dioxide and waste products	22
Deviance	Unacceptable behaviour within a culture. Any behaviour that differs from the perceived social or legal norm is seen as deviant	147
Diastole	The relaxation phase of cardiac muscle where chambers fill with blood	23

Term	Definition	Page(s)
Direct force	A force applied through the centre of mass resulting in linear motion	90
Dislocation	The displacement of one bone from another out of their original position	74
Dissociation	The release of oxygen from haemoglobin for gaseous exchange	32
Distance/time graph	A visual representation of the distance travelled plotted against the time taken	90
Drag	The force that opposes the direction of motion of a body through water or air	96
Drive	Directed, motivated or 'energised' behaviour that an individual has towards achieving a certain goal	119
Dynamic flexibility	The range of motion about a joint with reference to speed of movement	67
Eccentric force	A force applied outside the centre of mass, resulting in angular motion	92
Energy	The ability to perform work, measured in joules or calories	46
Energy balance	The relationship between energy intake and energy expenditure	48
Energy continuum	The relative contribution of each energy system to overall energy production, depending on the intensity and duration of the activity	36
Energy expenditure	The sum of basal metabolic rate, the thermic effect of food and the energy expended through physical activity	48
Energy intake	The total amount of energy from food and beverages consumed, measured in joules or calories	48
Enzyme	Biological catalyst that increases the speed of chemical reactions	46
Ergogenic aid	A substance, object or method used to improve or enhance performance	48
Erythropoietin	A naturally produced hormone responsible for producing red blood cells	41
Ethics	Rules that dictate an individual's conduct. They form a system of rules that groups and societies are judged on. An ethic in sport would be that an athlete sticks to the spirit of the rules of the game	147
Excess post-exercise oxygen consumption (EPOC)	The volume of oxygen consumed post-exercise to return the body to a pre-exercise state	38
Extrinsic feedback	Feedback that comes from external sources, for example a teacher or coach	112
Extrinsic risk factor	An injury risk or force from outside the body	76
Fats	Triglycerides that provide the body with fatty acids for energy production	46
Fixator	A muscle that stabilises one part of a body while another part moves	16
Frank-Starling mechanism	Increased venous return leads to increased SV, due to an increased stretch of the ventricular walls and therefore force of contraction	25
Free body diagram	A clearly labelled sketch showing all the forces acting on a body at a particular instant in time	84
Friction	The force that opposes the motion of two surfaces in contact	84
Gaseous exchange	The movement of oxygen from the alveoli into the bloodstream and carbon dioxide from the bloodstream into the alveoli	28
Gene therapy	The use of genes and genetic elements to treat human disease	156
Globalisation	A process that involves sport as a worldwide business and features corporate brands, media coverage and freedom of movement of sport participants, officials and spectators	143
Golden triangle	The interdependence and influences of the three factors of sport, sponsorship and the media – each one influences the others	151
Gradient	The slope of a graph at a particular moment in time. Gradient = change in y axis/change in x axis	90
Group	A collection of people who share similar goals and interact with one another	124
Haematoma	Localised congealed bleeding from ruptured blood vessels	74
Heat therapy	Applying heat to an area before training for a therapeutic effect, such as increased blood flow	80

Term	Definition	Page(s)
High-density lipoprotein (HDL)	HDLs actively remove cholesterol from arterial walls and transport it to the liver	71
Hook	A type of sidespin used to deviate a projectile's flight path to the left	100
Humidity	The amount of water vapour in the atmospheric air	42
Hyperthermia	Significantly raised core body temperature	42
Hypoxic chamber	A sealed room that simulates high altitude	155
Intermittent exercise	Activity where the intensity alternates, either during interval training between work and relief intervals or during a game with breaks of play and changes of intensity	37
Intrinsic feedback	A type of continuous feedback that comes from the proprioceptors – nerve receptors found in muscles, ligaments and joints that pick up movement information	111
Intrinsic risk factor	An injury risk or force from inside the body	76
Joint	An area of the body where two or more bones articulate to create human movement	8
Knowledge of performance	Information about how well the movement is being executed, rather than about the end result	112
Knowledge of results	A type of terminal feedback that gives the performer information about the end result of the response	112
Low-density lipoprotein (LDL)	LDLs deposit cholesterol in the arterial walls	71
Lift force	An additional force created by a pressure gradient forming on opposing surfaces of an aerofoil moving through a fluid	98
Linear motion	Movement of a body in a straight or curved line where all parts move the same distance in the same direction over the same time	90
Macro-cycle	A long-term training plan, typically over a year, to achieve a long-term goal	55
Magnus effect	Creation of an additional Magnus force on a spinning projectile which deviates the flight path	100
Magnus force	A force created from a pressure gradient on opposing surfaces of a spinning body moving through the air	100
Massage therapy	A physical therapy used for injury prevention and soft tissue injury treatment	80
Match fixing	When a sports competition is played to a completely or partly predetermined result. This is against the law	149
Maximal	A high intensity of exercise above a performer's aerobic capacity that will induce fatigue	25
Mechanical advantage	Second-class lever systems where the effort arm is greater than the load arm. A large load can be moved with a relatively small effort	88
Mechanical disadvantage	Third-class lever systems where the load arm is greater than the effort arm. A large effort is required to move a relatively small load	88
Medial tibia stress syndrome (MTSS)/ shin splints	Chronic shin pain due to the inflammation of muscles and stress on the tendon attachments to the surface of the tibia	75
Memory trace	When the brain cells retain or store information	114
Meso-cycle	A mid-term training plan, typically over 6 weeks, to achieve a mid-term goal	55
Micro-cycle	A short-term training plan, typically over 1 week, to achieve a short-term goal	55
Motivation	'The internal mechanisms and external stimuli that arouse and direct our behaviour' (Sage 1974)	119
Motor (or movement) skill	An action or task that has a goal and requires voluntary body and/or limb movement to achieve that goal; it is learned rather than being innate	108
Movement pattern	A description of the action taking place at a joint	9
Muscle hyperplasia	Increased number of muscle fibres	65
Muscle hypertrophy	Increased muscle cell size	65

Glossary

Term	Definition	Page(s)
Myogenic	The capacity of the heart to generate its own electrical impulse, which causes the cardiac muscle to contract	23
Myoglobin	A protein molecule that, similarly to haemoglobin, helps with the transport of oxygen	37
Myosin filaments	Proteins that form the contractile units of skeletal muscles	16
Negative feedback	Information about an unsuccessful outcome, which can be used to build more successful strategies	112
Net force	The sum of all forces acting on a body; also termed resultant force. It is the overall force acting on a body when all individual forces have been considered	83
Non-parabolic flight path	A flight path asymmetrical about its highest point caused by the dominant force of air resistance on a projectile	97
Non-steroid anti-inflammatory drugs (NSAIDs)	Medication taken to reduce inflammation, temperature and pain following injury	79
Oxygenated blood	Blood saturated with oxygen and nutrients, such as glucose	22
Oxyhaemoglobin dissociation curve	A graph showing the relationship between pO_2 and percentage saturation of haemoglobin	32
Parabola	A uniform curve symmetrical about its highest point	96
Parabolic flight path	A flight path symmetrical about its highest point caused by the dominant weight force of a projectile	96
Parallelogram of forces	A parallelogram illustrating the theory that a diagonal drawn from the point where forces are represented in size and direction shows the resultant force acting	98
Parasympathetic nervous system	Part of the autonomic nervous system responsible for decreasing HR, specifically during recovery	25
Periodisation	The organised division of training into blocks, each with a goal and time frame	55
Personality	The patterns of thoughts and feelings and the ways in which we interact with our environment and other people that make us a unique person	117
Pharmacological aids	A group of ergogenic aids taken to increase the levels of hormones or neural transmitters	48
Physiological aids	A group of ergogenic aids used to increase the rate of adaptation of the body and thus increase performance	49
Physiotherapy	Physical treatment of injuries and disease using methods such as mobilisation, massage, exercise therapy and postural training	79
Plane of movement	The description of three-dimensional movements at a joint	9
Positive feedback	Feedback that reinforces skill learning and gives information about a successful outcome	112
Power output	The amount of work performed per unit of time, measured in watts (W)	62
Pre-capillary sphincters	Rings of smooth muscle at the junction between arterioles and capillaries, which can dilate or constrict to control blood flow through the capillary bed	27
Precision hydration	The monitoring of sodium loss during sweating, leading to more effective replacement of essential salts in the body	155
PRICE	Protocol for the treatment of acute injuries: protect, rest, ice, compress and elevate	78
Principles of training	The rules that underpin training programme design to ensure safe and effective fitness adaptation	54
Professionals	People who compete in sporting activities and earn an income by participating	138
Projectile	A body that is launched into the air, losing contact with the ground surface, such as a discus or a long jumper	96
Projectile motion	Movement of a body through the air following a curved flight path under the force of gravity	96
Propaganda	A type of communication that seeks to influence people towards a certain cause. The information given is biased towards a certain belief or set of values	144

Quick quizzes at www.hoddereducation.co.uk/myrevisionnotesdownloads

Term	Definition	Page(s)
Proprioceptive neuromuscular facilitation (PNF)	A stretching technique to desensitise the stretch reflex, whereby a performer completes a static passive stretch, isometrically contracts against the agonist, relaxes, then stretches further	68
Prosthetic	An artificial device that substitutes for or supplements a defective part of the body	155
Protein	Amino acids essential for the growth and repair of cells and tissues	46
Public school	A place of education of old standing that the sons of gentlemen traditionally attended in large numbers from 8 to 18 years old	138
Pulmonary circuit	Circulation of blood through the pulmonary artery to the lungs and pulmonary vein back to the heart	21
Reaction	The equal and opposite force exerted by a body in response to the action force placed upon it	83
Rehabilitation	The process of restoring full function after an injury has occurred	79
Resultant force	The sum of all forces acting on a body or the net force acting on a projectile	98
Rupture	A complete tear of muscle, tendon or ligament	75
SALTAPS	Protocol for the assessment of a sporting injury: stop, ask, look, touch, active movement, passive movement and strength testing	78
Saturated fatty acid	A type of fat molecule that is typically solid at room temperature and is mainly found in animal products	46
Selective attention	Relevant information is filtered through into short-term memory and irrelevant information is lost or forgotten	113
Self-efficacy	The confidence we have in specific situations	130
Self-esteem	The feeling of self-worth that determines how valuable and competent we feel	129
Self-serving bias	A person's tendency to attribute their failure to external causes (e.g. 'I lost the badminton match because the floor was too slippery') and their success to internal causes	127
Shin splints/ medial tibia stress syndrome (MTSS)	Chronic shin pain due to the inflammation of muscles and stress on the tendon attachments to the surface of the tibia	75
Six Rs	Protocol for recognition of concussion: recognise, remove, refer, rest, recover and return	79
Slice	A type of sidespin used to deviate a projectile's flight path to the right	100
Social facilitation	The positive influence on sports performance of others who may be watching or competing	123
Social inhibition	The negative influence on sports performance of others who may be watching or competing	123
Social loafing	Some individuals in a group seem to lose motivation. It is apparently caused by the individual losing identity when placed in a group. Individual efforts may not be recognised by those who are spectating or taking part	125
Soft tissue injury	Damage to the skin, muscle, tendon or ligament, including tears, strains and sprains	74
Somatic anxiety	Anxiety experienced physiologically, for example sweating	121
Spectatorship	The act of watching something without taking part; often related to sports spectators	149
Speed/time graph	A visual representation of the speed of motion plotted against the time taken	91
Sponsorship (in sport)	To support an event, activity or person related to sport, by providing money or goods	149
Sports confidence	The belief or degree of certainty individuals possess about their ability to be successful in sport	129
Sprain	Overstretch or tear in the ligament that connects bone to bone	74
State anxiety	An athlete's emotional state at any given time, variable from situation to situation	122

Term	Definition	Page(s)
Static active stretching	A performer moves the joint into its fully stretched position without any assistance and holds for 10–30 seconds	68
Static flexibility	The range of motion about a joint without reference to speed of movement	67
Static passive stretching	A performer moves the joint just beyond its point of resistance with assistance and holds for 10–30 seconds	68
Strain	Overstretch or tear in the muscle or tendon that connects muscle to bone	75
Streamlining	The creation of smooth air flow around an aerodynamic shape to minimise air resistance	84
Stress	Often linked to negative feelings; a psychological state produced and perceived by physiological and psychological forces acting on our sense of wellbeing	133
Stress fracture	A tiny crack in the surface of a bone caused by overuse	75
Subluxation	An incomplete or partial dislocation	74
Sub-maximal	A low-to-moderate intensity of exercise within a performer's aerobic capacity	25
Sub-routines	The elements or separate movements that make up a particular skill	104
Sympathetic nervous system	Part of the autonomic nervous system responsible for increasing HR, specifically during exercise	25
Systemic circuit	Circulation of blood through the aorta to the body and vena cava back to the heart	21
Systole	The contraction phase of cardiac muscle where blood is forcibly ejected into the aorta and pulmonary artery	23
Tapering	Maintaining the intensity but decreasing the volume of training by one-third to prepare for competition	56
Tendinosis	The deterioration of a tendon in response to chronic overuse and repetitive strain	75
Thermic effect of food (TEF)	The energy required to eat, digest, absorb and use food taken in	48
Thermoreceptors	Sensory receptors that sense a change in temperature and relay information to the brain	42
Thermoregulation	The process of maintaining internal core temperature	42
Torque	A measure of the turning (rotational or eccentric) force applied to a body	92
Trait anxiety	A trait that is enduring in an individual. A performer with high trait anxiety has the predisposition or the potential to react to situations with apprehension	122
UK Sport	An organisation whose aim is the development of the country's sportspeople. It is funded jointly by the government and the National Lottery	152
Unsaturated fatty acid	A type of fat molecule that is typically liquid at room temperature and is found in sunflower, olive and fish oils. They can help lower cholesterol	46
Vascular shunt mechanism	The redistribution of cardiac output around the body from rest to exercise which increases the percentage of blood flow to the skeletal muscles	27
Vasoconstriction	Narrowing of arteries, arterioles and pre-capillary sphincters	26
Vasodilation	Widening of arteries, arterioles and pre-capillary sphincters	26
Vasomotor control centre (VCC)	The control centre in the medulla oblongata responsible for cardiac output distribution	27
Vasomotor tone	The partial state of smooth muscle constriction in the arterial walls	27
Velocity/time graph	A visual representation of the velocity of motion plotted against the time taken	91
Venoconstriction	Narrowing of the veins and venules	26
Venodilation	Widening of the veins and venules	26
Venous return	The return of the blood to the right atria through the veins	25
Vicarious learning	This happens when one person observes that a reward is given to another person for certain behaviours and learns to emulate that same behaviour	131

Quick quizzes at www.hoddereducation.co.uk/myrevisionnotesdownloads

Term	Definition	Page(s)
Violence	Intense physical force that is directed towards harming another individual or group of individuals and can cause injury and death	148
Vitamins and minerals	Essential organic and inorganic nutrients required for healthy body function	46
VO$_2$max	Maximum volume of oxygen inspired, transported and utilised per minute during exhaustive exercise	58
Weight	The gravitational pull that the earth exerts on a body. Weight (N) = mass × acceleration due to gravity	83

Now test yourself answers

Chapter 1.1a

1

Joint	Agonist	Antagonist
a) Wrist	Wrist flexors	Wrist extensors
b) Elbow	Biceps brachii	Triceps brachii
c) Shoulder	Anterior deltoid	Posterior deltoid
d) Hip	Iliopsoas	Gluteus maximus
e) Knee	Biceps femoris	Rectus femoris
f) Ankle	Tibialis anterior	Gastrocnemius and soleus

2 Sagittal plane: vertical – divides body into left/right. Frontal plane: vertical – divides body into anterior/posterior. Transverse plane: horizontal – divides body into upper/lower.

3 Agonist: a muscle responsible for creating movement at a joint. Antagonist: a muscle that opposes the agonist, providing a resistance for co-ordinated movement. Fixator: a muscle that stabilises one part of the body while another part moves.

4 Concentric: the muscle shortens to produce tension. Eccentric: the muscle lengthens to produce tension.

5 Motor neuron and its muscle fibres

6 Slow oxidative, fast oxidative glycolytic, fast glycolytic

7 Three from:

	Slow oxidative	Fast oxidative glycolitic	Fast glycolitic
Neuron size	Small	Large	Large
Fibres per neuron	Few	Many	Many
Capillary density	High	High	Low
Mitochondria density	High	Moderate	Low
Myoglobin density	High	Moderate	Low
Phosphocreatine store	Low	High	High

8 Three from:

	Slow oxidative	Fast oxidative glycolitic	Fast glycolitic
Speed of contraction	Slow	Fast	Fast
Force of contraction	Low	High	High
Fatigue resistance	High	Moderate	Low
Aerobic capacity	High	Moderate	Low
Anaerobic capacity	Low	Moderate	High

Chapter 1.1b

1 Diastole (relaxation phase); systole (contraction phase)

2 SA node, AV node, bundle of His, bundle branches, Purkinje fibres

3 Myogenic means having the ability to generate its own electrical impulse.

4 Heart rate (HR): the number of times the heart beats per minute.
Stroke volume (SV): the amount of blood ejected from the left ventricle per beat.
Cardiac output (CO): the amount of blood ejected from the left ventricle per minute. HR × SV = CO

	HR	SV	CO
Untrained	70–72 bpm	70 ml	5 l/min
Trained	50 bpm	100 ml	5 l/min

5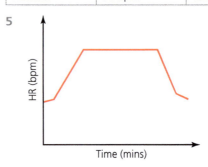

6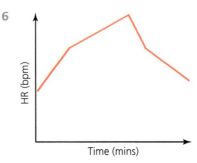

7 Medulla oblongata in the brain

8 Neural (proprioceptors, baroreceptors, chemoreceptors); intrinsic (temperature, venous return); hormonal (adrenaline and noradrenaline)

9 Muscle pump, respiratory pump, pocket valves, gravity, smooth muscle

10 Breathing rate: the number of inspirations or expirations per minute. Tidal volume: the volume of air inspired or expired per breath. Minute ventilation: the volume of air inspired or expired per minute. VE = TV × f (minute ventilation = tidal volume × breathing rate).
Breathing rate, tidal volume and minute ventilation all increase during exercise.

11 At rest: active process. External intercostal muscles between the ribs contract, pulling the chest walls

up and out. The diaphragm muscle below the lungs contracts and flattens, increasing the size of the chest.

During exercise: active process. In addition to the external intercostal muscles and diaphragm, the sternocleidomastoid lifts the sternum, and the scalene and pectoralis minor contract and lift the ribs more. Effect: the volume of the thoracic cavity increases, creating a larger concentration gradient between inside the lungs and outside the body, therefore more air enters the lungs more quickly.

12 At rest: passive process. External intercostal muscles between the ribs relax so that the chest walls move in and down. The diaphragm muscle below the lungs relaxes and bulges up, reducing the size of the chest.

During exercise: active process. In addition to the external intercostal muscles and diaphragm, the internal intercostal muscles contract and pull the ribs down and in, and the rectus abdominus contracts and pushes the diaphragm up. Effect: a decrease in the volume of the thoracic cavity increases pressure in the lungs, therefore air is forced out quickly because of the larger concentration gradient.

13 Chemoreceptors, thermoreceptors, proprioceptors, baroreceptors

14 Partial pressure (pp) is the pressure a gas exerts within a mixture of gases.

15 The difference between the high and low pressure in different areas is called the diffusion gradient.

16 A move in the oxyhaemoglobin dissociation curve to the right caused by increased acidity in the bloodstream.

Chapter 1.1c

1 ATP is adenosine triphosphate. This compound is the only immediately usable form of energy stored in our bodies. ATP is readily available as it is stored in the muscle cell.

2 We have limited stores of ATP in our body (enough for 2 seconds) and it is the usable energy currency in our body.

3 ATP/PC system, glycolytic system, aerobic system

4 Aerobic glycolysis, Krebs cycle, electron transport chain

5 The relative contribution of each energy system to overall energy production, depending on the intensity and duration of the activity.

6 The point at which an energy system is unable to provide energy and therefore energy production switches to another system.

7 OBLA is the onset of blood lactate accumulation – the point at which blood lactate values go above 4 mmol/l.

8 Fast alactacid component: 1 PC stores restored. 2 Replenishment of blood and muscle oxygen.
Slow lactacid component: 1 Elevated ventilation and circulation to maximise the delivery of O_2 and the removal of by-products. 2 Elevated body temperature which increases metabolic rate. 3 Removal of lactic acid.

9 Warm-up, active recovery, cooling aids, intensity of training, work:relief ratios, strategies and tactics, nutrition

Chapter 1.1d

1 Altitude is the height or elevation of an area above sea level.

2 As altitude increases, the diffusion gradient decreases.

3 Rate of oxygen diffusion decreases, reducing haemoglobin saturation and resulting in poor transport of O_2. Blood volume decreases – plasma volume decreases by 25% to allow increase in density of RBCs. Stroke volume decreases, which increases heart rate. Maximal cardiac output, stroke volume and heart rate decrease during maximum-intensity exercise.

4 Breathing frequency increases at rest and during exercise; there is a reduced aerobic capacity and VO_2max, impacting on the intensity and duration of an athlete's performance.

5 Acclimatisation benefits for the cardiovascular and respiratory systems are: an increase in red blood cell production, due to increased release of erythropoietin; stabilisation of breathing rate and ventilation, although they remain elevated at rest, compared to sea levels; reduction of SV and CO as O_2 extraction becomes more efficient; reduced incidence of altitude sickness, headaches, breathlessness, poor sleep and lack of appetite.

6 Cardiovascular drift is an upward drift in heart rate associated with a rise in body temperature (1 °C increases heart rate by 10 bpm).

7 Any three from: Cardiovascular system: dilation of arterioles and capillaries to the skin; decreased blood volume, venous return, SV, CO and BP. Respiratory system: dehydration and drying of the airways in temperatures above 32 °C make breathing difficult; increased breathing frequency to maintain oxygen consumption; high levels of sunlight increase the effects of pollutants in the air.

8 Pre-competition: 7–14 days of acclimatisation in the same conditions to increase the body's tolerance to heat OR using cooling aids such as ice vests to reduce core temperature and delay effects of dehydration.

During competition: pacing strategies to reduce the feelings of exertion at low-exercise intensities OR wearing suitable clothing to maximise heat loss OR rehydrating as often and as much as possible with a hypotonic or isotonic solution.

Post-competition: using cooling aids such as cold fans OR rehydrating using isotonic solutions to replace lost fluids, glucose and electrolytes.

Chapter 1.2a

1. Carbohydrates (CHOs), fats, proteins, vitamins, minerals, fibre, water
2. Saturated fatty acids (bad fats): solid at room temperature, typically animal products, associated with heart disease. Unsaturated fatty acids (good fats): liquid at room temperature, sunflower/olive/fish oil, can help lower cholesterol.
3. Energy is the ability to perform work, measured in joules or calories. Energy balance is the relationship between energy intake and energy expenditure: energy in > energy expenditure = weight gain; energy in < energy expenditure = weight loss; energy in = energy expenditure = weight stays the same.
4. Energy expenditure = BMR + TEF + physical activity energy expenditure. It is important as it will allow the athlete to plan their diet to facilitate effective training and performance.
5. Caffeine: benefits – increased nervous stimulation, increased focus/concentration, increased metabolism of fats, preservation of muscle glycogen, increased endurance performance. Drawbacks – diuretic effect = dehydration, insomnia and anxiety, gastrointestinal problems.
   Blood doping: benefits – increased RBCs, therefore more haemoglobin; increased O_2 transportation and aerobic capacity; increased intensity and duration of performance. Drawbacks – increased blood viscosity, decreased cardiac output, increased risk of blood clots and heart disease, risk of transfusion infections (HIV/AIDS).
   Cooling aids: benefits – reduced core body temperature; decreased sweating, dehydration and early fatigue; decreased injury pain and swelling; increased speed of recovery and repair; decreased DOMS. Drawbacks – difficult to perceive exercise intensity; ice burns and pain; may mask or worsen injuries; chest pain and decreased efficiency in older people; dangerous for those with heart and blood pressure problems.

Chapter 1.2b

1. Specificity, progression, overload, variance, moderation and reversibility
2. Macro-cycle is long-term, e.g. 4 years; meso-cycle is medium-term, e.g. 4–6 weeks; micro-cycle is short-term, e.g. 1 week.
3. Aerobic capacity: the ability of the body to inspire, transport and utilise oxygen to perform sustained periods of aerobic activity.
   VO_2max: maximum volume of oxygen inspired, transported and utilised per minute during exhaustive exercise.
4. Physiological make-up – the greater the efficiency of body systems to transport and utilise O_2 = higher VO_2max; can be determined by genetics. Stronger respiratory muscles, larger heart, higher SV, higher CO, increased number of RBCs, capillaries, SO fibres = higher VO_2max.
   Age – from age 20, VO_2max drops 1% each year. Efficiency is lost in elasticity of heart, blood vessels and lung tissue = lower VO_2max.
   Gender – females lower than males. Females have higher body fat, smaller lung volumes, lower haemoglobin levels = lower VO_2max.
   Training – aerobic training increases VO_2max up to 20%. Aerobic training causes long-term adaptations to heart, lungs, blood = higher VO_2max.
5. Similarities: both used to improve aerobic capacity; both use activities such as swimming, cycling and running.
   Differences: continuous – work interval is 20–80 mins; intensity is 60–80% max HR; low to moderate intensity; no breaks in activity. HIIT: 20–60 minutes; intensity is 80–95% max HR; high intensity; has recovery periods built in.
6. $60 + (0.70 \times (202 - 60)) = 159.4 = 159$ bpm
7. SO muscle fibre hypertrophy, increased size and density of mitochondria, increased stores of myoglobin, increased stores of glycogen and fats, FOG fibres become more aerobic, increased strength of connective tissue, increased thickness of articular cartilage, increased bone mineral density. Overall these increase the intensity and duration of performance and reduce the risk of injury, osteoarthritis and osteoporosis.
8. Cross-sectional area of muscle, age, gender, fibre type
9. Maximum strength: one repetition maximum test or grip strength dynamometer. Strength endurance: UK abdominal curl test. Explosive strength: vertical jump test.
10. Static flexibility: the range of motion about a joint without reference to speed of movement. Dynamic flexibility: the range of motion about a joint with reference to speed of movement.
11. Type of joint, length and elasticity of surrounding connective tissue, gender, age
12. Goniometry: 360-degree protractor; difference between starting angle and full range of motion calculated. Sit and reach test: test box placed against wall, straight legs at full stretch, best score is recorded.
13. Static stretching: can be active (on own) or passive (with partner); isometric stretching; proprioceptive neuromuscular facilitation (PNF); ballistic stretching; dynamic stretching.
14. It can: reduce blood lipids (fats) and cholesterol and increase the proportion of HDL to LDL cholesterol; prevent hardening and loss of elasticity in arterial walls, slowing onset of atherosclerosis and hypertension; decrease blood viscosity, preventing blood clots and reducing BP; increase coronary circulation; lead to cardiac hypertrophy, increased SV and lowered resting HR; decrease body fat,

reducing strain on the heart; increase blood flow and O_2 transport, reducing strain on the heart; reduce the risk of a stroke by 27% by lowering BP.

Chapter 1.2c

1 Signs: lying motionless/slow to get up, possible post-traumatic seizure, loss of consciousness, balance problems, disorientation/confusion. Symptoms: lying motionless/slow to get up, headache/dizziness, visual problems/light sensitivity, nausea/vomiting. Sporting example: a hockey player may suffer a concussion after being hit in the head by a hockey ball.
2 A stress fracture is a tiny crack in the surface of a bone caused by overuse. Shin splints are chronic shin pain due to the inflammation of muscles and stress on the tendon attachments to the surface of the tibia.
3 Fracture (e.g. a fracture of a bone in a boxer's jaw), dislocation (e.g. rugby player suffering a shoulder dislocation from a bad tackle).
4 Any two from: contusion/haematoma (e.g. impact from a tackle in rugby), sprain (e.g. a knee ligament tear after a bad tackle in football), strain (e.g. from lunging to return a drop shot in badminton), abrasion (e.g. from falling or slipping on an athletics track), blister (e.g. on the hands of gymnasts).
5 An acute injury is a sudden injury associated with a traumatic event. A chronic injury is a slowly developed injury associated with overuse.
6 Any two from: previous injury, posture and alignment issues, age, nutrition, poor preparation, inadequate fitness level, inappropriate flexibility level.
7 Any two from: poor technique and training; incorrect equipment and clothing; inappropriate intensity, duration or frequency of activity; warm-up and cool-down effectiveness.
8 Any three from: raising body temperature, preparing body physiologically, preparing body psychologically, minimising the risk of injury.
9 Maintaining heart rate, aiding the removal of lactic acid, aiding the healing process.
10 In the event of a sporting accident, to consider whether a player should continue.
11 Soft tissue injuries

Chapter 1.3a

1 First law, law of inertia: a body continues in a state of rest or uniform velocity unless acted upon by an external or unbalanced force. Second law, law of acceleration: a body's rate of change of momentum is proportional to the size of the force applied and acts in the same direction as the force applied. Third law, law of reaction: for every action there is an equal and opposite reaction.

2 Net force is the sum of all forces acting on a body; it is also termed resultant force. It is the overall force acting on a body when all individual forces have been considered.
3 Vertical forces: weight (the gravitational pull that the earth exerts on a body) and reaction (the equal and opposite force exerted by a body in response to the action force placed upon it). Horizontal forces: friction (the force that opposes the motion of two surfaces in contact) and air resistance (the force that opposes the direction of motion of a body through the air).
4 $5 \times 2.54 = 12.7$ N
5 $65/4 = 16.25$ m/s
6 Roughness of the ground surface, roughness of the contact surface, temperature, size of normal reaction
7 Velocity, shape, frontal cross-sectional area, smoothness of surface
8 Velocity – a sprinter has more drag than an athlete walking. Streamlining/shape – a ski jumper creates a flat shape, keeping their arms by their side, body leaning forward. Frontal cross-sectional area (FCA) – BMX riders make themselves as small/low as possible to reduce FCA. Smoothness of surface – elite swimmers wear swimming goggles under swimming hat, to ensure head surface is smooth.
9 Centre of mass is the point at which an object or a body is balanced in all directions. It is the point where the weight of the body tends to be concentrated.
10 Mass of the body, height of the centre of mass, size of the base of support, line of gravity
11 Any relevant example, such as: rugby – stability (in the scrum); instability (changing direction to dodge/step around a player). Similar examples can be detailed for netball, basketball etc.
12 Lever, fulcrum, effort, load
13 A second-class lever has the mechanical advantage to move a large load with a small effort, such as at the ball of the foot to vertically accelerate an athlete's whole weight easily. A third-class lever has the mechanical disadvantage, requiring a large effort to move a relatively small load, for example flexion of the elbow in an upward phase of a biceps curl.

Chapter 1.3b

1 Linear motion is the movement of a body in a straight or curved line, where all parts move the same distance in the same direction over the same time.
2 Linear motion results from a direct force being applied to a body, i.e. where force is applied directly to the centre of a body's mass.

3 Distance is the total length of the path covered from start to finish. Displacement is the shortest straight-line route from start to finish.

4

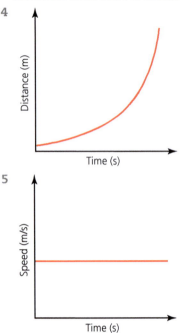

5

6 Angular motion is the movement of a body or part of a body in a circular path about an axis of rotation.
7 Angular motion results from an eccentric force being applied to a body, i.e. where the force is applied outside the centre of a body's mass.
8 Longitudinal, transverse, frontal
9 Moment of inertia: the resistance of a body to change its angular motion or rotation. MI = $\Sigma m \times r^2$, measured in kilogram metres² (kgm²).
Angular velocity: the rate of change in angular displacement or rate of rotation. Angular velocity = angular displacement/time taken, measured in radians per second (rad/s).
Angular momentum: the quantity of angular motion possessed by a body. Angular momentum = moment of inertia × angular velocity, measured in kilogram metres² per second (kgm²/s).
10 MI = $\Sigma m \times r^2 = 50 \times 1.5^2 = 112.5$ kgm²
11 Air resistance is the force that opposes the direction of motion of a body through air.
12 Drag is the force that opposes the direction of motion of a body through water.
13 Velocity, frontal cross-sectional area, streamlining and shape, surface characteristics
14 Speed of release, angle of release, height of release, aerodynamic factors (Bernoulli and Magnus)
15 Weight: if weight is the dominant force and air resistance is very small, a parabolic flight path occurs.
16 Air resistance: if air resistance is the dominant force and weight is very small, a non-parabolic flight path occurs.
17 The Bernoulli principle states that there is the creation of an additional lift force on a projectile in flight resulting from Bernoulli's conclusion that the higher the velocity of air flow, the lower the surrounding pressure.

18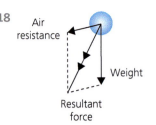

The resultant force is closer to the weight arrow, so the flight path will be more parabolic.
19 Topspin, backspin, hook (sidespin), slice (sidespin)
20 Magnus force is a force created from a pressure gradient on opposing surfaces of a spinning body moving through the air.
21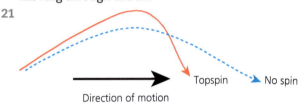

Chapter 2.1

1

Type of practice method	Classes of skill most suitable	Practical examples
Part	Low organisation, serial, complex	Backswing of a tennis serve
Whole	High organisation, low in complexity	Golf swing, sprinting
Progressive-part	Complex, low organisation, serial	Triple jump, trampoline routine
Whole–part–whole	Low organisation	Swimming strokes

2 Proactive transfer, retroactive transfer, positive transfer, negative transfer, bilateral transfer
3 Offer variable practice, make aware of transferable elements, give clear and concise demonstrations, ensure diverse childhood experiences
4 a) negative and proactive
  b) bilateral
5 Proactive transfer is when a skill learned in the past affects a skill currently being learned or to be learned in the future, whereas retroactive transfer is when learning a new skill affects a previously learned skill. Either could be positive or negative.
6 Operant conditioning, Thorndike's laws, cognitive theory of learning, observational learning/social learning theory
7 a) observational learning/social learning theory
  b) cognitive theory of learning
8 Stage 1: cognitive stage (initial) – performances will be inconsistent and full of errors, and will lack co-ordination and flow.
Stage 2: associative stage (intermediate) – learner attends to relevant cues, errors are fewer and smaller, big improvements in performance.

Stage 3: autonomous stage (final) – learner can execute skill with little conscious thought (automatically), so they can concentrate on other factors

9. Verbal, visual, manual and mechanical
10. Intrinsic, extrinsic, positive, negative, knowledge of results (KR), knowledge of performance (KP)
11. Knowledge of results (KR) is feedback about the outcome of our movements, e.g. whether the ball went into the net. Knowledge of performance (KP) concerns the movement itself and the quality of it, e.g. whether the shooting technique was correct.
12. Short-term sensory store (STSS): a limitless memory store for holding information for about 1 second, viewed as a subdivided part of short-term memory (STM).

    Short-term memory (STM): represents a 'working memory space' where information from the STSS and long-term memory (LTM) is received and brought together. STM has a limited capacity to store information – around seven items. The information is held for as long is attention is held.

    Long-term memory (LTM): contains well-learned, retained and permanent coded information collected over past experiences. It is limitless in capacity and length or retention, for example learning to ride a bike.
13. When the brain cells retain or store information
14. Rehearse information physically and mentally, ensure information is meaningful, associate information with already learned skills/tactics, avoid overload – only give a few key points, organise or chunk information, create a clear mental image.

Chapter 2.2

1. The patterns of thoughts and feelings and the ways in which we interact with our environment and other people that make us a unique person
2. Trait theories (type A/type B, stable/unstable and extroversion/introversion): Trait theorists do not believe that the situation or environment has any bearing on a person's behaviour. Behaviour is said to be consistent. Trait theory attempts to predict behaviour.

    Social learning theory: suggests that rather than being born with characteristics, we learn them from other people, especially from those we hold in high esteem.

    Interactionist theory: recognises that traits and social learning both have a role in determining behaviour and personality. It suggests that we base behaviour on inherent traits that we then adapt to the situation we are in.
3. A predisposition to act in a particular way towards something or someone in a person's environment
4. Any three from: Beliefs, experiences, ability, feeling fear or excited by the challenge, influence of others, experiencing stress or release from stress
5. Cognitive: what we know and believe about the attitude object (beliefs – e.g. that exercise is good for you). Affective: how we feel about the attitude object (emotion – e.g. enjoy exercise). Behavioural: how we behave towards, respond to or intend to respond to the attitude object (behaviour – e.g. take part in exercise regularly).
6. Intrinsic motivation is the drive from within, for example wanting to achieve mastery for its own sake. It includes feelings of fun, enjoyment and satisfaction. Extrinsic motivation comes from an outside source, for example a trophy or reward. It is a valuable motivator for the beginner but will eventually undermine intrinsic motivation.
7. Somatic arousal relates to the changing physiological state of the body, e.g. sweating, increased heart rate. Cognitive arousal relates to the changing psychological state of the body, e.g. worrying, overthinking, dwelling too much on something, increase in anxiety.
8. Drive theory, inverted U theory and catastrophe theory
9. Cognitive anxiety: anxiety experienced by the mind; symptoms include worry about failing, indecision, confusion, negative thoughts, poor concentration, irritability, loss of confidence, images of failure.

    Somatic anxiety: anxiety experienced physiologically; symptoms include increased BP, sweating, adrenaline boost, need to urinate, muscle tension, pacing, yawning, nausea, vomiting, diarrhoea, loss of appetite.
10. To ensure optimum performance/achieve the best results/form; for physical and mental wellbeing.
11. They are relaxed, confident and completely focused; activity is effortless; movements are automatic; they have fun and are in control.
12. Instinct theory: views aggression as being a natural response, innate and instinctive. Animalistic. Humans developed aggression as survival instinct.

    Frustration–aggression hypothesis: frustration will always lead to aggression. Any blocking of goals that an individual is trying to reach increases an individual's drive, thus increasing aggression and frustration. If success follows, aggression leads to catharsis.

    Social learning theory: aggression is learned by observation of others' behaviour. Imitation of this aggressive behaviour is then reinforced by social acceptance. If we see a teammate fouling an opponent and this stops the opponent from playing well, it is reinforced and copied.

    Aggressive cue hypothesis: for aggression to occur, certain stimuli must be present. These stimuli are cues for the performer which are subconsciously linked to aggression, for example baseball bats or ice hockey sticks. Frustration causes anger and arousal and this creates a readiness for aggression. E.g. a player sees a colleague fouled, then decides to join in.

13 The effect of having others present during performances can be either positive or negative: positive = social facilitation; negative = social inhibition.

14 A group is a collection of people who share similar goals and interact with one another.

Forming stage: group members are getting to know each other, individual roles are unclear, high dependence on leader for guidance.

Storming stage: team members are establishing themselves in the group, focus is clearer, leader has a more advisory role.

Norming stage: roles and responsibilities are accepted, much more agreement and consensus of opinion, strong sense of commitment and unity.

Performing stage: more strategies, a clear vision and aim, team does not need to be instructed or assisted, disagreements occur but are resolved within the team.

15 Actual productivity = potential productivity – losses due to faulty process

Potential productivity refers to the best possible performance of the group taking into account resources available and the ability of the players. For example, a non-league team losing 4–0 to Chelsea might well be reaching their full potential but are not winning due to their limited resources. Losses due to faulty processes are caused by two factors: (1) Co-ordination problems: if co-ordination and timing of team members don't match, team strategies that depend on them will suffer. For example, positional error or an ill-timed move. (2) Motivational problems: if individual members of a team are not motivated to the same extent, they will be 'pulling in different directions' and players will withdraw effort.

16 The Ringelmann effect occurs when individual performances decrease as group size increases. Group performance also suffers as group size increases – this is known as social loafing. Some individuals in a group seem to lose motivation. It is apparently caused by the individual losing identity when placed in a group. Individual efforts may not be recognised by those who are spectating or taking part.

17 Any three from: to direct attention, increase effort, increase persistence, increase motivation, help improve confidence/self-efficacy and control arousal/anxiety

18 Specific, Measurable, Achievable, Recorded, Time-phased

19 The perceived cause of a particular outcome

20 Locus of causality, stability, controllability

21 First attribution involves luck – this is an external, unstable, uncontrollable attribution. Second attribution involves ability/experience – this is an internal, stable, uncontrollable attribution.

22 Learned helplessness is the belief that failure is inevitable and that the individual has no control over the factors that cause failure. It can demotivate/lead to low confidence and make an athlete give up.

23 Mastery orientation is the view that an individual will be motivated by becoming an expert (master) in skill development. It can motivate and create high confidence, causing an athlete to persevere and succeed.

24 Performance, participation, self-esteem

25 [The components are numbered 1 to 6.] 1 Sporting context: the sporting situation a performer is in. E.g. gymnast doing a vault in a competition. 2 SC-trait: everyone has an existing level of sport confidence (SC). E.g. low levels of confidence in gymnastics (low levels of SC-trait). 3 Competitive orientation: everyone has an existing level of competitiveness. E.g. gymnast does not enjoy competitive situations. 4 SC-state: the confidence that can be shown in a specific situation in sport (SC-trait + competitive orientation). E.g. gymnast has combination of low confidence with a non-competitive orientation: low levels of SC-state, so not likely to be successful. 5 Behavioural response: response to the situation. E.g. vault is successful or not. 6 Subjective outcome: the emotion felt towards the behavioural response; these perceived feelings affect future SC-trait and competitive orientation: positive perceived feelings may increase confidence, while negative perceived feelings may decrease confidence. E.g. satisfaction if vault successful, leading to increased future confidence; disappointment if vault is not successful, possibly leading to decreased confidence.

26 Performance accomplishments, vicarious experiences, verbal persuasion, emotional arousal

27 A prescribed leader is someone appointed by people of a higher authority. An emergent leader becomes a leader through their hard work and determination. People who look up to and respect them help them to become a leader. They may be skilful in their sport and become a leader to show others how well they can do and to inspire teammates.

28 a) autocratic
   b) democratic
   c) laissez-faire

29 Stress in sport is more often linked to negative feelings and can be seen as a psychological state produced and perceived by physiological and psychological forces acting on our sense of wellbeing. Stressors: competition, conflict, frustration, climate.

30 Centring, progressive muscular relaxation, biofeedback, breathing control

Chapter 3.1

1 Upper class: aristocracy or gentry who were hereditary landowners. Activities: real tennis and fox hunting – sophisticated activities with complex rules which required money to participate; pedestrianism – as patrons (sponsors) of lower-

class competitors – derived from putting wagers on footmen; cricket – played as 'gentleman' amateurs. Lower/peasant class: peasants who worked manually, mainly on the land. Activities: mob football, dog fighting, prize fighting – simple activities, often violent with few rules; pedestrianism – as competitors, racing (walking or running) – derived from footmen racing and beating others; cricket – played as 'player' lower-class professionals.

2 Post-industrial Britain – 1850 onwards – due to the trade and manufacturing opportunities created by the Industrial Revolution. The middle class included professionals, factory owners and managers who did not own big estates and were not born into aristocracy. Many members of the middle class went to public schools, which were influential in the development of sports such as rugby and football.

3 Education and literacy: the vast majority of the working classes had very little interest in education because it was perceived to be of little relevance. Child labour was still common practice; working-class families were reluctant to give up the earnings of their children for the benefits of education. The employment of children continued to increase even after 1850. The 1870 'Forster Act' modernised education in England. Elementary education became free with the passing of the 1891 Elementary Education Act. Education became more accessible to the working classes, allowing them to understand more sophisticated rules in sport. Sport became widespread.

Law and order: the development of laws affected the types of activity undertaken, especially for the lower (working) class. Laws led to a decline in blood sports, e.g. animal baiting and cock fighting. Upper classes held onto their sports, such as fox hunting. Lawmakers were from the upper and middle classes, so it was in their interest to support the sports these classes enjoyed.

4 Class, gender, law and order, education, availability of time, availability of money, availability of space, transport

5 Children between the ages of 5 and 16 must receive an education. Examinations and qualifications are now available in physical education and sport, including sports science. GCE A-level, GCSE, Cambridge National, BTECs and Cambridge Technical qualifications are available in PE/sport. Universities offer a wide range of PE/sport-related degrees.

6 The globalisation of sport is a process that involves sport as a worldwide business and features corporate brands, media coverage and freedom of movement of sport participants, officials and spectators. The key factors that facilitate the globalisation of sport are: freedom of movement for performers, greater exposure of people to sport and media coverage.

7 To promote development of the physical and moral qualities of sport; to spread Olympic principles, creating international goodwill; to bring together athletes of the world every 4 years; to educate young people through sports in a spirit of better understanding between each other and of friendship, thereby helping to build a peaceful world.

8 Excellence, respect, friendship

9 Any three from: Berlin 1936 – Third Reich ideology; Mexico City 1968 – Black Power demonstration; Munich 1972 – Palestinian terrorism; Moscow 1980 – boycott led by the USA; Los Angeles 1984 – boycott led by the Soviet Union.

Chapter 3.2

1 Deviance is unacceptable behaviour within a culture. Any behaviour that differs from the perceived social or legal norm is seen as deviant. In sport this may be in the form of illegal performance-enhancing drugs, doping, violence, match fixing, bribery or illegal sports betting.

2 Pressure to succeed affecting a performer's judgement and decision making, pressure from rewards for winning and lucrative sponsorship deals, thinking 'everyone else is doing it'.

3 Any three from: desire to win so overwhelming it leads to violence, nature of activity – physical sports like ice hockey more prone to violence, frustration of events, alcohol and social drugs or performance-enhancing drugs, rivalries, the media increasing tensions, perception of unfairness or poor officiating, deindividuation.

4 Match fixing is when a sports competition is played to a completely or partly predetermined result. This is against the law. Match fixing involves contacts being made between corrupt players, coaches and team officials.

5 Television: terrestrial, satellite and pay-per-view; radio: local and national stations, dedicated sports stations; printed press: newspapers and magazines; the internet; social media; cinema

6 A commodity is an article that can be traded. In this case, sport is the article that can be sold to different media outlets or companies that wish to associate their brand with a particular sport.

7 Six Nations Rugby (sport), Guinness (sponsor), BBC (media)

8 Identifying potential talent; supporting an athlete's lifestyle; supporting an athlete's coaching; supporting through research, sports science and sports medicine; providing a World Class Programme or pathway to success

9 Any two from: 1 Most HE institutions offer university sports scholarships or bursaries. This enables access to special support services. 2 Many top sports facilities are located at universities, so HE is increasingly involved in the development of sporting excellence in the UK. 3 The Talented Athletes Scholarship Scheme (TASS) and, in Scotland, the Winning Students Scheme (WSS) are both government-funded sport programmes,

delivered through a partnership between universities and NGBs. 4 Some universities host centres of sporting excellence, which can be linked to a National Sports Institute.

10 The main role of UK Sport is to invest National Lottery funds and income from central government to maximise the performance of UK athletes in the Olympic and Paralympic Games and global sporting events. Success is measured by medals won and the number of medallists developed.

11 Any four from: 1 Assessment of whether someone has the potential to be an athlete, e.g. assessing bone density and internal body fat. 2 Health screening devices. 3 Prosthetic devices (e.g. Springlite). 4 Wheelchair devices with slanted back wheels allowing tennis players to move across the court quickly. 5 Improved access to buildings, e.g. specialist hoists at swimming pools. 6 Rehabilitation and elite training facilities with state-of-the-art equipment. 7 Various simulated competitive environments, e.g. surf simulators. 8 Improved sports surfaces and artificial lighting. 9 Provision of equipment for elite athletes. 10 Use of composite material in racquets and protective gear, making them lighter. 11. Improvement in the design of trainers and sports footwear. 12 Development of the hypoxic chamber. 13 Precision hydration techniques. 14 More effective physiological laboratory testing for athletes. 15 Gait analysis in runners to help avoid injury. 16 Heart rate monitors and GPS watches, helping to monitor activity and motivate performance.

12 Any two from: 1 Most professional sports use instant replay to help officials make the right decision. 2 Improved detection of doping. 3 Improved detection of foul play. 4 Better timing devices.

13 Any two from: 1 It has increased entertainment through the use of action-replays and slow-motion playback. 2 During live sports events, giant screens show the action and also replays. 3 In some sports, officials are able to access video replays to make key decisions. This increases entertainment for fans, who wait on the edge of their seats until the replay call is announced. 4 Multiple camera angles allow spectators to enjoy every aspect of performance and see whether officiating decisions are correct. 5 Performance is analysed at intervals by pundits, using motion-capture analysis. 6 Mobile phones and 4G/5G mean sport as entertainment is available 24/7. 7 Constant interruptions can interfere with the flow of an event and can irritate viewers. 8 It could reduce the numbers of people attending live sport events.

Exam practice answers

Chapter 1.1a

1 [2 marks] Movement: plantar flexion; agonist: gastrocnemius/soleus.
2 [1 mark for each] A ball and socket; B (middle) deltoid; C latissimus dorsi/pectoralis major; D concentric.
3 Upward [sub max 2 marks from]: 1 It is the agonist or prime mover. 2 It causes extension or movement (of the elbow joint). 3 This is a concentric contraction/it shortens under tension.
Downward [sub max 2 marks from]: 4 It is (still) the agonist or prime mover. 5 It controls flexion or movement (of the elbow joint). 6 This is an eccentric contraction/it lengthens under tension.
4 [4 marks from] 1 High/higher proportion of slow twitch or type 1 or SO muscle fibres most likely to perform successfully in or choose aerobic or endurance or low-intensity, long-duration activities. 2 Any suitable example of endurance activity, e.g. marathon running. 3 High/higher proportion of type 2a or FOG muscle fibres most likely to perform successfully in or choose speed endurance activities or team games. 4 Any suitable example of speed endurance activities, e.g. 400 m, 800 m, 1500 m. 5 High/higher proportion of fast twitch or type 2b or FG muscle fibres most likely to perform successfully in or choose anaerobic or explosive or high-intensity, short-duration activities. 6 Any suitable example of explosive activity, e.g. throwing event, 100 m sprint. 7 (More even) mix of muscle fibre types may perform successfully in both aerobic and anaerobic activity/ they may be good at team games (with varying intensities of activity). 8 Type 1, 2a and 2b (for mix)/ any suitable example of aerobic and anaerobic activity, e.g. 'can do both sprinting and long-distance runs'.
5 [4 marks] [sub max 2 marks from] 1 Small neuron size and stimulate few, small muscle fibres. 2 This results in a low force of contraction (contract intermittently). 3 This is appropriate for a marathon runner as the intensity is moderate. [sub max 2 marks from] 4 They have a high mitochondria, myoglobin and capillary density. 5 This results in a high aerobic capacity and resistance to fatigue. 6 This enables a marathon runner to complete a long-distance endurance event which can last hours.

Chapter 1.1b

1 [5 marks from; sub max 4 marks for contraction phase] (Contraction phase) 1 (SA node) Sinoatrial or SA node or SAN receives or initiates or sends an impulse. 2 (Atria contract/impulse spreads across atria) This causes atrial systole or contraction of atria/atrial depolarisation. 3 (Blood to ventricles) This causes the remaining blood (in the atria) to be pushed (actively) into the ventricles (during ventricular diastole). 4 (AV node) Impulse reaches atrioventricular or AV node or 5 (Purkinje) impulse distributed or continues down the bundle(s) of His/ impulse distributed throughout or to the Purkinje fibres (and only if point 4 or 5 awarded or BofH or Purkinje fibres identified) 6 (Ventricles contract) This causes ventricular systole or contraction of ventricles/ventricular depolarisation/blood pushed or ejected from ventricles.
[sub max 1 mark for relaxation phase] (Relaxation phase) 7 (No impulse) Repolarisation occurs/there is no impulse. 8 (Atria fill) Atria fill with blood (during atrial diastole). 9 (Atrial pressure) (pressure builds in atria) Blood travels (passively) into the ventricles.
2 [3 marks from] 1 HR is controlled by the CCC (located in the medulla oblongata). 2 Proprioceptors detect that movement has increased. 3 Chemoreceptors detect decrease in blood pH. 4 Increase in lactic acid. Increase in CO_2. Baroreceptors inform of changes in blood pressure.
3 [2 marks] 1 (Combines) with or in haemoglobin/as oxyhaemoglobin or HbO_2. 2 (Dissolved) in plasma.
4 [3 marks from] 1 Oxygen diffuses or moves from the alveoli to the blood/oxygen diffuses down the diffusion or pressure or concentration gradient/oxygen travels from high partial pressure or concentration to low partial pressure or concentration. 2 There is a high partial pressure or concentration of oxygen or pO_2 in the alveoli. 3 (During exercise) muscles use more oxygen. 4 (So) there is a low(er) partial pressure or concentration of oxygen or pO_2 in the blood. 5 There is a large(r) or steep(er) or increased diffusion or pressure or concentration gradient of oxygen. 6 More oxygen diffuses or moves (from the alveoli) to the blood/increased or faster rate of diffusion of oxygen (from the alveoli) to the blood.
5 [4 marks from] 1 (Active) Expiration becomes active. 2 (Muscles relax) External intercostals and diaphragm relax. 3 (Additional muscles contract) Internal intercostals or rectus abdominus or transverse abdominus or obliques contract. 4 (Rib cage) (This) pulls the rib cage or ribs down and in 5 (Diaphragm) (and) forces the diaphragm up (further or with more force). 6 (Thoracic cavity volume) Decreasing the volume of the thoracic cavity/decreasing the volume in the lungs. 7 (Thoracic cavity pressure) Increasing the pressure within the thoracic cavity or in the lungs. 8 (Air) Forcing (more) air out of the

lungs/increasing tidal volume/increasing volume of air expired/increasing rate of breathing or expiration.

6 [3 marks from] 1 (At the start of exercise) Increase in CO_2 levels/acidity/decrease in O_2 levels/pH/chemoreceptors. 2 (When exercise starts there is) Movement of joints/tendons/mechanoreceptors/proprioceptors. 3 (Information from chemoreceptors/proprioceptors is sent to) Vasomotor centre/medulla oblongata. 4 (Activation of) Autonomic/sympathetic nervous system/(nor)adrenaline. 5 (Opening of) Pre-capillary sphincters/rings of circular/smooth muscle. 6 Vasodilation to areas needing blood/muscles. 7 Vasoconstriction of areas not needing so much blood/kidneys/liver/gut.

Chapter 1.1c

1 [3 marks from] 1 The only usable form of energy in the human body/energy currency that powers all forms of biological work. 2 High-energy phosphate compound/the phosphate bonds are high-energy bonds/a store of potential energy. 3 When the phosphate bond is broken, energy is released/ATP is broken down to release energy/ATP → ADP + P + energy. 4 An exothermic reaction/facilitating enzyme is ATPase. 5 Can be resynthesised (via the energy systems/with or without oxygen). 6 The breakdown and resynthesis of ATP is a reversible reaction.

2 [4 marks from] 1 A coupled reaction is where the product of one reaction is used in another reaction. 2 Reactions are linked and interdependent. 3 One reaction is exothermic and the other is endothermic. 4 PC is broken down into P + C + energy. 5 This energy is then used to resynthesise ATP. 6 Energy + ADP + P → ATP

3 [6 marks] (Advantages of ATP/PC system) [sub max 2 marks from] 1 No fatiguing by-products are produced. 2 Allows for the quick resynthesis of ATP. 3 Doesn't need oxygen/few reactions. 4 PC can be quickly resynthesised/50% recovery in 30 seconds/100% recovery in 180 seconds. 5 PC is readily available in the muscle. (Disadvantages of ATP/PC system) [sub max 2 marks from] 6 Only small amounts of fuel stored in muscle cell (PC). 7 Low energy yield/only 1 ATP resynthesised. 8 Can only provide energy for short period of time/2–10 seconds. (Advantages of glycolytic system) [sub max 2 marks from] 9 Large potential fuel store of glycogen available (stored in muscles and liver). 10 Requires few reactions/can work anaerobically/in the absence of oxygen. 11 Can provide energy quickly/faster/more quickly (than the aerobic energy system). (Disadvantages of the glycolytic system) [sub max 2 marks from] 12 Produces the by-product lactic acid/reduces pH/inhibits enzyme action. 13 Causes pain/stimulates pain receptors/causes fatigue. 14 (Relatively) low yield of ATP (in comparison to aerobic system).

Chapter 1.1d

1 [5 marks] [sub max 4 marks from] 1 Decrease in (atmospheric) pressure causes increase in breath frequency or breathing or ventilation rate. 2 Partial pressure of oxygen or of pO_2 in the (atmospheric) air or the alveoli is low or reduced or less (than at sea level). 3 This reduces or gives low(er) concentration or diffusion gradient of oxygen at the alveoli or between the alveoli and blood. 4 Less oxygen diffuses into the capillaries or blood. 5 Less oxygen combines with haemoglobin/haemoglobin not fully saturated (at lungs)/less oxygen is transported/less oxygen in the blood. 6 This reduces or gives a low(er) concentration or diffusion gradient of oxygen at muscle or tissue or between blood and muscle or tissue. 7 Less oxygen diffuses into the muscle (cell) or tissue or myoglobin. 8 Less oxygen available for (aerobic) respiration. 9 Hypoxia or hypoxic conditions at high altitude/impact on overall performance while at altitude. [sub max 1 mark from] 10 Performance (of endurance events) deteriorates or decreases at altitude/performers fatigue faster/accelerated OBLA/decrease in VO_2max or aerobic capacity/reversibility occurs/increase muscle fatigue. 11 Increased altitude can cause hyperventilation which will decrease performance.

2 [6 marks] [sub max 2 marks from] Explanation of altitude training: 1 Altitude is usually classed as a height over 2000 m/8000 feet above sea level. 2 3–5 days (1000–2000 m); 1–2 weeks (2000–3000 m) 3 2+ weeks (3000 m+) 4 4+ weeks (5000–5500 m). 5 Partial pressure of oxygen is lower/less oxygen available at altitude. 6 Body produces erythropoietin/EPO/hEPO. 7 Alternative methods now available, e.g. hypoxic tents/altitude tents/oxygen tents/apartments/train low, live high. [sub max 3 marks from] Improves performance: 8 Increased number/concentration of red blood cells. 9 Increased concentration of haemoglobin/myoglobin. 10 Increased capacity to carry oxygen. 11 Delayed OBLA. [sub max 3 marks from] Hinders performance: 12 Altitude sickness. 13 Training at same intensity difficult/reversibility may occur/loss of fitness. 14 Benefits lost within few days back at sea level. 15 Psychological problems linked to travel/time away from home.

Chapter 1.2a

1 [4 marks from] 1 Method used = glycogen loading/CHO loading. 2 Starts 1 week before competition. 3 Day 1: intense exercise (deplete glycogen stores). 4 Days 2–3: high-protein/high-fat diet. 5 Day 4: intense exercise (deplete glycogen stores further). 6 Days 5–7: high-CHO diet and tapering training or rest. 7 This super-compensates and muscles store more CHO than usual.

2 [4 marks from] 1 Named aid – HGH, anabolic steroid or EPO. Benefits: 2 (HGH and anabolic steroid) increased muscle mass and strength. 3 Increased

recovery rate. 4 Increased intensity and duration of training. Risks: HGH 5 Abnormal bone and muscle development. 6 Enlargement of vital organs. 7 Increased risk of cancer and diabetes. Anabolic steroids: 8 Liver damage. 9 Heart failure. 10 Acne, hormonal disturbances. EPO: 11 Increased blood viscosity. 12 Decreased cardiac output. 13 Increased risk of blood clots and heart disease.

3 [3 marks from] 1 Increased body temperature/overheating. 2 Reduced sweating/reduce blood flow to skin. 3 Increased blood viscosity/blood becomes thicker/reduction in blood plasma. 4 Increased heart rate/cardiovascular drift. 5 Lower blood pressure. 6 Lower cardiac output/stroke volume/venous return. 7 Transportation of oxygen/carbon dioxide less efficient. 8 Loss of electrolytes/possible cramp. 9 Headaches/dizziness/fainting. [Do not accept 'dehydrated' as 'hydrated' is in the question stem.]

4 [3 marks] [1 mark from] 1 Sufficient/enough/correct amount of each component. 2 Idea of correct rather than lots. [2 marks from] 3 Sufficient carbohydrates for energy. 4 Sufficient fats for energy. 5 Sufficient protein for (muscle) growth/repair development. 6 Sufficient minerals for bone formation/muscle function/increased (energy) metabolism/electrolyte balance/blood formation/equivalent. 7 Sufficient vitamins for increased (energy) metabolism/blood formation/equivalent. 8 Sufficient water – medium for reactions/lubricant/regulate temperature/avoid dehydration.

Chapter 1.2b

1 [3 marks from] Identification of adaptation and explanation (both needed to gain mark). 1 Muscle hypertrophy/muscles bigger – muscles therefore stronger. 2 Hyperplasia/more fibres/fibres split – muscle fibres therefore generate more force. 3 Increase in mitochondria/increase in myoglobin stores – more oxygen transported within muscle cell/increases endurance capability/delays fatigue/delays OBLA. 4 Increase in glycogen/fat stores – more food fuel for aerobic respiration/medium-/low-intensity work. 5 Increased efficiency of lactic acid system/anaerobic glycolysis. 6 Increase in ATP/PC stores – more fuel for anaerobic respiration/high-intensity work. 7 Increased buffering capacity – greater tolerance to lactic acid/delays threshold. 8 Recruitment of more motor units – generates greater strength of contraction. 9 Improved co-ordination of muscle fibre recruitment – FOG/FG motor units can be recruited faster/allowing for a larger force in a shorter space of time.

2 a) [2 marks] Test A – (NCF) multi-stage fitness test/Queens College step test/Cooper 12-minute run test. Note: any suitable test that gives a 'predicted' VO$_2$max score, so direct gas analysis would be incorrect. Fitness component B – muscular/strength endurance.

   b) [3 marks] Answers **must** be explained. Both heart and muscles must be addressed. [sub max 2 marks for either] Heart: 1 Large/strong heart/hypertrophy able to contract with more force/contractility of myocardium – improved/greater efficiency at pumping blood/O$_2$ to the muscles. 2 Low resting heart rate/bradycardia – greater efficiency at pumping blood/oxygen to the working muscles. 3 Larger stroke volume/(maximal) cardiac output – more blood/oxygen pumped per beat into the systemic circulatory system/per unit of time. Skeletal muscle: 4 Large myoglobin stores – more efficient transport of oxygen (from the blood capillaries to the mitochondria). 5 Many mitochondria allow greater use of aerobic respiration/less time spent on anaerobic respiration. 6 High enzyme activity – increases rate of glycogen/fat breakdown (making aerobic system more efficient). 7 Large stores of glycogen/fats – more fuel available to break down for ATP/resynthesis/energy. 8 Large number of SO muscle fibres – more suited to aerobic/endurance work.

3 [4 marks from] 1 Stiffening of blood vessels. 2 Blocking of blood vessels (atherosclerosis). 3 Reduction in blood flow. 4 Increase in blood pressure/hypertension. 5 Increase in heart rate. 6 Increase in stroke volume. 7 Heart has to contract more forcefully to do the same work/is put under increased strain. 8 Can lead to stroke/heart attack or other CV diseases. 9 Formation of blood clots/thrombosis.

4 [6 marks from the following; even numbered point can only be accepted if corresponding odd numbered point is given; sub max 3 odd numbered points]

1 Increased myofibril response/hypertrophy	2 Increased strength/power/force production of contraction
3 Increased levels of ATP and PC within the muscle	4 Athlete can exercise for longer before feeling effects of fatigue
5 Increased activity of enzymes responsible for breakdown of ATP and PC/more anaerobic enzymes	6 Increased anaerobic capacity
7 Increased ROM	8 Reduction in injury risk
9 Increased anaerobic metabolism	10 Athlete can perform anaerobic exercise for longer
11 Increased capillary network	12 Better delivery of oxygen

Chapter 1.2c

1 [6 marks] 1 Cool-down lasts 20–30 minutes. 2 Gradually decreases in intensity. 3 Has several stages: moderate-intensity activity, to maintain HR, aid venous return and remove waste; and stretching exercise to reduce muscle tension and lower temperature. 4 Maintains heart rate – to maintain

blood flow and metabolic activity, flushing muscle tissue with oxygenated blood. 5 Aids the removal of lactic acid – enhancing future performances, delaying fatigue and injuries. 6 Aids the healing process.

2 [4 marks] [1 mark for definition] Definition: rehabilitation is the process of restoring full function after an injury has occurred. [3 marks from] 1 Rehabilitation depends on an accurate diagnosis and specialist treatment. 2 Early stage: gentle exercise encouraging damaged tissue to heal. 3 Mid stage: progressive loading of connective tissues and bones to develop strength. 4 Late stage: functional exercises and drills to ensure the body is ready to return to training.

3 [2 marks] A compound fracture is when bone (hard tissue) breaks the skin. It happens suddenly after a traumatic event.

4 [4 marks from] 1 Seek medical attention. 2 PRICE. 3 Support using strapping/a brace. 4 Anti-inflammatory and pain medication. 5 Physiotherapy to strengthen surrounding connective tissue and restore range of motion. 6 Hydrotherapy to maintain fitness without weight bearing. 7 Arthroscopy surgery can be used to reshape and resurface torn cartilage.

Chapter 1.3a

1 [6 marks from] (Newton 1 law of inertia) 1 (ball) The tennis ball remains in the server's hand until they apply a force to the ball to toss it. 2 (ball) The tennis ball will continue to travel vertically up or down (from the toss) until the force of the racquet head changes its direction. 3 (player) The player needs to apply a force to the ground to allow them to stretch up or jump to hit the ball. (Newton 2 law of acceleration) 4 (ball) The harder the player hits the ball, the faster it will travel in the direction it has been hit. 5 (player) The greater the force applied to the ground, the faster or further the player will jump into the air. (Newton 3 law of reaction) 6 (ball) The racquet strings apply a force to the ball and the ball applies an equal and opposite force to the strings (or vice versa). 7 (ball) When the ball is bounced before the serve, the ball exerts a downwards force on the ground and the ground exerts an equal and opposite force on the ball. 8 (player) To jump to hit the ball, the player applies a (downward or action) force on the ground.

2 [5 marks from; sub max 4 marks with no example] 1 (height of CofM) The lower the centre of mass or gravity, the more stable or balanced/the higher the centre of mass or gravity, the less stable or balanced/(low CofM) performer has higher inertia or can resist external forces. 2 (e.g.) A (rugby) player lowers their centre of mass or gravity to prepare for a tackle. 3 (line of gravity) Line of gravity or centre of mass within base of support creates a balanced or stable position/line of gravity or centre of mass moving away from centre of base of support reduces balance/line of gravity or centre of mass outside base of support creates an unbalanced or unstable position. 4 (e.g.) A gymnast performing a handstand keeps line of gravity or centre of mass within base of support to remain balanced or stable/sprinter moves their centre of mass or gravity in front of the body/close to hands in the 'set' position to enable a faster start. 5 (base of support) A wide(r) base of support allows greater movement of centre of mass or gravity, giving better stability or balance/allows greater margin for error before unstable position reached/or vice versa. 6 (e.g.) In a headstand a gymnast will be able to remain stable (or not overbalance) for longer (than a gymnast in a handstand). 7 (angular motion) By moving the centre of mass or gravity outside line of action of force, a performer can create an eccentric force or rotation or spin or angular motion. 8 (e.g.) A gymnast leans forward before applying force at feet (that travels outside centre of mass) to perform forward roll. 9 (linear motion) By moving the centre of mass or gravity inside line of action of force, a performer can create a linear or direct force or linear motion. 10 (e.g.) A performer will apply force that travels through centre of mass to perform a vertical jump. 11 (take-off) By raising the centre of mass or gravity at take-off, a body can remain in the air longer or gain more height. 12 (e.g.) A high jumper raises arms at take-off to raise the centre of mass or gravity to gain more height/a long jumper raises their arms to raise the centre of mass or gravity to remain in flight for longer.

3 [6 marks: 1 mark for each formula and 1 mark for each correct calculation and units]

weight = mass × acceleration due to gravity = 98 × 10 = 980N

acceleration = (final velocity − initial velocity)/time taken = (8 − 0)/2.6 = 3.08 m/s/s

momentum = mass × velocity = 98 × 8 = 784 kgm/s

Chapter 1.3b

1 [6 marks from] 1 (Axis of rotation) Longitudinal. 2 (Concept 1) Analogue of Newton 1 states that an athlete will continue to rotate with constant angular momentum 3 unless acted upon by an unbalanced/net/external torque/moment of force. 4 (Concept 2) MI/Moment of inertia is the body's resistance to rotate/change angular motion. 5 (Concept 3) Angular velocity/speed/is the rate of spin of a body. (Start of rotation). 6 Generate angular momentum 7 by applying moment of force/torque to athlete. 8 Friction/force at feet being applied outside axis of rotation/longitudinal axis. 9 Large MI/body parts/arms and leg a long way from axis of rotation. 10 Small angular velocity/rate of spin. (During throw) 11 Reduce MI/bring body parts/arm and leg/towards axis of rotation. 12 Increases angular velocity/rate of spin. 13 Release speed of discus is greater/discus is thrown further.

2. [2 marks] 1 (Action) force/F (from edge of ball). 2 Weight/W/mg (from CM).

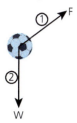

3. [4 marks from] [1 mark max for identifying two of Newton's laws] (Points must relate to correct law) 1 (Newton 1) The ball remains stationary until it is kicked/force applied. 2 (Newton 2) The ball's acceleration/rate of change in momentum is proportional to the size of the (resultant) force acting upon it/larger the force the further/faster it will go. 3 The ball will accelerate in the direction of the (resultant) force. 4 (Newton 3) The foot applies a force to the ball, therefore 5 the ball applies an equal and opposite force to the foot.

4. [3 marks] [must have sporting example to gain mark] 1 Longitudinal (top to bottom), e.g. spinning skater or equivalent. 2 Transverse (side to side), e.g. somersault or equivalent. 3 Frontal (front to back), e.g. cartwheel or equivalent.

5. [4 marks; sub max 2 marks for centre of mass] 1 CM is the point at which a body is balanced in all directions. 2 It is the point at which weight appears to act. 3 Its position depends on the distribution of mass/can change position when body shape changes. 4 It follows a predetermined flight path/height that CM reaches is predetermined at take-off. [sub max 3 marks from (Fosbury Flop) 5 Due to arching/hyperextension of back/shape of FF 6 CM can be positioned outside the body. 7 Therefore, CM can pass underneath the bar as body goes over it 8 whereas in other techniques/straddle/western roll 9 where CM stays within body 10 CM has to pass over the bar.

6. [4 marks from] 1 Discus is an aerofoil shape. 2 Takes on an appropriate angle of attack to the direction of motion. 3 Air has to travel further over the top of the discus. 4 Air travels faster over the top of the discus. 5 This creates a low-pressure area on top of the discus 6 called the Bernoulli principle. 7 Air tries to move from high to low pressure (creating the lift force). 8 Makes flight path non-parabolic/asymmetrical. 9 Lengthens flight path/discus travels further/is in air for longer.

7. [5 marks from] 1 Fluid friction (acting against swimmer moving through water). 2 Acts in opposite direction of motion. 3 Increases as swimmer's speed increases. 4 Swimmer needs to reduce forces to achieve a higher speed/velocity. 5 Reduce friction by streamlining. 6 Creating smooth flow around swimmer/drag reducing profile drag/turbulence behind. 7 Reduce frontal/forward cross-sectional area. 8 Reduce fluid friction by wearing specialist smooth clothing/hat/shaving hairs.

8. [6 marks from] 1 Body forms an aerofoil shape 2 Creating angle of attack. 3 Air travels further under cyclist. 4 Air travels faster under cyclist. 5 Creates low pressure under cyclist. 6 Bernoulli force formed from high to low pressure. 7 Bernoulli force downwards/down force.

9. [5 marks from]

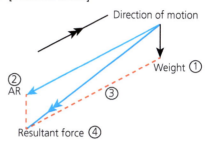

[Diagram, see above – sub max 4 marks] 1 Weight acting downwards. 2 Air resistance acting opposite to the direction of motion and significantly larger than weight. 3 Use of parallelogram law. 4 Resultant force. [Explanation – sub max 4 marks] 5 RF shows the direction of acceleration. 6 Acceleration is (almost) in the opposite direction to motion, therefore shuttle will decelerate/slow down (rapidly). 7 Makes flight path asymmetrical/non-parabolic. 8 Shortens flight path.

10. [5 marks from] (Generation of spin) 1 Eccentric/off centre/moment of force must be applied. 2 Force applied outside CM of the ball. 3 Gives ball angular momentum/motion. (Effect of spin on bounce) 4 Topspin makes ball shoot forward/accelerate off surface/move at a smaller angle to the surface. 5 Backspin makes ball sit up/decelerate off surface/move at a greater angle to the surface. 6 Sidespin has little or no effect on bounce of the ball/allows ball to keep on swerving in same direction.

Chapter 2.1

1. [4 marks; 1 for each explanation and 1 for each example] 1 (Simple skill explanation) One or few stimuli to process/limited information to process/one or few decisions to make/skill with few sub-routines/limited cognitive demand/limited perceptual requirements/less feedback/limited decision making. 2 (Example of simple skill) Swimming/running/sprinting/sprint start; (closed skills e.g.) throwing/kicking/jumping (in a closed situation). 3 (Complex skill explanation) Many stimuli to process/lots of information to process/many decisions to make/increased perceptual requirements/more feedback/skill with more or many sub-routines. 4 (Example of complex skill) Batting or bowling in cricket/basketball dribble/tennis serve/hitting a ball/gymnastics routine/somersault/high jump/triple jump/golf swing; (open skills e.g.) receiving a ball/delivering a pass (in an open situation).

2. [6 marks; sub max 4 marks for any one phase; at least 1 mark from each phase needed for max marks]

(Cognitive/first/beginner phase) 1 Visual – demonstration/video/poster (of a movement)/gives mental picture/gives idea of what skill should

look like. 2 Verbal – giving (basic) information of what needs to be done/positive feedback/positive reinforcement/to correct errors/keep verbal guidance simple/to focus on key points. 3 Manual – (physically) supporting movements to increase safety or confidence or timing/to reduce risk/to learn basic body position/to get feel of movement/to develop kinaesthesis. 4 Mechanical – using a mechanical aid/stabilisers on a bike/swimming float/to increase safety or confidence/to reduce risk/to learn basic body position/to get feel of movement/to develop kinaesthesis/helps understanding/helps performer understand what they need to do.
(Associative/second/intermediate phase) 5 Visual – demonstration of more difficult or new movements or skills. 6 Verbal – feedback to refine or correct or develop skills/to introduce tactics or strategies. 7 Manual – for more specific or more advanced body position or movement/for safety or confidence/should be gradually or completely removed. 8 Mechanical – twisting belt in trampolining or bowling machine in cricket (or equivalent) to practise more complex actions or to groove skill.
(Autonomous/third/advanced phase) 9 Visual – demonstration of difficult moves/as reminder of basic moves/show video of a top-class performer/video analysis/allows analysis. 10 Verbal – (advanced) tactics or strategies/technical detail/discussing outcomes/negative feedback as well as positive/predominant or best method (at this stage). 11 Manual – for highly complex or difficult moves/limit manual at this stage to encourage kinaesthesis or kinaesthetic awareness/used less in this stage. 12 Mechanical – a bowling machine set at a difficult setting (to stretch and challenge).

3 [6 marks; 1 mark only for each numbered point] 1 (Short-term sensory store/STSS) STSS is where: information enters (from senses or display)/selective attention happens/important information filtered in/irrelevant information filtered out/capacity limitless/duration < 1 second. 2 (Example for STSS) Concentrating on the ball when hitting or catching/blocking out crowd noise/position of teammates or opponents, etc./other suitable examples showing contribution of STSS. 3 (Short-term memory/STM) STM is where: information is perceived or understood or judged or interpreted/incoming information compared to learned information/initiates movement/retrieves information (from LTM)/information organised or chunked or encoded/rehearsal helps transition to LTM/capacity 5–9 items/7+ or –2/duration < 30 seconds/duration increased if information rehearsed. 4 (Example for STM) Judging the speed of the ball/grouping information relating to skill or situation/other suitable example showing contribution of STM. 5 (Long-term memory/LTM) LTM is where: information or motor programmes or patterns of movement or schema are stored/information decoded/information sent back (to STM)/(current) performance associated with previous performances (to recognise strengths and weaknesses)/capacity limitless/duration permanent. 6 (Example for LTM) Having or remembering technique of netball shooting/storage of named MP or sporting technique/other suitable example showing contribution of LTM.

4 [4 marks] Cognitive; demonstration; inconsistent; positive

5 a) [1 mark] A type of continuous feedback that comes from the proprioceptors/kinaesthesis. **Do not accept** internal feedback.

  b) [3 marks from] 1 Movements can be corrected immediately. 2 Helps motivate performers. 3 Helps build self-esteem and confidence. 4 Allows performer to be clear which aspect needs improvement. 5 Allows performer to know what good performance feels like.

6 [4 marks from] 1 Making sure the individual understands the similarities and differences between the two skills (e.g. footwork in netball and basketball)/Giving clear and concise demonstrations (e.g. javelin demonstration is easy to understand). 2 Making sure that the basics of the first skill are well learned so that they transfer more easily into the second skill (e.g. skill of throwing – transfer to arm action of tennis serve). 3 Making practice sessions similar to match situations to ensure a larger, generalised motor programme (e.g. a squash player who takes up tennis may find it difficult to learn not to use their wrist during shots). 4 Allowing positive transfer by offering variable practices which imitate game situations. 5 Making performer aware of transferable elements (e.g. teacher highlights that javelin is like throwing a rounders ball – arm position is the same). 6 Ensuring diverse childhood experiences as they enhance probability of transfer.

Chapter 2.2

1 [6 marks; sub max 2 marks for each personality type] Extroverted: seeks social situations, likes excitement, lacks concentration, confident. Introverted: does not seek social situations, likes peace and quiet, good at concentrating. [sub max 2 marks from] Coaching considerations: consider arousal levels, consider type of feedback, consider environmental conditions (crowd, noise levels).

2 [4 marks; 1 mark for definition] Attitude is a pre-disposition (mixture) of beliefs or feelings or behaviours towards an (attitude) object/something/someone (e.g. training or participation in sport). [3 marks] 1 Cognitive element which is a belief about training/playing well/participation/health. 2 Affective element which is an emotional aspect such as enjoyment/positive feelings/hostility/negative feelings towards training/playing well/participation/health. 3 Behavioural element which is behaviour towards training/playing/health/shows commitment/persistence/sticking to the task/trying hard/avoidance behaviours/giving up.

3 [2 marks; 1 mark for each type] Type A: Practical example showing high personal stress levels/anxious/high arousal/apprehensive/intolerant/

impatient/works fast/ambitious/aggressive/highly competitive, for example football player being very anxious and wound-up about playing. Type B: Practical example showing low personal stress/low arousal/cool under pressure/confident/tolerant/relaxed/passive/less competitive (than Type A), for example an athlete being very confident or calm when preparing for a race.

4 [4 marks] Aggression: 1 Definition/explanation – aggression is intent to harm or injure outside the rules of the game. 2 Practical example – e.g. throwing a punch at the opposition in a rugby match. Any other suitable example acceptable. Assertion: 3 Definition/explanation – assertion is forceful behaviour within the laws of the event. 4 Practical example – e.g. an athlete shoulder-pushing another on the final bend in a 1,500 metre race. Any other suitable example acceptable.

5 [4 marks] Trait anxiety: 1 Definition/explanation – trait anxiety is a trait that is enduring in an individual. A performer with high trait anxiety has the predisposition or the potential to react to situations with apprehension. 2 Practical example – e.g. a person who is often anxious in most situations will be anxious before their first swimming competition. Any other suitable example acceptable. State anxiety: 3 Definition/explanation – state anxiety: an athlete's emotional state at any given time is variable from situation to situation. 4 Practical example – e.g. if a swimmer is experienced and has competed in many races, they may no longer be anxious at the start of a race. Any other suitable example acceptable.

6 Levels mark scheme:
At Level 3 [8–10 marks] the candidate explains fully the positive and negative influences of an audience on performance. There is very good use of psychological theories and terminology. Many relevant practical examples are used.
At Level 2 [5–7 marks] the candidate explains, but is at times descriptive. There are few psychological theories and psychological terminology is rarely used. There are few relevant practical examples.
At Level 1 [1–4 marks] the candidate is mostly descriptive with few or no psychological theories. Very few or no practical examples are used.
Indicative content: 1 (Drive) Arousal/drive/anxiety increased (drive theory/dominant response/Zajonc's theory. 2 (Drive) Dominant response/habit more likely to occur/learned responses automatic/motor programmes are run. 3 (Zajonc/inverted U) Weaker players'/novices' performance deteriorates/incorrect dominant response. 4 (Drive/inverted U) Good performances from well learned/stronger/elite/correct dominant response produced. 5 Extroverts likely to perform better with an audience/reticular activating system (RAS) favours extroverts when audience present. 6 Introverts likely to perform worse with an audience/reticular activating system (RAS) does not favour introverts when audience present. 7 (Home/away) If audience in familiar setting performance helped/advantage/disadvantage if away/unfamiliar/hostile environment. 8 (Evaluation apprehension) Anxiety raised by being judged/perceived judgement of others/evaluation apprehension/the nature of the audience/who is in the audience. 9 (Proximity) Proximity of the audience/how close the crowd is to the player. 10 Distractions/widening of attentional focus/utilisation of too many cues. 11 Attention narrows for those who are used to audiences/high levels of ability/optimum cue utilisation. 12 Gross skills are helped by high arousal, therefore an audience can facilitate performance. 13 Fine or complex skills are more desirable at lower levels of arousal so an audience could inhibit performance.

7 [4 marks from] 1 Can give focus/target that gives sense of direction. 2 Lowers arousal/calms you down. 3 Sharing goal setting can give shared responsibility/can lower anxiety. 4 Goal setting can include goals that are attainable/success more likely and therefore lower anxiety. 5 Measured goals can give evidence of improvement/gives reward/positive reinforcement that can improve confidence/lower anxiety. 6 Goal setting that is timed correctly or appropriately can give sense of control/steps towards success that can control anxiety. 7 Exciting/inspiring goal setting can motivate and enthuse/encourage/be enjoyable which may control anxiety. 8 Recorded goals attained gives sense of achievement/progress which controls anxiety. 9 (Negative view) Poor/irrelevant/inappropriate goal setting can lead to high anxiety.

8 [6 marks from] 1 (Situational characteristics) Effective leadership will take into account the situation. Or the environmental circumstances may dictate a certain strategy of leadership to encourage participation. Or, for example, dangerous environment so autocratic style needed. 2 (Leader characteristics) Effective leadership is related to the personality of the leader. Or the personality/experience/ability of the leader will influence whether a person participates or not. 3 (Member characteristics) Effective leadership is related to the nature/type/motivation of group members. Or they may be friendly and therefore encouraging. 4 (Required behaviour) The style of leadership that is suitable/appropriate will either motivate or demotivate to participate. 5 (Actual behaviour) The leader's behaviour can have a direct impact on participation. 6 (Preferred behaviour) What is wanted from group members. Or if you lead the way/style that the group members want you to, then you may motivate/win hearts and minds and increase participation. 7 Consequences are good/more participation/more satisfaction/enjoyment if the needs of the group match the leader's behaviour. 8 Consequences are good/more participation/more satisfaction/enjoyment if the situational demands are met by the leader's behaviour. 9 Leaders should be flexible/can change/can adapt to differing styles (to accommodate

the differing needs to improve participation and enjoyment). 10 You are more likely to participate if you are satisfied/pleased/see the value with the leader/see leader as a role model.

9 [4 marks from] 1 (Attribution) Encourage attribution of any previous failure or learned helplessness to controllable/internal factors or unstable factors or don't blame self/give other reasons for past failures, for example lack of effort/inappropriate goals in netball. 2 (Reinforcement) Give verbal persuasion, encouragement/praise/reward, positive reinforcement, for example the coach praises a young volleyball player's serve to raise confidence. 3 (Control arousal/stress management) Control arousal, give them anxiety or stress management strategies, emotional control or control arousal, imagery or mental practice/rehearsal or visualisation, positive thinking/self-talk or negative thought stopping, somatic strategies to calm down, e.g. biofeedback or PMR, for example encourage the sprinter to imagine winning the race. 4 (Vicarious) Vicarious experience/see others achieve/show others of similar ability succeeding/show role models to inspire: for example, the diver lacked confidence but saw another diver of a similar ability dive off the top board and this raised their confidence. 5 (Success) Performance accomplishments/give early success to raise confidence/encourage small achievable goals at first/goal setting, highlight previous success/practice/train hard/learn skills/strategies, for example remind the discus thrower that they have reached a certain distance before. 6 (Educate) Educate or inspire or teach appropriate skills or tactics, show what the player can do to enhance performance: for example, the coach teaches the hockey player new stick skills to beat an opponent. 7 (Others) Show others who are less good or who are less able or who also lack confidence/show them that they are not abnormal or that lack of confidence is not something to be ashamed of, for example show a tennis player a video of other players who have been successful but who show low confidence levels.

10 [4 marks; 1 mark for leadership style] Task-centred/task-orientated/autocratic leadership style. [Sub max 3 marks from] 1 Leader respected by group. 2 Leader has good relationship with group. 3 Group highly motivated. 4 Group high ability/highly successful. 5 Clear task/goal/roles. 6 Good support network. 7 Good resources/equipment/facilities. **Do not accept** 'cohesiveness of the group' or 'easy task'.

11 [4 marks from] 1 (self-serving bias) Correct use of attributions to protect self-esteem/self-efficacy/self-confidence/avoid learned helplessness. 2 Attributing success to internal causes – stable factors/ability. 3 Attributing success to internal causes – unstable factors/effort. 4 Attributing failure to controllable factors. 5 Attributing failure to internal causes – unstable factors/effort. 6 Attributing failure to external causes – stable factors/task difficulty. 7 Attributing failure to external causes – unstable factors/luck.

Chapter 3.1

1 [4 marks from] 1 Upper class were aristocracy/gentry/were hereditary landowners. 2 Lower/peasant class were peasants who worked manually/mainly on the land. 3 (Upper class took part in) Real tennis/fox hunting: these were sophisticated activities with complex rules or required money to participate. 4 Pedestrianism as patrons (sponsors) of lower-class competitors. 5 Cricket as 'gentleman' amateurs. 6 (Lower class took part in) Mob football/dog fighting/prize fighting: these were simple activities/often violent/with few rules. 7 Pedestrianism as competitors, racing and beating others. 8 Cricket as professional/'player'.

2 [4 marks from] 1 Amateurs were not paid. 2 Cricket: Amateurs and professionals played in the same team. 3 Social distinction was preserved through different changing rooms. 4 The lower-class professionals bowled and cleaned the kit. 5 Soccer and rugby: The growth of socially mixed northern teams led to broken-time payments, where lower classes were paid in order to miss a day's work to play. 6 These payments were against the amateur principles of the upper classes. 7 Golf: Before 1861 there were separate Open Championships for amateurs and professionals. 8 The professionals did not fit in with the image of the gentlemanly game.

3 [2 from] Both identification and description needed for each mark. 1 Munich 1972, Games used to bring attention to a terrorist incident. 2 Moscow 1980, boycott of the Games by several countries, led by the USA, due to the invasion of Afghanistan by the Soviet Union. 3 Los Angeles 1984, boycott led by the Soviet Union due to alleged lack of security and over-commercialisation of the Games.

4 [3 marks from] 1 Participation of women in physical recreation had dropped dramatically in 1900. 2 Crowds at professional soccer and rugby league became male-dominated. 3 Professional sport was mainly watched by male skilled workers, with only a few women. 4 Working-class women were excluded from professional sport by the constraints of time and money.

5 Levels mark scheme

At Level 3 [8–10 marks] responses are likely to include: detailed discussion of political, sporting, social and economic factors in hosting a global sporting event; detailed explanations of advantages and disadvantages of hosting a global sporting event; a number of relevant sporting examples.

At Level 2 [5–7 marks] responses are likely to include: satisfactory discussion of political, sporting, social and economic factors in hosting a global sporting event; satisfactory explanations of advantages and disadvantages of hosting a global sporting event; a few relevant sporting examples.

At Level 1 [1–4 marks] responses are likely to include: basic discussion of political, sporting, social and economic factors in hosting a global sporting event; basic explanations of advantages and disadvantages of hosting a global sporting event; few or no relevant sporting examples.

Indicative content: (Sporting impacts – advantages) 1 Raises the profile of the sport; may lead to increased participation. 2 New or upgraded venues are built. 3 Event can focus on minority sports, which may inspire participation. 4 Increase in funding for sports involved. (Sporting impacts – disadvantages) 5 New facilities can end up not being used after the event. 6 Lesser-known non-global sports can suffer. 7 Sports deviance is likely to be highlighted by media at global events. (Social impacts – advantages) 8 More money brought into city or country, which can be used to benefit local population. 9 Events can give pride to the host nation or city and help with 'nation-building'. 10 Improved use of sport facilities by local communities. 11 Can improve transport systems. 12 Accommodation built for the event can be used by the community (Social impacts – disadvantages) 13 Some areas of the country may not get the same benefits as the host city. 14 Some areas of the host country do not benefit from improved infrastructure and transport. 15 Local inhabitants may have to vacate land being used for sport venues. (Economic impacts – advantages) 16 Increased income leads to positive economic impact. More money is brought to host city by those who participate or spectate. 17 More jobs created through building of facilities and creation of transport infrastructure and other support for the event. 18 Increase in tourism and related economic benefits during and after the event. 19 Commercial benefits related to goods sold in the area of the event and also to the sale of event-related goods. (Economic impacts – disadvantages) 20 Bidding to host an event can be expensive. 21 Events can cause an overall economic loss. 22 Benefits to employment and long-term jobs are often exaggerated. 23 If events or participants are linked with failure, it can lead to loss of revenue in merchandising sales. (Political impacts – advantages) 24 Individual political parties and their leaders can gain credit and therefore more votes if a bid is successful. 25 Staging an event can bring unity to a country and a sense of purpose. 26 The country or city can be used as a 'shop window' for its culture and commerce, therefore raising its status in the eyes of the world. (Political impacts – disadvantages) 27 If the cost is too high or over budget, it can lead to political disadvantage, losing votes and decreasing economic resources. 28 If something goes wrong, e.g. a terrorist attack, politicians have to shoulder responsibility. 29 If host nation does poorly, it can reflect badly on the political party. 30 Negative environmental impacts can decrease political popularity. 31 If legacy of event is negative, this can be politically damaging. 32 Protest by athletes or spectators can be politically embarrassing.

Chapter 3.2

1 [2 marks from] 1 Sports performers are high profile/role models so behaviour might be copied. 2 Sport reflects society, so if there is violence in sport it is because that is what some people 'want'/ because society is violent/has violence. 3 Violence in sport by performers can lead to violence among spectators. 4 Violence may put parents off letting their children participate in sport.

2 [6 marks; sub max 4 marks each for positive and negative aspects] Positive: 1 Can improve sports performance. 2 Can make sports safer for performers or spectators/fewer injuries. 3 Sports can be more exciting/entertaining/enjoyable with technology advances. 4 Can help make fairer decision/a fairer contest. 5 Can help spectators see/experience more when watching sport. 6 Can make sports more accessible. Negative: 7 But can take away the personal effect/more about the technology than the individual. 8 Technology gives those with money an advantage in performance. 9 Can increase the chance of injury/harm. 10 Can take away the element of chance. 11 Can make some sport less of a spectacle/more predictable.

3 [5 marks from] 1 Growing public interest and spectatorship. 2 More people now play sport at least once a week. 3 There has also been growth in the numbers that spectate. 4 More money is attracted to sports – the greater their spectatorship. 5 More media interest/leading to companies wanting to sponsor events and their participants. 6 Increased professionalism/sporting professionals are now likely to attract sponsorship from commercial organisations. 7 Increased advertising. 8 Opportunities to sell more goods and use sports as a 'billboard'. 9 Increased sponsorship/support of events or performers by providing money or goods.

4 [5 marks; sub max 4 marks each for positive and negative effects] Positive: 1 Increased income: BMX will receive money from television rights. 2 Increased sponsorship: more sponsors will be attracted by greater media coverage. 3 Raised standards: the money from media and sponsorship will improve facilities, coaching, equipment, standard of play. 4 Raised profile: increased interest/popularity/awareness/status. 5 Participation: increased participation/role models. 6 Player income: elite players earn more money. Negative: 7 Reliance: BMX may become reliant on increased media coverage. 8 Withdrawal: media may withdraw interest at any time. 9 Change of nature: BMX may have to alter its characteristics to attract media. 10 Alienation: traditional riders/spectators may be driven away. 11 Pressure: pressure on elite players to be successful to retain media interest. 12 Media control: media may control match times/highlight negatives.